Reviving the City

towards sustainable urban development

Dr Tim Elkin and Duncan McLaren
with
Dr Mayer Hillman

Published by

Friends of the Earth
26-28 Underwood Street
London N1 7JQ

with the

Policy Studies Institute
100 Park Village East
London NW1 3SR

ISBN 0 905966 83 X

Laserset by Policy Studies Institute
Printed and bound by Lithosphere
82-90 Queensland Road
London N7 7AW

Printed on recycled paper

A CIP catalogue record of this book
is available from the British Library

Acknowledgements

As ever, there are far too many debts for them all to be recognised personally, but the authors would particularly like to thank those who gave liberally of their expertise and guidance and whose ideas and writings inform much of the substance of this book, especially John Adams, David Cadman, Jeff Cooper, Gerald Dawe, Nigel Dudley, Frank Duffy, Malcolm Ferguson, Hugh Freeman, David Goode, David Hutchinson, Mike Jacobs, Tim Lang, James Robertson, Francis Tibbalds, Andrew Warren, Michael White and Peter Willmott. We must also acknowledge the advice and assistance of Matt Gandy, David Gee, Roger Higman, Andrew Lees, Janet MacKinnon, Jonathon Porritt, William Solesbury and Jeremy Vanke. As ever, responsibility for any errors remains with the authors.

We would also like to thank Sara Huey and Athena Lamnisos of FoE and Nicholas Evans, Clare Morgan and Karin Erskine of PSI for their work to ensure that the book actually made it to publication. And last, but not least, thanks are due to Margaret Cornell for her meticulous and rapid editing.

Friends of the Earth gratefully acknowledges the generous financial support of Godfrey Bradman, which made possible the researching and production of this book.

The Authors

Dr Tim Elkin has a batchelor's degree in engineering (Imperial College, London, 1971), master's degrees in Urban and Regional Planning (Liverpool University, 1976) and Environmental Management (Imperial College, London, 1981) and a PhD in Ecology (Waterloo University, Ontario, Canada, 1987). At Waterloo he prepared Canada's first municipal environmental audit. He has worked extensively in Britain and North America, as an engineer in Northern Canada, as a planner with local government in England, in academia and more recently as a consultant to Environment Canada, and to Friends of the Earth for whom he researched the first UK municipal State of the Environment study in the Metropolitan District of Kirklees.

Duncan McLaren has a batchelor's degree in Geography (Pembroke College, Cambridge, 1986), and a master's degree in Rural Resources and Environmental Policy (Wye College, London, 1987). He worked for some time as a research assistant in environmental and land-use consultancy, during which time he worked on projects for bodies including the Nature Conservancy Council and the Countryside Commission. Since 1988 he has been employed by Friends of the Earth, currently as a Senior Research Officer specialising in urban development and land-use policy issues.

Dr Mayer Hillman has been a Senior Fellow at the Policy Studies Institute (formerly Political and Economic Planning) since 1970, and is Head of its Quality of Life and Environment research programme. He has been principally engaged in policy orientated research on transport, energy and health issues, and is the author of many publications in these fields.

Contents

Foreword

The last decade began with explosions of unrest in many of our cities. Since then, the quality of urban life has deteriorated further, despite the recommendations of inquries into the riots, the Government's half-hearted 'Action for Cities' initiative and widespread criticisms of our built environments.

Whilst concern for environmental issues has increased dramatically since 1988, the environmental movement has paid little attention to cities. Urban sprawl has been condemned and urban development described as a 'cancer on the landscape' but there has been no attempt to examine critically the urban environment as a whole, not even in the Government's recent Environment White Paper. Yet cities are where some 90% of our population live, often in unpleasant or degraded environments.

As the last decade of this millenium begins, Friends of the Earth has produced *Reviving the City* as an initial contribution to what we hope will be considerable debate and action on sustainable urban development for the 21st Century. It is aimed at politicians and planners, architects and engineers, developers, financiers and, of course, at citizens themselves.

We hope that it will help restore confidence in our abilities to create cities that are based on beauty, equity, participation and conservation and which meet the needs of both present and future generations.

David Gee
Director, Friends of the Earth
November 1990

List of Tables

List of Figures

Introduction and Overview

What is sustainable development?

Sustainable development was firmly placed on the global agenda in 1987 by the report of the Brundtland Commission[1] in which it was defined as 'development which meets present needs without compromising the ability of future generations to achieve their needs and aspirations'. The report also argued that the process of development in less developed countries must be geared to sustainability rather than to growth and that it is the responsibility of the developed nations to enable this process to occur.

The UK Government's response to the agenda set by Brundtland has been limited, but included the commissioning of a report from David Pearce and his colleagues, published as *Blueprint for a Green Economy* in 1989.[2] This attempted to suggest how the constraints of sustainable development could be introduced into the UK economic system. However, the UK Government's Environment White Paper published in September 1990[3] offered no further progress, simply reiterating existing policies on economic and urban development. Nor did either Pearce or Brundtland explore the practical implications of sustainable development. The World Conservation Strategy,[4] and the UK non-governmental organisations' response to it,[5] as long ago as 1980 actually went into greater detail.

The European Commission produced a green paper on the urban environment in June 1990,[6] which began to consider policies to deal with the underlying causes of urban environmental problems and the wider impact of urban areas. The paper calls for research to explore in detail the implications of sustainable development for urban environmental management. In the present report we hope to discuss, in practical

1

terms, how cities, and in particular, UK cities, might develop towards sustainability into the twenty-first century.

The changes that are discussed fall into a framework of sustainable urban development which rests on four principles. The first two are the primary principles of sustainability:

i) **Futurity**. In any human activity, the effects of that activity on the ability of future generations to meet their needs and aspirations must be considered. To ensure that the needs of future generations are not compromised, at least a minimum environmental 'capital' stock must be maintained, including the environmental support systems of the planet as a whole as well as stocks of more conventional renewable resources, such as forests.

ii) **Environment**. In any human activity, whether or not it takes place in economic markets, the full and true environmental costs of that activity must be taken into account. This can be effected through regulation, market-based incentives or a combination of both.

Our ability to identify the minimum environmental capital stock is limited. However, it is clear that current rates of environmental degradation and resource depletion are likely to carry us beyond that level. The concept of sustainability constraints is of value here. These define limits to human activity in environmental terms. Although we cannot always define exactly where they lie, we can at least identify the direction of change needed to avoid breaching them. As our information improves we shall be able to identify them more closely. For example, in pollution terms the concept of *critical loads* is valuable. These are based on the environment's capacity to absorb pollution and can be defined in terms of rates of pollution per unit area or volume. In wildlife conservation we can attempt to identify the minimum levels of habitat that must be conserved to maintain species diversity.

However, because sustainability constraints are difficult to define, it is the main aim of this report to outline the development paths which will not breach constraints. Often, such paths can be identified by applying the *precautionary principle* that, where scientific doubt exists, the benefit of that doubt is given to the planet and its people. Our policies are therefore most often defined in terms of methods and techniques which can be applied in the absence of absolute scientific evidence, often in terms of 'minimisation' or 'reduction'. However, it must be clear that such policies cannot guarantee sustainability: that requires human activities to remain within the sustainability constraints.

Combined with these principles of sustainability are the secondary principles of development. Improving the lot of the least privileged in society is a conventional goal of development, but in the context of sustainability this requires increased equity and increased participation in both decision-making and the process of development.

iii) **Equity**. The principle of futurity can also be described as *inter-generational equity*; that is, a commitment to equitable access to resources between generations. However, a greater degree of equity within the current generation (*intra-generational equity*) is also required. Even the average Western rate of resource consumption cannot be achieved by the entire global population without ecological catastrophe, yet that is the aspiration of most developing nations. And, as the Brundtland Report demonstrated, the effects of poverty in less developed countries are also ecological degradation. The only solution therefore is more equitable access to resources.

iv) **Participation**. The problems of 'economic development' without democratic participation have been made manifest time after time. Unless individuals are able to share both in decision-making and in the actual process of development, it is bound to fail.

These four principles are intended to provide only a crude framework, but one in which attention is focused on the over-arching needs of environmental protection and resource conservation. Nevertheless, we cannot ignore the need to enhance democracy and reduce discrimination, since these social goals are not only desirable in themselves but are, at least in part, essential to long-term environmental sustainability.

The importance given to the 'long term' is a key feature that distinguishes sustainable development in broad planning terms. If one of our key goals is to carry forward at least a minimum stock of environmental capital, then the short-term planning that characterises modern development and the modern city must be rejected. Within the context of sustainable development the 'short term' means within the present generation, rather than months or years, while the 'long term' means, maybe, five generations into the future.

Urbanism

Before discussing how we apply the theory and practice of sustainable development to cities it is important to consider exactly what constitutes a city. The physical city (the mass of buildings, streets and people) is just the visible focus of the complete urban system. The social and economic impacts of the contemporary urban system are of truly global extent. Urban centres are crucial to the functioning of the world economic order: they are centres of production, exchange and consumption.

Table 0.1: Examples of major urban areas and populations

	Area ('000 ha)	Population ('000)	Density (people/ha)
Amsterdam (NL)	14	812	58.0
Hamburg (FRG)	39	1,645	42.2
Hong Kong	17	4,986	293.3
London (UK)	119	6,713	56.4
Los Angeles (USA)	473	9,479	20.0
Melbourne (Australia)	166	2,723	16.4
Paris (France)	209	10,094	48.3
Singapore	29	2,414	83.2
Tokyo (Japan)	110	11,597	105.4
Toronto (Canada)	54	2,137	39.6
West Berlin (FRG)	31	2,001	64.5

Note: Figures for 1980
Source: Newman, P. and Kenworthy, J., *Cities and Automobile Dependence,* Gower Technical, Aldershot, 1989.

The urban system includes the physical and economic hinterland of the city, although this is not included in the areas given in Table 1. In the case of the largest cities, like London, this economic hinterland extends beyond national boundaries, over physical boundaries and even into other continents. It is only in this context that the social and economic dynamics of the city (see Chapter 7) can be understood. However, the physical fabric of the city can also be said to house the motor of socio-economic change. Not only does it house decision-makers in politics and industry, but it is also where people and social groups principally interact and new styles and movements evolve.

The relationship of the city with the 'countryside' is complex. Suffice it to note here that the dynamic of the city tends to determine the pattern of change in the countryside rather than vice-versa. We must take note of the long history of this relationship in our analysis of how urban systems can be expected to develop in the absence of intervention in the ways set out in this report.

Over much of the planet the city is also the arena of most individuals' daily experience. Table 2 shows the proportion of the population of selected countries that lives in urban areas. The scale of those urban areas is also increasingly vast (see Table 1).

Table 0.2: Urban population as a proportion of total population

	Population (millions 1989)	% Urban (Estimate for 1990)	% in cities over 100,000 population (1985)
Australia	17	85.5	73.1
Canada	27	76.2	55.0
France	55	73.8	46.3
Germany (FR)	60	86.4	54.1
Japan	123	76.9	45.6
Netherlands	15	88.5	39.6
UK	56	92.1	67.8
USA	246	74.1	56.5
Europe	497	71.6	n/a
Africa	626	29.7	n/a
South America	292	72.8	n/a
Asia	3009	29.9	n/a

Source: World Resources Institute and International Institute for Environment and Development, *World Resources 1986* and *World Resources 1988-89*, Basic Books, New York, 1986 and 1988.

Urbanism and sustainability

Throughout their history, cities have never been free of problems, whether social or environmental. Indeed cities have never been 'sustainable'. The process of urbanism in antiquity has frequently been linked with desertification in the hinterland. Cities have always exploited the surplus food and materials produced in their hinterland, and thus interfered with previously more cyclical ecological systems.

More recently, the genesis of local authorities in the Public Health Acts of the nineteenth century was a response to severe environmental problems specifically in cities. The problems of contemporary urbanism are also severe, both in general, and specifically in terms of the environment. Cities have a concentration of polluters – from industry to cars to litterbugs and can in fact be seen as the location of one extreme of environmental degradation. Most importantly, now that the urban economic system is global in extent, cities and the exploitative activities generated by and in them are able to disturb the planetary support systems on which humanity depends. Disruption of the carbon cycle is the most threatening example, as the expected consequence is global warming.

However, previous efforts to tackle the environmental problems of cities have concentrated on the superficial environment; tree-planting, landscaping and the provision of open space. While these can be valuable to urban residents, they do not address the fundamental problems and cannot alone produce sustainable development. The Garden Cities movement is another response based on a similarly deterministic analysis and is also ineffectual. The opportunity costs of garden cities are in fact 'lost' improvements to existing cities. Also garden cities have rarely, if ever, drawn a socially balanced population, thus leaving the large cities with increasing social problems and a lower tax base on which to fund action. Some of the greatest contemporary problems of cities are social: deprivation in the inner city and on fringe housing estates, exacerbated by economic problems resulting from the rapid restructuring of urban economies.

Solving the problems caused by cities, as well as solving the problems of cities, is a massive challenge. This report outlines a possible solution.

Overview

Sustainable urban development is a new goal. It re identification of environmental constraints to human activit. related to cities and the adoption of methods designed to keep the results of our activities within those constraints. These goals can be achieved through an appropriate mix of regulation and incentive. This report concerns itself with practical solutions, based on existing cities: it sees no place for grandiose planning and social engineering. On the other hand, it assumes that some form of planning is vital to achieve sustainable development, though it does not prescribe specific tools for planning, except where the form of tool is clearly of relevance to our environmental concerns.

The city must be treated as a whole. The built form of the city is merely the tip of the iceberg of the urban system. The influence of urban activities on economic and ecological systems spreads far wider. Yet cities are not integrated into ecological systems. In particular, flows of energy and resources travel in only one direction, into the city and thence into waste disposal systems. Unfortunately the disposal media are generally unable to cope with current rates of disposal. Thus a priority is to reduce pollution flows into all media (air, water and land) to levels below local, regional and global critical loads and to eliminate emissions of dangerous, persistent and bio-accumulative substances (see Chapter 6). Much apparent waste can be re-used or recycled, but one particular priority is to close the nutrient cycle through effective return of nutrients from urban waste to agriculture and horticulture as compost (see Chapter 6). This would simultaneously allow agriculture to maintain production levels but reduce its dependence on chemical fertiliser. Combining this with improved cultivation practices could reduce the impact of nitrate pollution from agriculture on the quality of drinking water (see Chapter 5). In addition, the pollution problems caused by sewage treatment works and sludge disposal, and the risks of methane accumulation in landfill could be greatly reduced (see Chapter 6).

The built form of the city also interferes with ecological systems on a smaller scale. The lack of open space means that the hydrology of the area is greatly disturbed. Buildings disrupt the local climate. These

7

problems can be eased through increasing the proportion of greenery and open space (see Chapter 1). If this is achieved through the creation of 'naturalistic' greenspace then wildlife too will benefit (see Chapter 4). Ecological resources can also be used more effectively within and on the fringes of the city, for food production (allotments and market gardens) (see Chapter 5), for timber and recreation (urban forests) and pollution control (reedbeds and woodland) (see Chapter 4).

There are human activities which are likely to breach sustainability constraints wherever they take place, but which are particularly concentrated in cities. General strategies to guide those activities can be applied. The current use of finite material and energy resources is generally at too rapid a rate. Increasing re-use and recycling of materials such as paper, glass, timber, metals and plastics and increasing the use of the recycled products reduces both the rate of resource depletion and the rate of waste accumulation (see Chapter 6). Improved regulations and incentives for energy conservation in domestic and industrial processes, in space heating and in transport are vital to reducing energy resource depletion and, equally importantly, slowing the rate of accumulation of greenhouse gases and other pollutants in the atmosphere (see Chapter 3).

Improved design of buildings can reduce energy use and consumption of material resources through increased lifespan, and reduce the impacts of the building on the local climate (see Chapter 1). Improving the environment for walking and cycling and ensuring provision of secure, clean and rapid mass transit will greatly reduce energy use in transportation and pollution from vehicle emissions. The use of private motorised transport can be discouraged by traffic restraint. Moreover, improved standards of fuel economy and emission controls on vehicles will ensure that the impact of those which are used is minimised (see Chapter 2).

We must finally address the form of the city. Here fundamental changes in direction are needed to meet the goals of energy conservation and pollution reductions necessary to bring development within sustainability constraints. We have outlined alternative transport, but the built form of the city dictates the overall demand for transport, which can be reduced. The maintenance of high 'urban' densities of population alongside integrated land use can achieve this while providing the social interaction that makes cities desirable. In addition, if population densities fall local services and facilities often become less economically viable.

However, in the larger cities high densities and mixed land use cannot alone achieve these goals. The development of nodes within the urban fabric, a process the Danes call *decentralised concentration*, can allow for necessary levels of accessibility (see Chapters 1 and 2). Such development must be paralleled by policies which ensure that economic activity focuses on such nodes and on internalising circulation of capital to meet local needs with local resources, thus again reducing transport demands (see Chapter 7). Nodal development also allows effective rail-freight links for transport of necessary resources (see Chapter 2). Dense nodal development can also be efficiently provided with energy through combined heat and power generation. In this way the pollution impact of energy provision can be reduced. More widely, cleaner production techniques and renewable energy sources need to be developed (see Chapter 3).

Cities can be made more sustainable. It requires commitment and participation from all sectors of society but most importantly it requires governmental recognition of the potential for environmental damage that is present in urban systems and of the need to attempt to locate our sustainability constraints. Government must also take immediate precautionary action to establish a framework in which all sectors can contribute to the achievement of sustainable urban development.

The future of our cities, and indeed our planet, rests in our collective hands. The potential for progress, for true *development*, is great; yet so is the potential for disaster. If cities are to contribute to global sustainability, rather than wrecking our hopes, the solutions sketched out in this report must form some of the central planks of our bridge to the environmentally sustainable future.

A note: cities outside the 'developed' world

This report is relevant almost exclusively to the 'developed countries'. This is not because we consider urban development in 'less developed countries' to be of less importance, but merely because of the constraints of time and other resources. Moreover, to address the problems of urban development in 'less developed countries' first would be to fall prey to cultural imperialism. We must therefore first define the desirable course of development for the cities of the developed world. Further research is of course vital, to identify the paths of sustainable urban development for the 'less developed countries'. But it is already clear that, in the face of global environmental problems, the 'less developed countries' should be aiming to develop, not to where the 'developed countries' are now, but to where they and their cities *should be*.

The structure of the report

This report is divided into two sections. The first examines six topic areas in relation to sustainable urban development: the built environment (Chapter 1), transport (Chapter 2), energy (Chapter 3), the natural environment (Chapter 4), food and agriculture (Chapter 5) and finally waste and pollution (Chapter 6). In each chapter the current problems that prevent sustainable development will be discussed and some of the potential solutions examined.

The second section discusses broader issues relating to the socio-economic problems and organisation of the city (Chapter 7). This is followed by a summary of the importance of resource economy in sustainable urban development and a discussion of the parallel policy issues of equity and of quality of life in terms of the ways in which they can be promoted through sustainable urban development (Chapter 8). In conclusion, the roles of different sectors in making practical progress towards sustainability are outlined, and some broad recommendations are made for government action (Chapter 9).

References

1. The World Commission on Environment and Development, *Our Common Future*, OUP, Oxford, 1987.

2. Pearce, D., Barbier, E. and Markandya, A., *Blueprint for a Green Economy*, Earthscan, London, 1989.
3. *This Common Inheritance*, Cm1200, HMSO, London, 1990.
4. International Union for the Conservation of Nature, *The World Conservation Strategy*, IUCN, Gland, 1980.
5. World Wildlife Fund (UK), Nature Conservancy Council, Countryside Commission, Countryside Commission for Scotland, Royal Society of Arts and Council for Environmental Conservation, *The Conservation and Development Programme for the UK*, Kogan Page, London, 1983.
6. Commission of the European Communities, *Green paper on the urban environment*, COM (90) 218 final, Commission of the European Communities, Brussels, 1990.

Chapter 1: The Built Environment

Introduction

Sustainable urban development must aim to produce a city that is 'user-friendly' and resourceful, in terms not only of its form and its energy efficiency, but also its function, as a place for living. The city must be of a form and scale appropriate to walking, cycling and efficient public transport, and with a compactness that encourages social interaction. We share Sherlock's conception of the city:[1]

> Take away the high concentration of people and activities, together with the diversity and vitality which go with them, and there is no longer any point in living in a city.

The present

Despite strong planning policies, urban areas have grown in size, with a general reduction in the density of new development. The hearts of many cities have been torn out in comprehensive redevelopment schemes, and even today regeneration is more often based on large-scale (resource-inefficient) redevelopment that fails to retain existing features, buildings, employment and populations. Public spaces, especially streets, have become more dirty and dangerous, mainly as a result of the segregation of land uses and increasing levels of traffic.

Table 1.1: The regional distribution of dwellings in poor environments

	Proportion of dwellings in 'poor' environments	
	Number	%
Region		
North	121,000	9.7
Yorkshire & Humberside	252,000	13.0
North west	390,000	15.4
East Midlands	116,000	7.5
West Midlands	157,000	7.8
South west	143,000	7.7
East Anglia	25,000	3.1
Inner London	298,000	26.2
Outer London	222,000	13.3
Rest of South East	281,000	6.9
England	2,005,000	10.6

Source: Department of the Environment, *English House Condition Survey 1986*, HMSO, London, 1988.

The degradation of the built environment in the UK is demonstrated in Table 1.1 (and Figure 1.1) which show the proportion of dwellings in poor environments, as assessed in the *English House Condition Survey* of 1986. The criteria for 'poor' environments included the need for action to repair roads or pavements, to repair fences, gardens and common areas around dwellings, to improve lighting, tree-planting or landscaping, to provide public green space or to tackle intrusive traffic.

Physical environmental degradation is a widely recognised problem, but it is far from being the worst environmental problem relating to the built environment. Existing land-use patterns are the legacy of a period of abundant fossil fuel which permitted a marked trend towards lower population densities and greater physical separation and de-agglomeration of activities. The results are high environmental costs in terms of energy and resource demands. Equally, little thought has

Figure 1.1: Map showing distribution of dwellings in poor environments

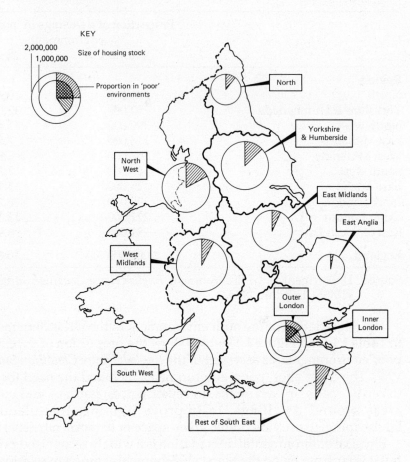

KEY

2,000,000 — Size of housing stock
1,000,000

Proportion in 'poor' environments

North

Yorkshire & Humberside

North West

East Midlands

East Anglia

West Midlands

Outer London

Inner London

South West

Rest of South East

F.O.E.   FIG 1-1

Source: Department of the Environment, *English House Condition Survey 1986,* HMSO, London, 1988.

14

been given to the implications of building design in terms of resource use or abuse.

Current UK Government policy is to encourage voluntary labelling schemes for buildings and building materials. Although the Environment White Paper of September 1990 did indicate that statutory labelling would be incorporated into the next revision of the Building Regulations, there was no indication of the timing that might imply. The 1990 revision of the regulations was the first for five years.

Shifting the development of the built environment towards sustainability requires consideration of the key issues of density and design.

Urban density

Much of the argument over density and the desirability of the compact or dispersed city centres on the provision of public open space. Jacobs claims that the idea of parks as lungs is science fiction.[2] She argues that it has led to dispersal, which in turn leads to the greater use of cars and therefore to more carbon monoxide in the atmosphere. Sherlock argues that greenness is best provided in urban areas by trees and shrubs in paving, be it in streets, in squares like London's Sloane Square, or in the haphazard spaces between buildings which can make or mar our surroundings. In particular, streets should be reclaimed from traffic to return to a role as meeting places and places where children can play:[3]

> Instead of frittering away valuable urban land as a palliative to those who suffer a poor environment, we would be better off using our resources to improve the appearance and safety of the whole urban environment while, at the same time, maintaining the concentrated form of the city.

However, there is a minimum level of provision of open space. Sherlock suggests that every urban borough or district needs one substantial park with plenty of forest trees, and an area of grass large enough to survive universal use; and formal recreational spaces in every neighbourhood. Goode points to London 20 years ago, before the recent property spate, when the population size was similar to the present but the amount of green space was considerably greater.[4]

The problem is therefore one of declining densities within urban areas, as well as erosion of existing open space. The city is being suburbanised by redevelopment and infilling of open space at suburban densities, particularly for housing. The advantages of intensive use of space are being lost. Compactness goes hand-in-hand with the goal of livability, and works to prevent commuting, one of the most wasteful and frustrating aspects of city living today.[5]

Intensification of the use of space in the city can minimise transport of water, energy, materials, products and people. Spatial intensification benefits bicycle traffic, for example. There is an inherent conflict between lower densities and a good transport system. Lower densities encourage car use, the effects of which on urban environments are discussed in Chapter 2 on transport. It is still only a small proportion of commuters who travel to city centres by car, but they are the major cause of urban congestion. Reducing this congestion would free urban roads for public service and delivery vehicles. Urban public transport services need to be increased and car traffic in central areas restrained.

Major commercial areas must be at the centre of gravity of the public transport system. All shopping centres, major leisure activities and public institutions need to be close to frequent train or bus services. The concept of 'decentralised concentration', practised by Danish planners, and adopted in principle, if not in name by the London Planning Advisory Committee (LPAC), provides a useful framework. Policies include the strengthening of small- to medium-sized local centres, integration of land uses, high densities and direction of growth to appropriate centres. The concept aims to concentrate those uses which are the focus of urban activity, particularly employment, in nodes: only one in the centre of small urban areas, more in larger cities. LPAC suggest 33 nodes in London.[6] The number of commercial nodes would vary from the number of industrial nodes or retail nodes. However many nodes exist, activity can be effectively focused on transport nodes by the planning system, using this concept.

Such an approach can also combat some of the problems caused by escalating land values in existing central areas. These not only force non-specialised uses outwards, but also trigger demolition and redevelopment before the end of the useful life of a building, stimulate the use of infill sites, thus removing valuable open spaces, and encourage the holding (un-used) of derelict land because it acquires inflated value expectations.

Commercial areas can also contribute to increasing residential densities. Most British cities have large amounts of unoccupied space in the buildings in their central areas, which are unlikely to have any commercial or industrial use in the foreseeable future. Converting these to residential occupation would be economical of resources and would have immense social advantages. Schemes to convert such space to residential use are currently operating in cities such as Norwich, Ipswich and Cambridge under the slogan of 'living over the shop'.

Overall, housing densities in towns and cities ought to be at a level equivalent to the typical three-and-four-storey urban street: a level at which it is still possible to provide each dwelling with its own front door on to a public street, and to provide gardens for all family dwellings. Figure 1.2 shows the potential for the design of high quality housing at densities 50% greater than those typical of new urban housing. Densities in the central area for those without families can be higher. There is already plenty of suburban housing around our cities for those who prefer it; and there is no reason to dilute the inner-city areas by suburbanising them as well. Indeed there are stronger arguments for increasing densities in the suburbs too. Retaining 'urban' densities of housing would ensure the survival of local facilities like shops, pubs, primary schools, doctors' surgeries and bus-stops within walking distance of everyone's front door.

In such a scenario our streets could be treated first and foremost as places rather than routes. In primarily residential areas it could be made safe for children to play outside their front doors and to cycle to school. In shopping and commercial centres, even when they are on a main road, first consideration could be given to the pedestrian. The person who lives or who has business in an area would always have priority over the person passing through.

Figure 1.2: High quality design for high density housing

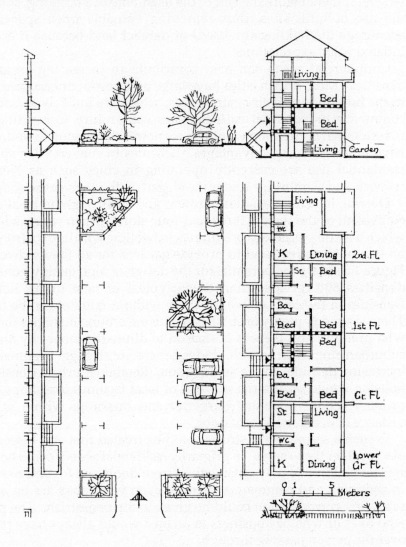

Source: Sherlock, H., *Cities are good for us*, Transport 2000, London, 1990.

Freeman calls for the reversal of the:[7]

> overwhelming preoccupation that planners, architects, and
> local governments have had for many years with reduction
> of high urban density ... [which] ... is actually essential for
> the positive qualities of towns and cities, such as cultural life
> and specialised professional services; the low densities of
> suburbs make these facilities difficult to provide without
> imposing a degree of car travel which is both
> environmentally damaging and unjust to the more
> disadvantaged sections of society.

This is not to say that high density cannot be a contributory factor to
housing stress. The Milner-Holland Committee into housing reported
in 1965 that Islington had the worst housing crisis in London, with
sub-standard private-rented accommodation at a density of 300 or more
people per acre in some wards. It was calculated that in order to bring
housing standards up to an acceptable level, 30 per cent of the borough's
population would have to be rehoused in outer London boroughs, the
new towns, or elsewhere. Despite Islington's 22 per cent population
decline between 1971 and 1981, it remains the most densely populated
borough and has less open space per head of population than any other
borough.[8]

Nevertheless, a number of studies have shown that, except in low-rise
housing estates, there is no direct correlation between high density and
dissatisfaction with living conditions. Low-rise is cheaper to build,
however, and developers' profits, at all but the highest land values, can
be maximised by high density low-rise development which is the least
satisfactory for residents.[9] Medium-rise high density housing should
therefore be encouraged on resource conservation grounds, while
attention should be paid through housing policy to other issues which
contribute more to residents' dissatisfaction, such as management,
heating and other facilities. Planning briefs can be used by local
authorities to ensure suitable densities and effective provision of open
space. However, existing policies setting maximum densities should be
revised upwards, with both minimum and maximum densities set for
particular areas.

Thus high density is in no sense synonymous with high-rise living. Community architecture* has come about largely as a response to previous approaches to designing the built environment, which produced acknowledged disasters in high-rise housing.[10] This movement now recognises that it is important to progress slowly but with innovation, to respect tradition, and most importantly, to respect local democracy, to provide what people need by involving them in the planning, design and management of their built environment.

In order not to make the dense city unnecessarily dependent on large-scale technical infrastructures, ways must be found of using the existing infrastructures more efficiently. The obvious example here is the need to manage our existing road system more effectively rather than building more roads in our cities, but other systems could also be better managed. Deelstra suggests a number of other examples: logistical measures, such as computer control of public transport; cascade systems such as fishponds behind water purification installations; time-linked activities and multi-purpose spaces, such as community forests used for both forestry and recreation.[11]

Some range of densities within the city is probably necessary to suit different family circumstances. Yet overall we have to challenge the assumption that more space is always available. This has permitted trends of increasing space per person in houses** in offices, and even in retailing where much new development has been single-storey. Land must be much more clearly recognised as a limited resource than it is at present. This is the situation in West Berlin, where, despite available open land, strong planning is used to force the decontamination of contaminated sites at additional costs of at least £80,000 per hectare.[12]

There should be a clear edge to the dense land-use patterns of the city in order to avoid incremental sprawl. At or beyond this edge, open space is needed for more extensive land uses such as horticulture or

---

* Community architecture is a development process in which people are involved in shaping and managing their environment. See Wates, N. and Knevitt, C., *Community Architecture*, Penguin, Harmondsworth, 1987.

** Now further encouraged by policies such as the replacement of rates by the community charge.

woodland, and urban development should not be provided for. Urban economic processes can be integrated with natural processes, and use made of nature's regenerative powers. Examples include marshy areas which can purify contaminated water and the use of reedbeds to treat sewage effluent. Space is also required for regenerative natural processes like solar and wind energy. In an ecological urban model the open space beyond the built-up area is part of the city, used for hydro-economy, waste management and energy production, as well as food production.

Urban design

Environmental issues present several challenges to urban design, not least how, at the strategic level, to recreate a diverse pattern of land use in our cities, and how, at the local level, to provide safe and friendly streets. The two are clearly connected. Central areas that are half-deserted, because of an over-concentration of office accommodation, are not only dull but can also be downright dangerous. On the other hand, nothing enhances a city's reputation more than friendly streets where there is plenty happening. It is therefore imperative that the central areas of our cities have a diversity of activities which, because they take place at different times, ensure that there is always something going on.

Diversity of activity is essential to community life, and the health of the city. This is strongly argued by Tibbalds:[13]

> Mixed uses are important. In 'commercial schemes' planners must insist that residential, shopping and recreational uses are also included. An example here is Jubilee Hall in Covent Garden: it houses a gym, a market, shops, offices and flats. The local community made that happen. What is needed [to replicate such success] is a strong planning system.

Mixed use means placing retail functions in residential areas and residential functions in retail areas and local industry in residential areas (with segregation only of the worst neighbours).* Local shops must therefore be retained and encouraged to improve. The tendency for retail outlets to become larger, fewer and further away must be resisted. Large out-of-town stores threaten existing shopping centres and generate traffic congestion as well as imposing higher infrastructure provision costs. There should be a general presumption against them in planning guidance. Other out-of town commercial developments such as warehousing and science parks involve similar environmental costs and require similar treatment by the planning system.

A proportion of space in the central area should be allocated to low-cost housing, shopping and service industries which may not be able to pay market rents but which are nonetheless necessary to the prosperity of the centre. This could be achieved through the extension of policies which already protect open space, historic buildings and certain shopping frontages, or alternatively by a thorough revision of the Use Classes Order which would ensure that changes in use which could be detrimental to this mixture were subject to detailed scrutiny under the development control system.**

Mixed use of space can bring renewed life back to many parts of the city, and in turn enhance security in public spaces for disadvantaged groups. Many of the city's security problems can be related to separated land uses, quite simply the loss of a social milieu. We need a built environment which encourages social interaction, while discouraging crime. As Cadman points out, it is the social interaction, the 'good-hearted, swarming, jostling' city, that gives life to the place.[14] On

---

*   Improved pollution control and discouragement of car access would reduce the bad neighbourliness of many businesses.

**   In the UK town and country planning system many changes in the use of land or buildings are permitted without the owner or occupier having to apply to the planning authority. These are regulated by the General Development Order, which defines general types of development which are 'permitted' and the Use Classes Order which defines groups of uses, within, and in certain cases, between which, changes of use are 'permitted'. Under the current Order valuable social facilities tend to be lost to more profitable uses as this is not seen as a concern of the planning system.

the smaller scale, the benefits to the street from removing or calming traffic are discussed in the following chapter, while in design terms the benefits of frequent doors and entrances at ground level, rather than long blank walls (or reflective office windows), are that the street becomes much safer and more welcoming.[15]

Yet much new residential development is typified by design for privacy such as walls with only occasional gates, which maintain exclusiveness and exaggerate the division between public and private space in the city. Taken alongside the lack of investment in public space, and the dirty, uncared-for state in which it is often found, this aspect of cities reflects 'public squalor and private affluence'. The challenge, however, is to increase the level of personal responsibility felt by individuals for 'public' space. This can be assisted by design of the public realm such that it is both secure and attractive. This requires enhanced security in most public space, and degrees of privacy in shared spaces.

Designing with nature

Chapter 4 on the natural environment argues that nature should be integral to the design of our cities because people both enjoy and need to be close to nature. Urban tree planting also contributes to the absorption of air pollution and to the visual coherence of the 'reborn' inner city areas. The concept of greening the city depends on a general acceptance of the need to plant trees not only in parks and public spaces, but also along roads, both renewing and extending existing 'greenery'. It may even be appropriate on a wider scale to require a proportion of the ground-level area to be allocated to planting trees appropriate to the local climate and ecology.

One of the greatest advantages of designing with nature is that it can provide a solution to the problems of run-off and flooding in our cities. Such problems typify the narrow perspective given to the natural environment in the design of the built environment. Rather than viewing rainfall as a resource, an essential part of the hydrological cycle, it is directed into the drainage and sewer system, and discharged into local watercourses. This is an engineered solution to run-off which requires the culverting of all watercourses to contain great fluctuations in water levels during storms. It both increases the likelihood of their becoming polluted and results in the loss of their natural setting. The alternative approach would be both less costly and more straightforward. A city can reduce the run-off problem by increasing the area of permeable land.

This can be achieved by introducing natural areas (including roof gardens), wherever possible, and through the use of permeable surfaces in locations such as car parks, to allow absorption of water, as is commonly done in the Netherlands. In this way, a city can successfully design with nature, keeping its watercourses relatively undisturbed. In Köln in West Germany the river's flood-plain has been retained as a recreational resource in much of the city. In parts of North America, a partial solution has been provided by introducing storm water basins and retention ponds, which are attractive in their own right, as well as providing for wildlife conservation and simulating natural hydrological processes.[16]

Resource conservation

Land is the basic resource that is wasted in cities. Not only must the tendency towards lower densities be countered, but derelict and under-used land must be put to good use. Temporary car parks (the most common use at present) not only have a blighting effect in themselves but also attract more traffic and therefore exacerbate congestion.

Chisholm and Kivell report that 46 per cent of derelict land is classified as urban:[17]

> Allowing for the fact that the urban authorities are, on the whole, very much smaller in area than rural authorities, there is clearly a high concentration of dereliction in the cities.

The 1988 derelict land survey indicated that urban derelict land had risen to 50 per cent of the total (see Table 1.2 and Figure 1.3).

24

Although the quantities of officially classified derelict land are small in relation to the total urban area, estimates of the total area of wasteland suggest that there may be up to 110,000 ha of wasteland in the urban areas of England and Wales (or almost 5 per cent of urban Britain), and a further area of under-utilised land.[18]

Table 1.2: Derelict land remaining (1988)

	Derelict Land Remaining (ha)		
	Inner city	Other urban	Total
Type of Dereliction			
Colliery spoil heaps	498	2,075	4,695
Metalliferous spoil heaps	199	451	4,769
Other spoil heaps	265	925	2,430
Excavations and pits	415	1,510	5,958
Military dereliction	67	183	2,576
Derelict railway land	1,047	2,127	6,413
Mining subsidence & land affected by underground mining operations	378	269	1,035
General industrial dereliction	3,135	3,702	8,482
Other forms of dereliction	1,028	1,798	4,131
Total	7,032	13,040	40,489

Note: Totals include dereliction in rural areas
Source: Department of the Environment, *Review of Derelict Land Policy*, DoE, London, 1989.

Table 1.3 shows the limited net effect of the restoration that took place in major urban areas in England in the period 1974-82. Similar information is not available for the 1982-88 period except on a regional scale. Although in that period greater emphasis was given to the reclamation of urban dereliction, the only class of derelict land which saw a further net increase in area over that time was the residual class 'other forms of dereliction' into which most urban industrial dereliction falls.[19]

Table 1.3: Dereliction and restoration in major urban areas, 1974 and 1982 (hectares)

	Area derelict		Area restored
	1974	1982	1974-82
Metropolitan counties			
Greater London	324	1,954	422
Greater Manchester	3,405	4,035	1,727
Merseyside	529	1,716	390
South Yorkshire	1,565	1,110	871
Tyne & Wear	1,314	1,458	834
West Midlands	1,535	1,833	1,000
West Yorkshire	2,857	2,640	1,104
Sub-total	11,529	14,746	6,348
Urban districts over 200,000 population			
Bristol	7	90	31
Derby	96	35	24
Hull	196	304	27
Leicester	41	0	5
Nottingham	101	36	58
Plymouth	26	26	7
Southampton	0	12	0
Stoke-on-Trent	517	312	616
Sub-total	984	815	768

Note: The figures for 1974 and 1982 are not fully comparable as the 1982 assessment was more comprehensive.

Source: Department of the Environment, *Survey of Derelict Land in England*, DoE, London, 1974 and 1982. Table reproduced from Chisholm and Kivell, *Inner City Waste Land*, 1987.

Figure 1 .3 Map showing regional distribution of derelict land by type

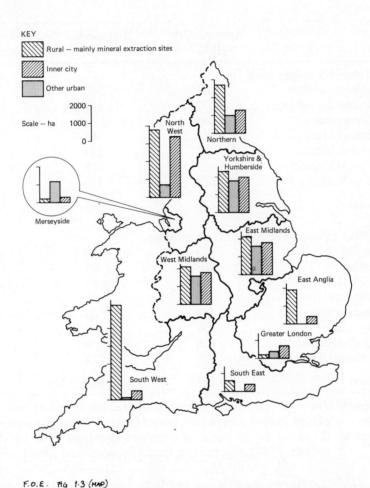

KEY

Rural — mainly mineral extraction sites

Inner city

Other urban

Scale — ha

F.O.E. FIG 1·3 (MAP)

Source: Data from Department of the Environment, *Review of Derelict Land Policy*, DoE, London, 1989.

Table 1.4: Vacant land on the public land register in major urban areas in 1987

Area in hectares

	Area vacant 1987	Disposed of 1984-7[1]	Brought into use 1984-7[1]
Metropolitan counties			
Greater London	1,896	947	394
Greater Manchester	2,173	461	200
Merseyside	1,399	64	33
South Yorkshire	1,543	63	13
Tyne & Wear	1,657	263	130
West Midlands	96	328	91
West Yorkshire	2,002	113	20
Total	11,630	2,239	881
Urban districts over 200,000 population			
Bristol	353	60	13
Derby	205	43	4
Hull	524	41	23
Leicester	330	18	25
Nottingham	164	22	24
Plymouth	222	36	15
Southampton	38	6	9
Stoke-on-Trent	219	17	8
Total	2,055	243	121

Note 1: The figures for land disposed of and brought into use refer to the period 1984-7, except for Greater London where the period is 1982-7.

Source: Department of the Environment computerised Land Register, February 1987, reproduced from Chisholm and Kivell.

Table 1.4 shows the stock of publicly owned vacant land in 1987, and the amount that has been disposed of and brought into use in the period since 1984. Chisholm and Kivell comment:[20]

> If we assume that all the land disposed of is in practice brought into use expeditiously, the rate at which land was

re-developed over the period 1984-87 implies that, even if
no further land became vacant, it would take almost 12 years
to clear the 1987 stock of publicly owned land in the major
cities. In practice, the rate at which land appears to have
become vacant has roughly balanced the rate of
redevelopment. So an alternative interpretation of the data
on the registers is that, on average, *publicly owned vacant land
remains idle for 12 years.*

However, some classes of vacant public land should not generally be
brought into permanent use. These are those areas which have a clear
future strategic role, particularly the derelict rail heads and yards in
inner urban areas. Such areas will be required again in the future as the
true environmental costs of road transport are revealed. In some cases
development may be justified on the grounds that in certain cases such
sites are especially accessible by public transport. However, the balance
between the need to retain land for rail use, to service existing and
potential industry, and the demand for accessible office development is
currently not being struck. In fact the area of 'derelict railway land' has
been reduced by over 20 per cent.[21]

Table 1.5 (and Figure 1.4) show changes in land use recorded by the
Ordnance Survey. Overall this data reveals a continuing conversion of
rural and vacant urban land to developed uses, with some acceleration
of the conversion rate over recent years. However, vacant land has
generally constituted less than a quarter of land developed, despite the
large stocks, and it must be noted that not all the vacant land that has
been used was classified as derelict.

The Council of Europe recommends that, in their management of
urban resources and definition of an industrial policy, local authorities
should give preference to the re-use of derelict land and better use of
under-used industrial land rather than the creation of new industrial
estates, and generally adopt a policy for using land prudently in the
development process.[22] These policies are reflected in the European
Commission's Green Paper on the Urban Environment.[23] If this is to be
effectively achieved in the UK the emphasis in planning policy given to
a presumption in favour of development must be revised. A
presumption against development on greenfield sites and sites

29

Figure 1.4: Land-use change in England 1987-9

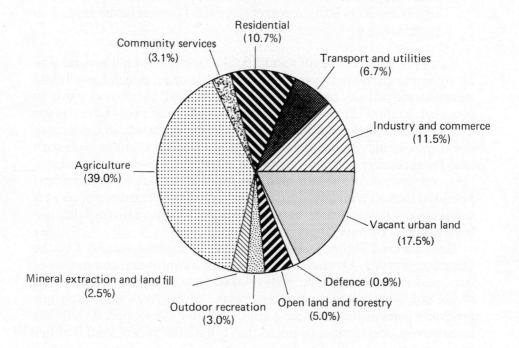

Sources of land for urban use

F.O.E. FiG 1.4.

Source: Data from *Land Use Change in England*, DoE Statistical Bulletins 87(7), 88(5) and 89(5).

designated as of importance for conservation and amenity would shift pressure towards derelict land, simultaneously diverting development pressure to the more deprived regions. Alternatively a market mechanism in the form of a tax or levy on greenfield development could be used to achieve a similar effect. The latter would also yield funds for reclamation of dereliction where absolute retrospective 'polluter' liability could not be enforced. Greenfield areas where the tax or presumption did not apply could be designated through the development planning system.

Instead, the UK relies on a programme of derelict land reclamation, to make derelict land attractive to developers and ease pressure for development elsewhere:[24]

> In urban and urban fringe areas, reclamation of dereliction should complement policies and strategies for economic and environmental regeneration and enhancement, including the role of green belts.

However, despite such exhortation, derelict land policy has not produced results in terms of the conservation of land. At the same time, it has been responsible for the destruction of many sites of interest for nature conservation as a result of 'reclamation' for development. However, the Department of the Environment's review of the policy proposes a shift in emphasis to allow for increased use of derelict sites for nature conservation and amenity purposes. But if sustainable development is to be promoted, the grant assessment procedure must include a full assessment of the environmental impacts, not just of the reclamation process, but of the proposed end-use.

Several obstacles have contributed to the problems of the derelict land policy, not least that private owners hold sites in the hope that their market value might increase, for example, as the result of development on surrounding sites. There are few direct costs in holding such sites: they are not liable for rates; but they can still be used to secure borrowing. In practice, local authorities are currently unable to force the development of privately owned derelict sites, or even to identify their owners.

Table 1.5: **Land-use changes to urban uses (annual average hectarage 1986-8)**

| | Resi-dential | New use | | | | |
		Transport & Utilities	Industry & Commerce	Community Services	Vacant	Total
Rural	4,155	1,660	905	455	470	7,645
Agriculture	3,508	1,345	670	285	105	5,920
Forestry & open land	310	215	100	50	80	755
Minerals & landfill	60	40	55	10	210	380
Outdoor recreation	240	50	45	95	30	450
Defence	35	10	35	15	50	140
Urban	3,445	890	1,740	390	1,065	7,530
Residential	1,230	60	90	50	190	1,625
Transport & utilities	75	470	185	15	270	1,020
Industry & commerce	335	55	825	25	515	1,750
Community services	190	10	30	185	55	470
Vacant	1,610	300	605	115	35	2,660
All uses	7,600	2,550	2,645	840	1,535	15,175
Net change in land in particular use						
1986	5,700	2,415	865	320	-1,480	6,410
1987	5,770	2,465	640	340	-1,560	6,620
1988	6,255	2,775	850	400	-1,675	7,190

Note: Figures may not sum to totals owing to rounding.
Source: As Figure 1.4 above.

The UK Government is considering some measures to improve this situation. These include improved powers for local authorities to recover the costs of reclamation from private landowners and the imposition of a financial disincentive on the holding of derelict land, but no firm proposals have been made. Legislation was passed in 1988 to allow the opening of the English and Welsh Land Registry to public inspection but it did not take effect until December 1990. As only current ownership is recorded, it will remain difficult to identify previous owners responsible for dereliction or contamination. Although local authorities have the power to 'tidy-up' sites that are 'detrimental to amenity', it is rarely used as the costs must be borne by the authority until the owner can be traced and charged. In extreme cases this process could cost more than the reclamation itself.

Development and the design and construction of buildings

Built development clearly cannot be treated as a homogenous phenomenon. Its environmental impacts depend upon its density and pattern. Individual buildings are equally diverse. Urban buildings are significant for resource conservation in several ways. They directly consume raw materials and energy. The structure and management of services associated with urban buildings, especially water supply and sewerage, also affect the rate at which resources are consumed and wasted.

Building materials

The environmental problems associated with building materials are widespread. They include the production of brick, stone and aggregate, the manufacture, use, and disposal of paints, solvents and timber treatment products, the release of chlorofluoro-carbons (CFCs) and other ozone depleting chemicals (particularly in insulation and refrigeration) and the use of tropical hardwoods.[25]

Building materials production makes significant impacts. The production of aggregates (crushed rock, sand, and gravel) alone is estimated to have involved land-take exceeding 2,000 ha per year since 1987.[26] The production of brick and building stone adds to this figure. There are then the environmental costs involved in transporting 165 million tonnes of aggregate from quarries and pits to building sites. Transportation is equally troublesome in regard to the importation of building materials into Britain. It is estimated that Britain spends £8,000 per minute (£12m. per year) importing building materials, mainly engineered products, from abroad.[27]

Paints and timber treatments figure prominently in the specification of building products. The environmental risks associated with them fall into two broad categories: health risks and environmental damage. Health risks are presented to construction workers and occupants. Environmental damage can be caused by various forms of pollution during a toxic product's production, application, use and disposal. Even the disposal of treated timber is a problem since this can release preservatives into the environment. In West Germany, treated timber is defined as toxic waste and has to be buried in a licensed tip. In Canada, it has to be wrapped and sealed for transport and disposal. In Britain, little emphasis is given to minimising such hazards, and even where they arise, the reclamation of contaminated sites is to standards related only to the intended use, rather than to absolute levels of hazard.

The construction industry has been a significant user of CFCs in refrigeration and air conditioning, some insulation materials and fire protection. Many alternative insulation products without CFCs already exist. To match the thermal efficiency of CFC products, certain alternative insulation materials require more thickness which will alter the design and detailing of buildings.[28] In the vast majority of circumstances it is possible to substitute these alternatives and many architects and developers have already amended specifications to exclude CFC use. For air conditioning (which is estimated to account for 27 per cent of the CFCs used in the industry) it is preferable to avoid designs which are dependent on artificial systems. Buildings in urban areas tend to have higher demands for air conditioning owing to the urban heat island effect and design standards therefore need to be higher.

Britain is one of the largest consumers of tropical hardwoods in the developed world and the largest importer in Europe. In 1988 it was estimated that 50 per cent of tropical hardwood imported into the UK was used by the construction industry.[29] Joinery products including windows and panelled and flush doors have replaced softwood with an increasing reliance on tropical hardwood. Over two million doors were imported into Britain from tropical countries in 1989. Yet less than 0.2 per cent of all tropical moist forests are being managed sustainably.[30]

34

Architects and the construction industry need to be educated about the endangered tropical forests. They should diversify the materials used, specifying tropical timber only from sustainably managed sources, and where possible substituting temperate hard and soft woods. The Royal Institute of British Architects (RIBA) is promoting a certifications and labelling system for building materials.[31]

The European Parliament has agreed a series of pro-active measures to help protect tropical forests by controlling the timber trade. It is proposed that imports of timber from tropical countries which do not have a management and conservation plan should be phased out. Other controls and quotas are being considered to change the market conditions for timber products.[32]

Building design

The most effective mechanism for reducing many of the environmental impacts associated with building materials is to design for durability. Davidson and MacEwen argue for long-life, high-quality buildings that require little maintenance and are renewed at long intervals rather than low-quality structures involving high maintenance that are replaced more frequently.[33] It is acknowledged that the former will normally mean a higher capital cost and there may be a limited role for short-life building, using renewable and recyclable materials wherever possible. Although on conventional criteria there may be overriding advantages in demolishing a building before the end of its useful life, these have to be reconciled with the long-term interests of society in resource conservation.

Energy too can be conserved by the improved design, operation and durability of buildings. The variance in occupancy cost (the annual cost per unit area of running a building) can be a factor of three from the least to the most expensive design of a building. Running costs can also be reduced through extended use of development control criteria, building regulations, tax incentives and energy pricing policy. The criteria used in the development control process could include promotion of solar gain in individual buildings and in the development as a whole, the construction of arcades around buildings, and the provision of shelter against wind.

Yet, not only are buildings being built with short planned life-spans but existing buildings are deteriorating faster than they are replaced or rehabilitated. During the 1980s, private sector developments like those in London's Docklands, the limited number of housing-association projects and the more extensive public-sector programme of up-grading inter-war council estates have not kept pace with the deterioration of ageing buildings. Davidson and MacEwen called in 1983 for a major rehabilitation programme for older housing (in the face of a current emphasis on demolition) which would not only serve the interest of resource conservation but also be in line with social needs. Their arguments have been reflected more recently from several quarters, including the Association of District Councils.[34] However, public investment in new and rehabilitated housing has fallen during the decade, largely as a result of restrictions on capital expenditure by local authorities. The revitalisation of UK urban housing cannot be delayed for much longer. The *English House Condition Survey* of 1986 showed a marginal overall improvement in the housing stock from 1981, but this was largely the result of demolition of the worst properties and the addition of new properties, rather than resulting from effective action on improvement and rehabilitation.[35]

The issue of rehabilitation in the commercial and industrial sectors is more troublesome. Here there is a clear preference for new buildings. The problem is that the scope for re-use of redundant commercial and industrial buildings, most of which are located in the inner city, is limited. Many of them are multi-storey and it is improbable that they can be converted to accommodate firms of the size and type that abandoned them in favour of more floor space and a single-storey structure. The main hope for re-use of such properties lies with small industries, particularly as inner-city districts contain a high proportion of these firms. That successful regeneration of this type is possible is demonstrated by a number of projects such as Dean Clough Mill in Halifax, derelict in 1980 and now housing a range of uses including warehousing, banking and an arts workshop. The Civic Trust regeneration campaign is promoting similar small-scale initiatives in many towns. Residential uses are also possible as has been shown by the successful conversion of warehousing to residential use on Merseyside.

The Royal Institute of Chartered Surveyors (RICS) emphasises the potential value of the community enterprise approach whereby action is initiated by local people to generate economic development for the benefit of the local area. The RICS also argues that, although the costs of rehabilitation may be less, rebuilding can offer a longer building life, more lettable floor space and a higher rent.[36] However, the RICS has recognised the utter waste of constant rebuilding and does promote new building for long-life. In 1974 it gave a boost to the recycling of buildings in what became known as the 'long life, loose fit, low energy study'.[37] Adaptability in buildings is central to this approach, combining maximum adaptability with minimum need to replace.

Even today, few commercial developers show any interest in this aspect of building design. This is because it is relatively easy to demolish the shell and to rebuild to new specifications in 10 to 15 years time. A similarly wasteful attitude exists towards energy saving, which receives less than 1 per cent of total expenditure of such businesses.[38] Low-energy building can take many forms, the main aim being to reduce the reliance on fossil fuels and make the maximum use of natural energy sources. Traditional design principles include admitting sunlight (especially the winter sun), retarding heat loss through insulation, building in materials (like brick) which can retain heat, and using natural means of cooling and ventilation. This topic is further discussed in Chapter 3 on energy.

Increasing artificial heating and cooling are only part of the increasing mechanical control of the internal environment of sealed buildings. But this has been linked to the 'sick building syndrome' and has therefore raised questions of its implications for the health of the occupants. Artificial dry air conditioning systems use CFCs as a refrigerant, and their leakage contributes to ozone depletion. Wet air conditioning, on the other hand, can be linked to legionella, and recently the Chartered Institute of Building Services Engineers spoke out in favour of decreasing dependence on what it suggested were unnecessarily high levels of use of artificial air conditioning.[39]

The environmental problems posed by building materials and design can be addressed to a significant extent through the extension of building regulations (relating to both design and materials) to cover environmentally damaging materials and issues such as energy efficiency and building life-span.*

In addition, the regulations must be extended to cover all new buildings while existing buildings should be brought within the system but at lower thresholds. The regulations could be applied at sale or other transfer.

The development process

A wasteful attitude towards buildings is very much part of the current urban value system, which promotes rapid change in an accelerating cycle of redevelopment. While recognising that professionals are under pressure from their clients to produce an economic building style, there is an opportunity also for education of the client. The process is complex, and many interests are involved, including those of investors, developers, owners, tenants and users. The decisions of all these groups influence the quality of a building and how well it is maintained. The fragmented nature of the development process, which often separates design, construction and assembly, further complicates the application of a long-life approach.

Translated into costs, the long-life approach implies buildings whose capital costs are high in relation to their running costs in maintenance and energy use. At present, in the trade-off between capital and running costs, decisions favour low capital costs. The division of interest in the building process in part accounts for this. Investors and landlord owners are relatively unconcerned about running costs (unless these are so high that a building is unlettable or unsaleable) and are more interested in keeping initial costs down. The public sector, for different reasons, is also under pressure to reduce capital costs. Life-cycle costing, which trades off the capital against the running costs of buildings, should be integrated into this process. Current costing

---

*   During 1990 the Buildings Research Establishment has brought forward proposals for a system of environmental labelling of buildings, but the standards proposed are neither statutory nor adequately stringent.

methods, based on high discount rates, reduce the value of the future benefits compared to the present costs. Pearce and his colleagues argue that a compensatory factor should be introduced into project appraisal where future environmental costs are involved.[40] This condition is met in building construction in that environmental costs such as high energy use or frequent demand for more building materials result.

A recent phenomenon is that both tenants and users of commercial buildings are demanding a greater say in the development process with the result that the developers are becoming increasingly responsive to end-user demands. In Sweden, Germany and Holland, the developer has no effective power at all, being almost wholly responsive to the consumer. In Sweden, for example, every employer has to consult his workforce through the works council, providing them with the opportunity to comment on the design of their building. This process tends to favour designs with lower running costs and those which minimise hazards to the user. However, it cannot be guaranteed to produce the best environmental design (for example, in terms of timber specification) and thus this consumer-led approach needs to be complemented by regulation.

Resource conservation is not the only reason for conserving existing buildings. Buildings of architectural and historic interest are a valued part of the existing building stock. The Council of Europe argues strongly for rehabilitation of buildings for new uses as a way of conserving the historical heritage.[41]

Although the Environment White Paper of September 1990 gave emphasis to heritage conservation and a higher priority to buildings in historic town centres, this only involves a shift of priority within the grants made through English Heritage for repair and restoration.

A general emphasis on rehabilitation rather than rebuilding on the other hand would not only reduce direct threats to the built heritage but make it more likely that historic buildings survive in a harmonious setting. Frequent rebuilding is also disturbing in social and functional terms. City dwellers have made it plain over the last few decades, in their opposition to redevelopment schemes and new roads, that familiar surroundings, the known network of schools, shops and community ties, are of intrinsic value. A desirable characteristic of sustainable urban development would therefore be robustness, respecting the need for continuity in our urban surroundings.

The city also needs older buildings because of the need to provide the venue for the many 'downtown' activities that are essential to its commercial vitality but which cannot support the market rent of new accommodation.[42] Thus diversity needs to be maintained.

The policy framework

The existing policy framework for the built environment can be divided into two areas: planning policies and public investment policies, including housing and inner-city policy. None of these provide for planning the development of the infrastructure, yet much progress towards the sustainable development of the built environment can be achieved through the provision of an infrastructure which can guide the density and pattern of development.

Central government's policy on urban development is restricted geographically to fifty-seven Urban Programme authorities and ten Urban Development Areas (UDAs) which are perceived as having severe urban problems. Yet in these areas public money is being used to enhance and encourage the processes and forms of development criticised in this chapter and in Chapter 7 below. Urban Programme funding, distributed through local authorities, failed in most cases even to replace losses in rate support grant and, moreover, has been reduced during the 1980s. Its remnants have been directed at economic development rather than social goals.

Urban Development Corporations (UDCs) have a lamentable record in that they have consistently promoted development which fails to meet local needs, and which encourages car-borne journeys.[43] In the London Docklands Development area the UDC has promoted developments based on creating office accommodation including Canary Wharf and a large shopping centre. City Grant,* paid by central

---

*   The City Grant scheme was introduced in 1988, amalgamating three previous grant schemes. It is bid for by developers for private sector projects in inner cities which would 'not otherwise go ahead'.

government to developers, is used to promote similar schemes outside UDAs. The Docklands UDC's investment in transport infrastructure has been limited, but several major road-building projects have been justified in terms of improving Docklands' accessibility, including the controversial East London River Crossing and Britain's most expensive road: the two-mile Limehouse Link. Environmental criteria are rarely if ever used to assess grant applications under any of these programmes, and the introduction of such criteria, both to the process and to the end-use, should be a high priority.

Sherlock laments central government's lack of a comprehensive policy on urban development. He argues that while local government is decentralising certain Town Hall activities to neighbourhood offices, it is impossible for them to prevent the general trend towards centralisation of other activities, public and private.[44] To resist this trend, local authorities need both guidance and support from Whitehall. At present, the government is ambivalent, supporting local authority rejection of some projects which threaten local centres, allowing others to go through on appeal, and rarely giving guidance that is fully informed by environmental concerns.

On the other side of the coin, housing densities are being kept low, actively through planning policies and passively through increased emphasis on private sector provision. Low housing densities increase the impacts of the centralisation of other facilities primarily through increasing the relative attractiveness of car travel. The new unitary development plans now being drawn up by District and Borough Councils in the cities seem likely to continue to rule out developments at desirable densities of 150 people per acre, 50 per cent above the maximum permitted by many councils, thus removing the opportunity to regenerate close-knit urban communities and the local facilities that depend on high concentrations of people. UK Government policy is that:

> land in urban areas should be used to meet as much as possible of the demand for sites for new housing...(but this) should not mean the disappearence of the playing fields and green spaces which every town and city needs.[45]

Yet the issue of density is not even discussed.

Many aspects of sustainable urban development can be achieved only by planned intervention in the urban environment. However, at the strategic level, there has been far too little research to draw firm conclusions about the resource implications of different sized and differently planned settlements, or of alternative land-use patterns and densities.

Owens does, however, provide some pointers:[46]

> The most consistent feature of land use patterns found to be inherently energy efficient (in that they reduce the need for travel and space heating) is relatively low physical separation of activities, achieved by moderately high densities and some decentralisation and clustering of employment and services. These characteristics are also compatible with district heating and public transport (especially if high *linear* densities are used), and need not preclude the use of passive solar energy.

She goes on to specify one important caveat:[47]

> The land use patterns identified provide a necessary but not a sufficient condition for energy savings; it cannot be taken for granted that individuals will take advantage of the opportunity to travel less. ... The important point is that certain land-use patterns provide the *potential* for energy saving, whether or not this is realised, and are in this sense robust.

Brown and Jacobsen quote a study of US cities by Newman and Kenworthy which compares gasoline use per capita with an 'activity intensity' index (a measure of the number of residents plus jobs per hectare). These show a direct negative relationship:[48]

> Residents of Houston and Phoenix ... consume nearly twice as much gasoline per capita as do residents of New York, a

metropolitan area with double the number of people and
jobs per hectare.

An element of this use is explained by the increasing proportion of
commuters and more could be explained by the increased commuting
distances. The differences between inner cities and suburbs are even
greater. Denver's (suburban) residents use more than eleven times as
much gasoline as Manhattan's! Yet even the use in Manhattan is only
equivalent to an *average* European urban resident's consumption.

Such evidence therefore suggests that planners should aim for
compactness and integration of land uses, for some degree of
'self-containment' at the urban and intra-urban scale, and for
compatibility with a range of possible future energy supply options in
all developments. The changes to planning policy required are
fundamental but not difficult. The most effective change would be a
removal of the presumption in favour of development on greenfield
sites (including designated public open space in cities). This would
increase pressure to re-use derelict land and buildings, and assist local
authorities in guiding development to appropriate locations. It would
also act as an incentive to direct development towards less congested
cities. Development on greenfield sites would not be halted, but
controlled more effectively so that it did not threaten sustainable urban
development, particularly in terms of energy consumption.

In both the USA and Denmark, some serious attempts have been
made at integrating energy considerations into planning. In Portland,
Oregon and Davis, California, for example, land-use planning policies
aim explicitly at energy conservation through more compact
development, encouragement of public and non-motorised transport,
guiding growth to energy-efficient locations in the city or city region
and controls over spatial structure at the local scale involving siting,
orientation and lay-out.

Growth which does occur should be accommodated in settlements
that can accept it (in environmental terms), and where it can make
environmentally beneficial infrastructure investments more economical
because of increased population. This would be assisted by the change
in presumption, but stronger regional planning is also required. We
support the call made by Davidson and MacEwen for a new type of

framework at the strategic level to guide the development of towns and cities into a future of more uncertain resource supplies and to provide the basis for day-to-day urban management:[49]

> The new strategies would combine conventional Structure Plan policies for land use, economic and social development, transport and environment with policies for the conservation of energy and other resources used and wasted by urban areas. This would require some statutory change in the present Structure Plan remit to allow policy-making on the use of resources other than land. Techniques of resource-auditing and budgeting, already used by some local authorities, would need to be developed further to provide an information base for new style resource strategies ... The need is to disseminate much more widely the 'best practice' on linking development with resource-conservation.

Resource-conservation strategies and the assessment of planning proposals on grounds of 'conservation performance' could help to guide urban change towards sustainability and solve current conflicts between urban regeneration and the dispersal of people, investment and jobs from the larger cities. A new framework for planning and investment at regional and national levels is required to co-ordinate the approach to urban regeneration and the husbanding of resources through development plans with significantly expanded scope.

However, UK Government proposals for a new framework for development planning are based on a perceived need to streamline the system. The proposed changes are to a system of statutory district development plans, county structure plans simply outline county policies and regional guidance to coordinate approaches to strategic issues. Such a system could be compatible with the proposals outlined above, but there is little evidence of the political will needed to impose and resource appropriate statutory duties and to provide adequate national and regional guidance.

Such an extension of the scope of development planning should be paralleled by extended scope in development control decisions. It would be ludicrous if the development plan attempted to direct land use in ways that conserved energy, but the development control decision was unable to consider energy conservation as a 'material consideration'. This is the second fundamental change, in that planning legislation must be reformed to require development control to consider non-land-use matters, particularly those environmental concerns relating to design. One advantage of using the development control process to consider environmental concerns is that conditions can be applied which relate to the specific development. If these changes are to be effective, however, enforcement of planning control and conditions must be made more effective.

However, the demise of regional planning, the streamlining of strategic planning, the relaxation of development control and the lack of resources have left the planning system in a poor state to tackle the needs of sustainable urban development. Failure to correct this situation will leave us with resource-intensive and inflexible patterns of development in a future of resource constraints.

Conclusion

Cities have great capacity to be more resourceful. Yet contemporary cities have developed with densities, patterns and building designs that fly in the face of resource conservation. Cities are also about bringing people together. The city as a focus of social activity must retain its concentration of people and diversity of activities without which the whole point of urban living is lost.

The implications for design and planning are clear. High density and integrated land use not only conserve resources but provide for a compactness that encourages social interaction. Decentralised concentration can provide for the effective development of local centres. Buildings themselves require sensitive design, using materials that are less environmentally damaging and more energy efficient, and structures conducive to continuity and adaptability. Urban design integrated with nature can both save resources and allow city dwellers to enjoy a more natural environment.

References

1. Sherlock, H., *Cities Are Good For Us: The case for high densities, friendly streets, local shops and public transport*, Transport 2000, London, 1990, p53.
2. Jacobs, J., *The Death and Life of Great American Cities*, Pelican, London, 1965.
3. Sherlock, *op. cit.*
4. Goode, D., *Interview transcript*, June, 1989.
5. Sherlock, *op. cit.*
6. London Planning Advisory Committee, *Strategic Planning Advice for London*, LPAC, Romford, 1988.
7. Freeman, H., *Mental Health and the Environment*, Churchill Livingstone, London, 1984.
8. Milner-Holland, E., *Report of the Committee on Housing in Greater London*, Cmnd 2605, HMSO, London, 1965; Gandy, M., *A political geography of Islington*, Unpublished BA dissertation, Cambridge University, 1988.
9. Goodchild, B., 'Housing layout, housing quality and residential density', *Housing Review*, Vol. 33, No. 4, 1984.
10. Jacobs, *op. cit.*; Newman, O., *Defensible Space*, Macmillan, New York, 1972; Coleman, A., *Utopia on Trial*, Hilary Shipman, London, 1985; Thomas, M., 'A future turned sour', *New Ground*, No. 17, 1988.
11. Deelstra, T., 'An ecological approach to planning cities', *Town and Country Planning*, April pp. 105-7, 1988.
12. Auhagen, A., *Personal communication*, 1989.
13. Tibbalds, F., *Interview transcript*, July 1989.
14. Cadman, D., (ed.), *The Living City*, Routledge, London, 1989, 'Introduction'.
15. Hillman, J., 'The importance of the street': paper presented to Town and Country Planning Association conference on *British towns and the quality of life*, London, 28 November 1989.
16. Hough, M. *City Form and Natural Process*, Croom Helm, London, 1984.
17. Chisholm, M., and Kivell, P., *Inner City Waste Land*, Institute of Economic Affairs, London, 1987, p19.
18. Joseph, S., *Urban Wasteland Now*, Civic Trust, London, 1987.

19. Department of Environment, *Review of Derelict Land Policy*, DoE, London, 1989.
20. Chisholm and Kivell, *op. cit*, p56.
21. Department of Environment, *op. cit.*
22. Council of Europe, *Environment and Regeneration of the Industrial City in Europe*, Urban Renaissance in Europe Study Series No. 30, Council of Europe, Strasbourg, 1986.
23. Commission of the European Communities, *Green paper on the urban environment*, COM (90) 218 final, Commission of the European Communities, Brussels, 1990.
24. Department of Environment, *op. cit*, p.7.
25. Lorch, R., *What are you doing about the environment?*, Junior Liaison Organisation, London, 1989.
26. Based on figures from the British Aggregate Construction Materials Industry, *Statistical Yearbook 1988*, BACMI, London, 1989.
27. BBC TV *Panorama*, 'Built in Britain, Made Abroad', 26 June 1989.
28. Curwell, S.R., Fox, R.C., and March, C.G., *The use of CFCs in Buildings*, Friends of the Earth, London, 1988.
29. Counsell, S., *Good Wood Guide*, 2nd edn, Friends of the Earth, London, 1990.
30. *Ibid.*
31. Royal Institute of British Architects, *Environmental policy statement*, RIBA, London, 1990.
32. Counsell, *op. cit.*
33. Davidson, J., and MacEwen, A., 'The Livable City' in *The Conservation and Development Programme for the UK*, Kogan Page, London, 1983.
34. Association of District Councils, *Meeting Housing Needs*, ADC, London, 1989.
35. Department of the Environment, *English House Condition Survey 1986*, HMSO, London, 1988.
36. Royal Institute of Chartered Surveyors, *Rehabilitation or new buildings?*, RICS Report.
37. Gordon, A., 'Architects and resource conservation', *Journal of the Royal Institute of British Architects*, Vol. 81, No. 1, 1974.
38. Duffy, F., *Interview transcript*, July 1989.
39. 'Install natural ventilation where possible – CIBSE', *Heating and Ventilating News*, 13 May 1989.

40. Pearce, D., Markandya, A., and Barbier, E., *Blueprint for a Green Economy*, Earthscan, London, 1989.
41. Council of Europe, *Heritage and Successful Town Regeneration*, Architectural Heritage Reports and Studies, No. 14, Council of Europe, Strasbourg, 1989.
42. Sherlock, *op. cit.*
43. McLaren, D.P., *Action for People*, Friends of the Earth, London, 1989.
44. Sherlock, *op. cit.*
45. *This Common Inheritance*, CM1200, HMSO, London, 1990
46. Owens, S., 'Energy Demand: Links to Land Use and Forward Planning', *Built Environment*, Vol.11 No.1, 1985, pp. 33-44.
47. *Ibid.*
48. Brown, L. and Jacobsen, J., *The Future of Urbanization: Facing the ecological and economic constraints*, Worldwatch Paper 77, New York, 1987, p. 17.
49. Davidson and MacEwen, *op. cit.*, pp. 135-6.

Chapter 2: Transport

Introduction

Sustainable urban development must enable access to the facilities and services of the city while minimising the resultant external costs. A transport system *can* be developed which would make life more enjoyable through meeting travel needs while lowering the risk and fear of road accidents, limiting damage to the environment, conserving finite resources, giving value for money, extending opportunities for groups in the population with low personal mobility, and generally promoting healthy life-styles.

The present

The current intrusion of motorised traffic on living in the city cannot be overstated, whether it be in the form of noise, fumes or danger. Global warming is increasingly being fuelled by traffic emissions of carbon dioxide[1], while finite resources are depleted unsustainably to provide roads, vehicles and fossil fuel.

Nonetheless, it remains the conventional wisdom that the growth of road transport (and increase in the capacity of the country's infrastructure to accommodate this growth) reflects a quasi-natural evolutionary process, with high material benefits. It is further assumed that other improvements in the quality of life of the population come in the wake of this growth. This can be described as a demand-led and promotion-oriented approach to transport policy.[2] Table 2.1 and Figure 2.1 indicate the growth in road transport which has occurred since 1978, particularly when compared with that of rail. This is a continuation of

Table 2.1:   Passenger transport in Britain (1978-88)

Estimated billion passenger kilometres

	1978	1981	1984	1986	1988
Road					
public service vehicles	50	42	42	41	41
private transport[1]	378	410	441	471	523
pedal cycles	5	5	6	5	5
Rail	35	34	35	37	41
Air	3	3	3	4	5
Total	471	494	527	558	614

Note 1:   This includes cars, motorcycles and taxis.
Source: Department of Transport, *Transport Statistics, Great Britain, 1978-1988*, HMSO, London, 1989.

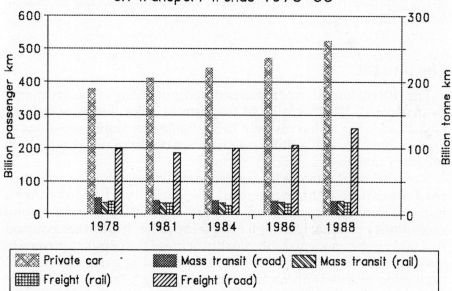

Figure 2.1
UK transport trends 1978–88

Source: As Table 2.1 above.

the general post-war trend and the Department of Transport predicts that these trends will continue.[3]

The Department's 'optimistic' high-growth forecast envisages an increase in road traffic of 142 per cent by 2025. The low-growth forecast envisages 83 per cent growth. These increases are comprised entirely of car and lorry traffic. No increase is forecast for public transport. A very small proportion of the increase is expected to result from increasing population, and most will be due to continued growth in the number and length of journeys made. Since 1962 the average length of journeys to work has increased by 40 per cent.[4] However, for some time the validity of Department of Transport forecasts has been widely questioned because of their suspect methodology and narrow perspective.[5]

The basic criticism of the forecasting models is that they are self-fulfilling, in that the construction of roads in response to a forecast encourages traffic to increase and fulfil the forecast.[6] The Department of Transport's forecasters envisage traffic growth stopping only when car ownership reaches 'saturation level'. However, continued road building after that point would actually encourage even more car *use*. If saturation were achieved there would be about twice as many cars in the country, and there would still be almost 20 million people without cars.

That road building encourages car use is accepted even by the Society of Motor Manufacturers and Traders:[7]

> A continuing major road-building programme is fundamental to our livelihoods and is one area of public expenditure which the Government could increase without damage to our economic recovery ... It would mean lower operating costs for the whole of industry, *more incentive for people to buy and use cars*, and more bypasses to keep lorries and other traffic away from congested towns and villages, and of course more jobs for the construction industry. (emphasis added)

Such a view confuses ends and means. Yet it is still largely shared by the Department of Transport. Although they no longer see their forecasts as targets, and argue that 'there will be cases where on economic or environmental grounds it is neither practicable nor desirable to meet the demand by road building, for example in city centres'[8], the principle of reducing road capacity for traffic is still outside their policy.

Adams provides a strong image based on the Department's growth expectations:[9]

> ... another 27.5 million vehicles would form a queue 104,000 miles long. This could be accommodated, if stationary, on a new motorway stretching from London to Edinburgh, if it were 257 lanes wide. [The need for parking] doubles the size of the new motorway/parking lot we require to 514 lanes. To accommodate existing vehicles as well would require 944 lanes ... [And] the national parking lot required by a Britain saturated with vehicles ... would require paving an area over twice the size of Berkshire.

The new traffic forecasts envisage a level of car ownership higher than that currently prevailing in Los Angeles. And it is inconceivable that this level of car ownership could be accommodated in Britain without Los Angeles-style land use. Whilst many engineers and planners still see traffic forecasts as inexorable, desirable traffic levels should be decided first and the transport system designed to produce those levels.

Increasing demands for access to goods and services have generated travel and, other things being equal, will continue to do so. There has been a strong relationship between gross domestic product (GDP) (resulting from aspirations for increasing consumption) and the amount of travel undertaken and generated. For many years the growth rates of GDP and tonnes-miles of freight in Britain have been almost identical.[10]

With economic growth, and more money to be spent, there come all sorts of desires which tend to blow the old, dense city apart as people want larger gardens, swimming pools and more space for both living and working. The danger is that these aspirations will continue to go unchallenged. As long as people can *pretend* that everyone can have these things without imposing costs on others, it appears that this is the course that they will continue to pursue. But these demands should not lead us to cater for increasing traffic levels. The modal split of transport can be altered to reduce its environmental impacts and, more fundamentally, the relationship between freight movement and GDP can be broken by increasing local economic self-reliance (this concept is discussed at greater length in Chapter 7) thus decreasing the distance travelled by goods.

The effects of traffic in the city

Large volumes of traffic, and the resulting noise and air pollution, do not just lower the quality of the environment for people living and working in the city. The demand for roads eats into the city's public open space.[11] Furthermore, in many urban situations traffic intrudes to the extent that it forces alterations in people's behaviour and attitudes.

The rising volume and speed of traffic has created an environment in which young children in particular have sustained a dramatic loss of independence as parents have increasingly felt obliged to impose restrictions on them. This is understandable in the context of the UK's pedestrian fatality rate for children, which is the highest in Europe.[12] It has resulted in a considerable loss of freedom for individuals, compared to that enjoyed by their parents and even more by their grandparents. At the same time, the need to be constantly under the supervision of an adult is limiting on the development of the child, infringing on its independence and autonomy which are so important in the early years of life. Hillman argues that:[13]

> able-bodied adults accompanying able-bodied children because of fear is one of the more disturbing and wasteful by-products of the motorised society.

The 10-14 age group, on the other hand, has managed to maintain independence from parents in its travel patterns. It is in fact the only group whose travel patterns have not altered significantly since 1945. It is also the only group whose accident rate has not been significantly reduced in the last decade.[14] This demonstrates the increased risk exposure associated with more (and in many cases faster flowing) traffic which has forced changes in most groups' travel patterns.

Pensioners are another disadvantaged group. Their generally low access to a car is reflected in a greater dependence on walking and public transport. As pedestrians they too are at great risk:[15]

> ... the fatality rate, both per head of population and per mile walked is many times higher among old people, alarmingly so among those over 75 years of age.

Hillman points to some of the difficulties faced by pedestrians:[16]

> The lives of pedestrians, especially children and old people, are put at risk by the fact that the 'pavement network' for them is interrupted at every road intersection. Few pedestrian precincts have been created, but in any case pedestrians are rarely confined in their movements to such restricted areas, and on major roads, detours to crossings, footbridges and underpasses, which are rarely cleaned or policed, are necessary. It is noteworthy that about one in seven pedestrian casualties occurs on pedestrian crossings.

It is not surprising that the effect of increasing traffic volumes is to decrease social contacts within streets. In a study of three similar streets in San Francisco, traffic levels were inversely correlated with the number of friends and acquaintances each person had within the street[17] (see Figure 2.2). And the impact of traffic is not just confined to the street: it intrudes right into people's homes, effectively dictating the allocation of rooms in a dwelling according to the outside noise level, and obliging people to keep their windows closed.[18] Hillman underlines the cost to community life from ever increasing traffic levels:[19]

> Wide roads and streams of motor vehicles destroy the function of the street as a locus for social interaction and break community ties ... the residential street used to be the traditional play space and social milieu for children and

Figure 2.2: Social effects of heavy traffic

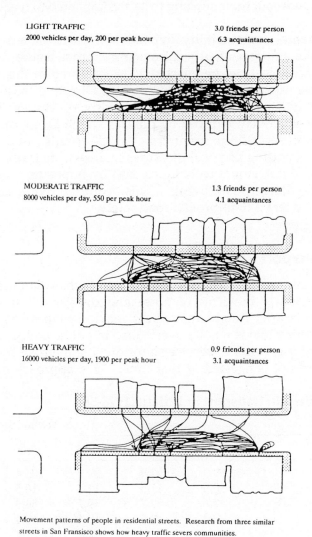

LIGHT TRAFFIC
2000 vehicles per day, 200 per peak hour

3.0 friends per person
6.3 acquaintances

MODERATE TRAFFIC
8000 vehicles per day, 550 per peak hour

1.3 friends per person
4.1 acquaintances

HEAVY TRAFFIC
16000 vehicles per day, 1900 per peak hour

0.9 friends per person
3.1 acquaintances

Movement patterns of people in residential streets. Research from three similar
streets in San Fransisco shows how heavy traffic severs communities.

Source: Appleyard, D., and Lintell, M., in *American Institute of Planners' Journal*,
March 1972, pp. 84-101.

provided an introduction for them to a world beyond their family, without their needing to be accompanied to reach it.

Environmental sustainability depends (in part) on reducing the environmental impacts of urban transport. Strict legislation on air pollution (and noise) can be enacted. The first step in this direction should be the rapid implementation of EEC Directives requiring the fitting of catalytic converters to new petrol-driven vehicles. Pollution can be more effectively reduced by policies which *reduce* car use and thus help to conserve finite resources. Vehicle speeds can be lowered substantially by using physical measures in area-wide traffic calming, by improved enforcement techniques, and by imposing more severe penalties for dangerous driving. This would provide significant by-products in terms of improved road safety.

Freight transport

The externalities of freight traffic are much higher than those of car travel, particularly in terms of noise and danger. It is therefore necessary to restrict freight movement inside urban areas to social hours, something that is wholly overlooked in public policy where it is assumed that it is better to service shops outside the rush hours since the roads are not congested at that time. This approach effectively

Table 2.2: Freight transport in Britain (1978-88)

(Billion-tonne-kilometres)

	1978	1981	1984	1986	1988
Road	99.3	92.9	99.9	105.4	130.2
Rail	20.0	17.5	12.7	16.5	18.0
Water[a]	47.6	52.7	59.7	54.8	60.9
Pipelines	9.8	9.3	10.4	10.4	10.8
Total	176.7	172.4	182.7	187.1	219.9

Note a: Inland waterway traffic comprises only a small fraction of this total.
Source: As Table 2.1 above.

means that lorries are travelling at night or early morning when people are sleeping. However, if the demand for personalised motor travel was reduced, roads would be freed for servicing shops at convenient times.

Table 2.2 and Figure 2.1 show the current national trends in freight transport. Although actual volumes of rail freight have increased since 1984 reflecting increased economic activity, the relative decline of rail use compared to roads has continued. Yet the environmental costs of road freight are high. Table 2.3 gives West German figures which show that environmental impacts in terms of pollution, danger and land-take are all higher for lorry use. (Figure 2.3 presents these figures graphically).

In fact, much of the transport of freight could be by rail, using small, quiet delivery vehicles only for transfer to shops and households. Retailers, however, are concerned only with transport costs, not with the type of vehicle which has to be employed. The argument of the

Table 2.3: The comparative impact of road (lorry) and rail freight (West Germany)

	units per tonne km	
	Road	Rail
Carbon dioxide	0.22kg	0.05kg
Oxides of nitrogen	3.60g	0.22g
Carbon monoxide	1.58g	0.07g
Hydrocarbons	0.81g	0.05g
Particulates (respirable)	0.27g	0.03g
Sulphur dioxide	0.23g	0.33g
Accidents (persons injured per billion tonne km)	248	10
Land-take (m^2 per tonne km per year)	0.007	0.0025

Note: The figures given are the average for West Germany in 1987: thus the rail figures relate to a mix of electrified and diesel trains and include the pollution impacts of electricity generation.

Source: Taufel, D., *The social costs of road transport of goods*, UPI report No. 14, Heidelberg, 1989.

Figure 2.3
Impacts of freight transport

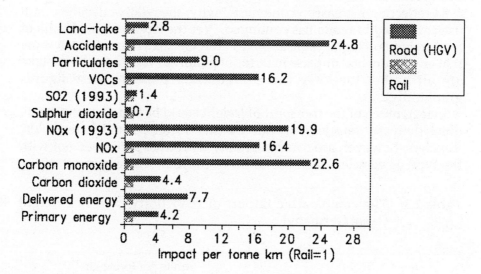

Source: As Table 2.3 above.

retailers is that by the nature of operations (big centralised depots, big lorries) they reduce lorry mileage. Adams comments:[20]

> The Department of Transport and the road haulage industry present bigger lorries as an environmental improvement. They say bigger means fewer. The department has just produced new forecasts which show that traffic levels for all sizes of lorry will increase, with the largest increase for the largest lorries. By the year 2025, there will be more than three and a half times as much juggernaut traffic as there is now.

These forecasts, however, may be underestimates. The effects of measures relating to the Single European Market, such as the removal of frontier controls and increased competition in the road haulage business, will be to reduce the relative costs of road freight. This could double road freight kilometres by the year 2000.[21] Measures to shift long-haul freight to rail must be made a high priority.

In cities the situation is more complex. Indeed, commercial vehicles are the life-blood of a city, but they must be designed to fit the streets in which they are collecting or delivering. They should be small city-friendly vehicles which can be given priority on the roads, perhaps by allowing them to use, in off-peak periods, bus lanes from which cars are excluded all day. Ideally, car traffic could be reduced even more. This could benefit industry: the Confederation of British Industry (CBI) claims that industry loses £15 billion per year as a result of delays caused by urban traffic congestion.[22] One dimension of city-friendliness is reduced noise levels. Manufacturers need incentives (whether by regulation, tax or subsidy) to bring forward lower-noise vehicles. The process has begun elsewhere in Europe with some success. In the Netherlands the testing method was tightened in 1984, and the manufacturers responded rapidly.[23]

Although transport costs have risen, they have risen at a slower rate than production costs have fallen. Companies that have embraced centralisation have largely increased their transport costs, but their overall production costs are much lower because of compensating savings in factors such as property and labour costs. The key is the differential costs between bulk haul – getting raw materials to the plant – and distribution of goods. With the development of the road network and bigger lorries, the relative costs of distribution have gone down vis-à-vis bulk haul and that has made it attractive to use fewer centres of production. There have been corresponding land-use effects with the advent of locations with cheaper land, labour and development costs, which also tend to be away from rail or water access. They must therefore be served by road for raw material delivery as well.

This situation is a direct result of government policy, which is aimed at reducing freight costs per mile. To reverse this trend the relative costs of distribution need to be increased by severe restrictions on lorries, except the small, specialised lorries suited to the urban environment.

However, for inter-city travel, the damaging effects of road transport of freight are relatively easily avoidable. Lessons can be learned from other countries on how to encourage the use of rail for freight: the proportion of goods carried by rail rather than road is nearly three times higher in France and Germany than in Britain. Although journeys are generally longer, the use of rail is encouraged in Germany by permitting the use of the largest lorries only if the majority of the journey is made by rail. In addition, the levels of public investment in railways are significantly higher. * Thus urban rail-heads, where transfers between modes would be made, need to be protected. The current habit of treating them as derelict, and offering public subsidies for their redevelopment, threatens their future strategic use.

In sum, whether freight or passenger transport, short-distance travel by rail should be cheap and attractive and the relative cost of longer-distance travel should increase at least linearly to fully reflect increasing environmental costs. Thus we require the reverse of the current situation where, as distance increases, cost per mile decreases.

Economic incentives

A great myth exists in regard to the taxes that road users pay. It is in fact untrue that they more than pay for what they take: account must also be taken of the cost of accidents and other forms of damage to society such as damage to buildings, contributions to acid rain, global warming, and so on. A recent German study showed that the costs which lorries impose on society in terms of pollution, noise, vibration, accidents and demands on road space outweigh their direct financial contribution by eight times.[25] As a result, economic disincentives to road use need to be increased.

---

*   British government estimated investment in 1989-90 is £689m. (0.2% of GDP); the French government's estimated investment for 1990 is £1,062m. (0.27% of GDP) and the West German government's estimated investment for 1990 is £1,662m. (0.34% of GDP).[24]

These should complement the effects of strong planning. The tax on fuel could be increased, as could the more generalised taxes on vehicles or vehicle use, import duties and other taxes payable on first registration, and annual licence fees. In the longer term there is much to favour a generalised approach, such as an increased fuel tax, in preference to the other method most often discussed, that of road pricing,* which is a selective approach designed to tackle a symptom of the traffic problem. Hillman believes that road pricing is advocated from[26]

> the point of view of congestion in the city centre; that [traffic restraint] is needed in the city centre or in central areas of the city, but not in the suburbs or in rural areas. This is not the case because the issue is not so much congestion as all the other externalities, danger, pollution and so on. Why only regard one element in the whole process, congestion, and say that that is why road pricing is required?
>
> Squeezing the car out of the inner city ... to the suburbs engenders a series of responses which ultimately result in a transport system whose external benefits will accrue mostly to motorists and whose external costs will bear most heavily on those without cars.

Such responses, notably corporate sector decentralisation, have been seen previously as a response to factors, including congestion, alongside the high costs of central locations. Increasing development of out-of-town retailing, employment and distribution centres has increased car use overall. In theory, however, road pricing, coupled with stringent development control in and around the suburbs, could reduce car use. However:[27]

---

* Road pricing involves charging the user of a road or roads (normally those of the central area of a city) an additional fee.

> If the squeezing is to stand any chance of increasing the use
> of public transport ... the most obvious way to ensure this is
> to make the squeezing pervasive, not geographically or
> temporally specific ... The main problem [in the city] is too
> many cars. The solution is to reduce their number, not to
> drive them out to the suburbs.

The city is the *focus* of a much larger hinterland. Therefore, the city's
transport problems cannot be addressed in isolation from the
surrounding transport system. Improved road links between cities
increase the pressure on urban areas. Ironically transport planners often
refer to people as captive to public transport. We may in the future have
to refer to the opposite, and worry about people who are captives to the
car, people out there in dispersed suburbia without access to affordable
petrol, and stranded in the absence of public transport!

While some advocate shifting all taxes on to fuel, there are advantages
in a double, vehicle and fuel, tax, if for no other reason than the problem
of parking the 50-odd million vehicles forecast. Lester has suggested
that in the short term both vehicle (ownership and use) and road taxes
are required as part of a strategic approach to traffic restraint.[28] Initially
it will prove difficult to raise fuel and vehicle taxes enough to affect
access problems within cities without disastrous short-term effects on
rural areas. Lester therefore argues that:[29]

> In the short term, road pricing offers the opportunity to
> address urban congestion, while at the same time starting to
> slowly increase fuel and vehicle taxes, recognising that these
> go hand-in-hand with land use changes, just as road pricing
> goes hand-in-hand with improvements in public transport.

Thus road pricing is only of value if it forms part of a package of
transport policy reforms which ensure that it does not simply shift the
undesirable impacts of traffic from one location to another. The other
elements may include increased taxation on fuel and on vehicles.

In Hong Kong in 1982 the government doubled the tax payable on the
first registration of a private car or motorcycle, and trebled the annual
licence fee for such vehicles. Today, the first registration tax is

comparable to the price of a new car and the annual licence fee amounts to roughly one tenth of this price. Since the increases were implemented the number of licensed private cars has fallen from over 190,000 to about 140,000, or about one car per 25 persons. (This compares with a level of about one car per three persons in London.) In Singapore additional licence fees have been introduced for the central area. The Organisation for Economic Co-operation and Development (OECD) estimate that between 1975 and 1982 this avoided the need for £420m. investment in road 'improvements' and restricted car ownership to 60 per cent of the level it would otherwise have achieved.[30]

Car ownership can also be directly discouraged. Denmark has doubled the price of a new car through increased taxes. Such taxes can be applied differentially to discourage people from buying larger cars. Smaller cars use less resources, take up less space and create less pollution.

While discussing economic incentives the issue of company cars must also be addressed. In 1982, almost 40 per cent of all car trips to central London were made by company cars, while over 70 per cent of such car trips received some form of company assistance. This is given an incentive by taxation policy which provides tax-relief on the cost of buying and running vehicles for 'business purposes'.[31] Despite reductions in these incentives in the 1988 and 1989 budgets, company car use is still encouraged. Removing such traffic from city centres, by reducing the incentives for its use and by restricting the availability of parking, could contribute significantly to improving the urban environment.

Whatever the measures adopted, particular complementary measures must be taken to ensure that people with mobility handicaps (who currently are exempt from Vehicle Excise Duty) are not discriminated against.

Car ownership and use

It is important to distinguish between car use and car ownership. We are not suggesting that ownership should be banned, but that over-use should be discouraged. Driving to work in the city represents the most obvious example of socially irresponsible car use. Nearly 50 per cent of all car mileage takes place on urban roads, and if urban motorway journeys were included, the figure would be higher. Apart from not being energy-efficient, urban driving is one of the most polluting ways of driving a car. Yet in the UK, company-car subsidies encourage such use of cars. In Paris, on the other hand, public transport season tickets are subsidised.

Discouraging car use is likely to lead to a decrease in car ownership, reversing the trend of increasing car ownership encouraging increasing car use and increasing expenditure on roads (which encourages further increased ownership and use):[32]

> In the last 20 years, the number of cars has risen by 80 percent. Nearly two thirds of households are now car-owning, and more than half of adults are licence holders. These changes are reflected in ... a marked increase in the average length *and* number of journeys with the result that the average distance that each one of us travels daily has risen by 40 per cent and car mileage on the roads has nearly doubled.

The greatly increased levels of car ownership (and thus of vehicle emissions) forecast by the Department of Transport have a global dimension in the light of the ecological imperative presented by global warming. The total number of cars in the world must be spread more equitably, as the levels of ownership enjoyed in the developed world cannot be achieved globally without ecological catastrophe. What is the global per capita level of car ownership now? That may be an appropriate level for Britain to treat as a target for car ownership in the process of sustainable urban development, as it implies that the contribution of cars to global problems will not be increased (see Figure 2.4).

Figure 2.4
Car ownership levels

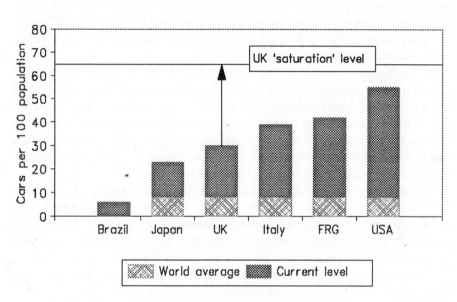

Source: Adams, J., 'Car ownership forecasting' *Traffic Engineering and Control*,
          March 1990.

Transport and land-use planning

Transport planning is required, not only to ensure that people's needs
are met by the least damaging forms of transport, but also that
increasingly those needs for transport are reduced.   Hillman
comments:[33]

> Positive planning policies directed towards minimising the
> mileage people have to, or choose to, cover in meeting their
> daily needs not only lead to a reduction of the undesirable
> outcomes but also make it more possible for walking,
> cycling and public transport to account for a higher
> proportion of journeys.

First, it is necessary to reduce the demand for transport by efficient planning, using both fiscal and land-use measures, and then to meet the residual demand by the most efficient, environmentally sound and equitable means possible. Planning can contribute by promoting scales and locations of facilities, and settlement patterns (densities and mixes of land uses) which are likely to enable people to lead more geographically self-contained lives.

In September 1990, in its Environment White Paper the UK Government announced a joint Department of Transport and Department of the Environment study on the relationship between development and travel patterns and ways of locating development to reduce travel distances and increase transport choice. This has been used to justify inaction in practice despite the clear evidence available from international comparisons on these issues.

Newman and Kenworthy demonstrate the extent to which the process of reducing population density (which has occurred alongside the development of car-oriented commercial facilities) can lead to increased car use in urban areas. They conclude that, alongside traffic restraint, improved public transport and orientation of transport infrastructure away from providing for cars, land-use measures based on increasing density and centralisation are needed.[34]

The city can be the ideal form for non-motorised travel if it is relatively compact. Considering that nearly three quarters of all commuting journeys in the UK are five miles or less in distance, the bicycle could come into its own for meeting journey needs that cannot be met on foot. Even if one takes a 4-mile radius it puts one in touch with most things; for example, school catchment areas are generally much smaller than this. And in employment, a wide range of job opportunities are available within that distance in most urban areas. For those that are not, we need to make land-use changes towards a system with many fewer highly centralised functions; in other words, those functions which require travel into the city centres of regional or national urban centres should be decentralised to more locations at appropriate nodes for public transport (the Danes call this 'decentralised concentration').

Any city can support a proper public transport system for those who do not want to walk or cycle, although with proper provision for these modes a much higher proportion of people would choose to get around in this way. Hillman argues that:[35]

> Cars are far more responsible than any of the other main methods of personal travel for a reduction in environmental quality and a distortion of preferred travel patterns, such as cycling. They also hinder the efficient and safe use of other methods and even their own use. Their use is associated with 60 per cent of all road deaths and serious injuries. They are among the most extravagant users of finite fuel. And they are available, on an exclusive basis, to only a minority of the population.

Much of the spread of urban areas and the extension of mileage that people travel in their daily lives has happened gradually with little, if any, regard to the transport implications. Local authorities have continuous scope for reversing this process, by including appraisal of these implications not only in their locational and land-use strategies but also in the planning control process.

When planning decisions have been made in spheres which influence transport patterns, whether in retailing or industry, or in relation to the provision of schools, hospitals, post offices or sports facilities, it has been fairly exceptional for the travel implications to feature in the balance sheet. For instance, the policies of major retailers, which reflect their commercial aims, suggest that it is more profitable to have fewer and larger outlets. Hillman points to the implications for transport:[36]

> The trend is particularly marked with food retailing where the number of shops has fallen by about 50 per cent in the last 20 years. Further changes in the pattern of retailing have included the establishment of outlets such as hypermarkets outside of the traditionally expensive areas of commercial activity. Much of this has been associated with the provision of parking facilities. It has led to changes in accessibility and thereby patterns of travel, and especially to an increase in car-borne shopping.

As a result of these developments, retailers impose on their customers an obligation to travel further to get a wider range of goods at lower cost, because their customers can disregard the impact of that longer travel on everyone else. Similarly, the retailer can draw the profits from imposing that additional burden of requiring people to travel further to do their shopping; and on top of this, imposing an even greater burden on those who do not have a car. One third of households, and many more shoppers, do not have a car because, even in households with a car, the working member of the family takes it to work, leaving the homemaker to shop without it or only at times when it is available.

The anti-social nature of this compromise constitutes a further problem. A recent CBI study which examined the issue of congestion suggested that the road problem could be solved by such initiatives as four-day working weeks, more flexible working hours and so on.[37] The thinking behind this approach is to keep the shops open later when there is spare capacity on the road system, ie roads are seen as a resource which must be maximised (like machines in a factory). The key issue which the study ignored is the social harm of rising volumes of traffic, which, in fact, would be spread over a much longer period.

Planning changes in cities should reduce the amount of traffic rather than increase it. The question should be asked, is this development going to generate more traffic overall? Because the issue is not considered by the development control system, it is overlooked. Thus, applications for new shopping centres are submitted, and the only traffic element which is considered is whether there is sufficient road capacity at the junction onto which the traffic is discharging. The strategic issue of traffic reduction is not even thought of.

Thus, in retailing (for example) if the planning control mechanism incorporated the criterion that the applicant had to establish whether the proposed pattern of shopping development would make it easier to make the journeys on foot or by bicycle, there would be a predilection for more numerous local shops and fewer more distant shops. What is required to enable due consideration to be given to this aspect of policy in proposals for planning and land-use changes is a traffic impact statement enabling it to be incorporated in the decision-making process. Such an initiative could look at the full implications of a planning proposal, for pedestrians and cyclists, public transport, safety, and so on. The government has an important role to play in providing planning guidance, and is therefore in a position to further influence the density and extent of cities.

Centralisation into fewer, larger locations, has occurred not just in retail operations, but in most other spheres. In education there has been a trend toward larger schools, so that children have to travel further and therefore adopt motorised travel. It is the same with hospitals. The argument has been that larger hospitals are needed to afford certain treatments. However, within the total pattern of treatment provision, these specialised treatments are only small elements and it would be preferable from the point of view of both patients and service provision if more and smaller outlets were available. Why oblige everyone to travel further when only a small group need the special facilities?

Hillman points to two broad decision-making processes which need to take these issues on board:[38]

> those concerned with *public planning* and the decisions determining urban form, and the location of development, and those concerned with *personal planning*, that is, decisions people make about where they live and work. Each year about 10 per cent of people change their jobs ... Each time this occurs, there are opportunities for influencing travel patterns.

He suggests a strategy:[39]

> ... to move towards maintaining and promoting compact, self-contained urban settlements; to avoid over-centralisation in metropolitan areas and to develop public transport corridors within them and their satellites; to discourage commuting; to encourage provision of small-scale public and commercial facilities, and where this is not possible, to locate them near public transport routes; to encourage the provision of local industry and other facilities; to encourage people to consider travel implications when choosing where to live; and to enable

them to live in locations with low travel requirements if they so wish.

Even Los Angeles with its sprawling network of freeways, frequently experiencing 12-hour traffic jams that paralyse movement, is preparing to face reality. Underground public transport over such a vast area is not feasible in the rocky terrain, therefore the vehicles and the users' lifestyles are to be adapted to meet both environmental and economic threats at the same time. Measures to be established by 1993 include restrictions on car-use, improvements in mass transit systems and measures to shift freight to rail. Other measures to be introduced include a ban on new 'drive-through' facilities, provision for employers to provide incentives for car-share and use of mass transit, stringent parking management and encouragement for the relocation of businesses nearer to where the bulk of their employees live. These measures are in addition to emission controls based on improvements in technology. By 2000, 40 per cent of passenger vehicles and 70 per cent of freight vehicles are expected to use 'low emitting' technologies.* The expected reduction in emissions if all targets are met is around 40 per cent of oxides of nitrogen, over 50 per cent of volatile organic compounds (hydrocarbons) and sulphur dioxide and 70 per cent of carbon monoxide by the year 2010, compared with a baseline of 1985, bringing air quality in the Southern Californian basin well inside Federal standards.[40]

The land-use planning process has a further role to play at the development control stage, in reducing the provision of parking at new developments. Coupled with reductions in the availability of public parking (at least centrally) and effective enforcement of on-street parking controls, this can provide a strong disincentive to car use in cities. In Paris 200,000 parking spaces are destined for removal, while

---

* Defined as at least equivalent to methanol in terms of emissions produced. Electricity is included, somewhat misleadingly, as a 'low-emitting' technology, but there is an associated package of measures proposed to reduce pollutive emissions from electricity generation.

in Oxford central car parking has been replaced by development and park-and-ride schemes introduced.

The UK Government has recently recognised the value of controlling both public and private car-parking [41], but has yet to even propose planning guidance to engender widespread action to replicate the success of local schemes.

Walking is transport (and so is cycling)

The number of walking trips is three times that made by public transport; 37 per cent of all journeys (by number) are made on foot or on cycle. This gives some idea of the significance of walking in individuals' lives, rather than in terms of provision of transport. In metropolitan areas the figure is even higher.[42]

Yet there is no national policy on walking and pedestrians and cyclists are struggling against the tide of motorisation with little support from government. 75 per cent of the population can cycle[43] and cycle ownership has continued to rise in recent years. Yet, as Hillman reports, central and local government annual expenditure for cyclists is equivalent to the cost of 200 yards of urban motorway.[44] Resources could be saved: production of a bicycle takes a tiny fraction of the energy and materials needed to produce a car. Even accounting for the greater distance travelled by a car in its lifetime, the average commuter car uses approximately 7.5 times more energy per passenger mile than a bicycle.[45] Some companies and local authorities are offering employees incentives to cycle rather than drive, but these are patchy initiatives.

There are clearly a variety of reasons why people are not prepared to make more of their journeys on foot. Hillman suggests that there are three important deterrents (other than the general attractiveness of car travel) outweighing many of the advantages of walking, such as the saving of the direct and indirect costs of motorised travel and the health benefits of exercise:[46]

• a lack of easily accessible facilities, thereby entailing time-consuming and tiring journeys;

- the unattractive environment for walking, owing to pavements being poorly maintained and rarely forming a direct route owing to the necessity of diversions to cross many roads;
- the danger to life and limb resulting from the growth in the volume and speed of traffic.

He continues:[47]

> Similar constraints discourage people from cycling ... the principal reported reason for not cycling is the entirely justified fear of accidents, the deterrent effect of which was found in a study to reduce commuting by as much as a factor of ten.

Change to a new system would be relatively straightforward: an incremental process whereby, once the order of priorities is accepted, highway authorities in urban areas would be encouraged and funded to give priority to pedestrians at road intersections. Intersections would be raised to pavement level and priorities reversed so that it is not the wheeled traffic that has the right of way but the pedestrian, and the intersection is, in effect, a wide 'sleeping policeman'; as traffic approaches it will substantially reduce its speed. Thus such measures act as a form of traffic calming, designed to reduce the speed of traffic.

These measures are already used widely in residential areas in German and Dutch cities, and were first developed as the Dutch *woonerf* concept. The Dutch *woonerven* aim to reduce vehicle speeds to walking speed throughout residential areas, including through routes with residential functions, by means of a combination of physical measures such as humps, tables and chicanes, measures to reduce visibility such as tree-planting and regulatory techniques providing for pedestrian priority (see Figure 2.5). Elsewhere the aims have seldom been so ambitious, but the principle of using physical measures to reduce speeds, and thereby simultaneously reduce the attractiveness of driving and increase the attractiveness of walking and cycling, has been maintained. As well as improving road safety and encouraging a significant shift in travel modes, such streets enhance social interaction.

Figure 2.5: Design principles for traffic calming in a residential street

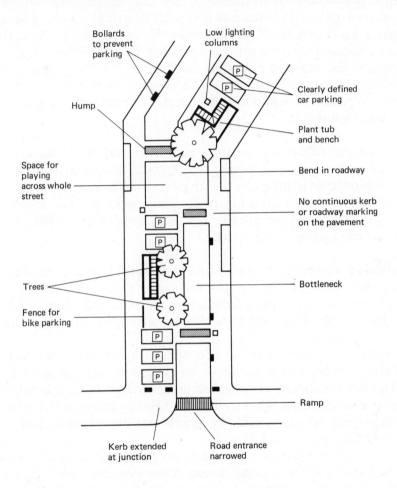

Bollards to prevent parking

Low lighting columns

Hump

Clearly defined car parking

Space for playing across whole street

Plant tub and bench

Bend in roadway

No continuous kerb or roadway marking on the pavement

Trees

Fence for bike parking

Bottleneck

Kerb extended at junction

Road entrance narrowed

Ramp

F.O.E. p. 5 REVISED VERSION.

Source: After Royal Dutch Touring Club AWNB, *Woonerf*, Den Haag, 1980

Excellent examples of residential environments in which priority is given to pedestrians can be found in Germany and Sweden where the pedestrian casualty rate has been dramatically lowered as a consequence.[48]   In the German case, Keller distinguishes three generations of traffic calming, beginning in residential areas, and moving to the scale of city-wide application.[49]   The Japanese have introduced some similar measures. In Osaka 'Community Roads' give priority to pedestrians and have physical traffic calming measures.[50]
Hillman notes that:[51]

> local authorities are now in a position to install speed humps on a wide scale, and there is no doubt that simply extending this concept to integrate it with pedestrian crossings would achieve the continuous pedestrian network that logic demands in order to cater for and promote the needs of people getting about on foot.

Suburban residents in the United States and Canada can demand speed limits down to 10 mph on their own patch, if they lobby city authorities. In the UK, consultation is expected shortly on the introduction of 20mph limits which are self-enforcing by means of physical measures.

A similar approach can be adopted with the cycle network, by providing routes either exclusive to cyclists or shared with motor vehicles that are subject to low speed limits. In Holland, cycle networks have been so successful that well over a third of journeys there (40 per cent in several cities) are made by bicycle and the cycle accident rate is far lower than it is in the UK.

Green space could be related closely to cycle- and foot-paths in many cities. Greenways and other linear space systems based on rivers, canals, disused railways, footpaths, bridleways and any other serviceable and coherent open landscape features, can provide routes for cycling, riding and walking. They provide routes for pleasure as well as for work, 'byways rather than highways'. They also operate as effective wildlife corridors, with the dangers of traffic and the effects of tight mowing removed. One of the most interesting greenway strategies is to be found in Leicester where Great Central Way, once a railway line following closely the course of the river Soar, will bisect the city from north to south when completed, providing a traffic-free route to the centre similar to those that already exist in many Dutch cities.

Mass transit

A shift away from individual motorised transport can be achieved by maintaining a good mass transit service with low fares, integrated ticketing (covering different modes) and a bus priority network. Recent UK government policy in this respect has been found wanting.[52] Public transport policies adopted by some local authorities in recent years, for example, the Greater London Council (GLC) and Sheffield District Council, have shown that cheap fares reverse the spiral of increasingly car-dependent activity. In London the GLC's 'fares fair' policy, combined with integrated fare and timetable systems, reduced car commuting by over 25 per cent.[53] In Freiburg in West Germany, an 18 per cent shift was achieved with no loss of revenue through a low-cost integrated season ticket.

But in the UK such support for public transport has now been abandoned as a result of central government pressure, and traffic congestion has increased in the city centres. Road building has again become the favoured option, but this can actually increase congestion. Competing public transport faced with decreasing patronage is forced to cut investment and services, which slows the service provided. The result is that congestion increases and both public and private transport provide less efficient services.[54]

This demonstrates the need for subsidised investment in public transport and illustrates a general principle. Car drivers perceive only the marginal cost of their travel and they tend to ignore the 'external costs' such as pollution. But unless public transport (such as rail investment) is subsidised in some way, users pay (and perceive) the full average cost of their travel. The most efficient use of national resources will only be made if this situation is rectified.[55] Writing off the cost of railway-building as is done with road-building would help, but drivers are still only directly aware of the cost of their petrol, rather than the full cost of car-use, and this difference needs to be accounted for through regulation or taxation. Interestingly, the CBI, recognising the problems that this unequal accounting causes for business, has recently called for equal treatment for rail investment, which currently has to make a profit, and road construction, for which notional time-savings provide the main accounted 'benefit'.[56]

Urban public transport comprises more than just buses. Although most new railways involve high capital cost, the light rail (or light rapid transit) option is one that larger urban areas could usefully explore.[57] As an alternative to the Metro model adopted in Newcastle and now being used for over one million passenger journeys per week, light railways can run in existing streets, sharing their use with pedestrians, cyles and even motor vehicles, and would reduce congestion, pollution and fuel consumption. Forty-eight UK cities are exploring this option at the moment, and it is likely that it would be more cost-effective than improving bus networks in the largest cities at least.[58] Yet the UK Government has committed funds to support only one proposal at present, that in Greater Manchester. Elsewhere in Europe, and in parts of the USA tram systems are still common. Typically light rail is used to provide a radial network in cities of 0.5-0.8m. population with routes 6-10 km long, although it is used in some larger cities such as Rotterdam, Vienna and Toronto as a feeder to the Metro system.[59] Germany provides an interesting model of how public transport promotion is integral to the social and economic well-being of the urban system as a whole.[60] See Table 2.4 for a comparison of different systems.

Light rail may have advantages over buses even with relatively low passenger flows. It is safer in streets shared with pedestrians as its route is rigidly defined. It also has a much better image. Taplin *et al.* cite as representative a case in Den Haag in Holland where in the first year after conversion of a bus route to light rail, passenger patronage increased by 22 per cent overall and by 32 per cent in off-peak periods.[61]

The viability of public transport, particularly in suburban areas, can be enhanced by making it more accessible. Bike-and-ride stations and facilities to carry bicycles on buses and rail systems have proved enormously popular in Denmark, Japan, the Netherlands and West Germany. In the Netherlands 35 per cent of rail passengers cycle to the station.[62] In the UK car access (park-and-ride) has been given priority by the transport planners. Renner reports that a US study has found

Table 2.4: Comparison of alternative forms of public transport

	Practical Passenger Flow/hour	Commercial Speed km/h	Noise Levels db(A)
Bus[a]	<6,000	21.4	89
Light Rail[b]	2-20,000	25.8	76-80
Metro[b]	15,000	29.4	81

Notes   a:Assuming bus lanes and priorities
b:Light rail is generally segregated from traffic for 40% or more of its route. Metro systems are 100% segregated.
Source: Taplin *et al.*, *Light Rail Transit Today*, Light Rail Transit Association, Milton Keynes (undated).

that improving bicycle access to public transport is the most cost-effective way to reduce vehicle emissions as well as to conserve fuel.[63] The Dutch government's national environmental plan includes road tolls and tax rebates to expand the use of public transport and bicycles.

By improving the alternatives to the car while increasing the costs of car use, a situation could be reached where the need for car use is dramatically reduced. People will recognise that there is no point in having a car, because it is used so little, and because it is expensive. If they do not own a car and have to hire one when necessary, use would fall still further.

The road lobby

The main obstacles to such progress are the political and vested interests which profit from our motorised society. Hamer describes the protagonists:[64]

> The road lobby is a network of vested interests: the people who make the cars that clog the roads; the people who fuel

77

these cars; the people who build the roads to relieve the traffic jams (and create them a few miles down the road); the people who own the lorries that cause the roads to crumble; and the people who patch them up. The road lobby exists for the sole purpose of influencing government policy, so that it can sell more cars, lorries, oil, rubber and concrete ... [Another element] is the motoring clubs, the AA and the RAC ... The road lobby does not just consist of big business. Its tentacles stretch into county halls throughout the land, and into the Department of Transport.

Mainly as a result of the road lobby's power, in the mid-1980s public expenditure on new roads was more than five times the investment in public transport, a figure which excludes another £1 billion spent on road maintenance. Hamer notes that:[65]

In 1984 the Society of Motor Manufacturers and Traders launched a 'motor industry promotion campaign'. In 1985 the campaign cost nearly £450,000. It has two main aims; cutting taxes and increasing road building. It has one motive: selling more cars.

Yet there are the beginnings of a division in this lobby. The Swedish managing director of the car makers, Volvo, announced in 1989 that he would be in favour of the removal of cars from city centres (although he did not go so far as to address the problem of cars outside the city).

Conclusion

Traffic is having a devastating effect on the quality of urban life, through noise, fumes, social severance and danger. Government forecasts predict more of the same. Catering for increased levels of traffic threatens the traditional dense city form and promotes waste of energy. Planning policies are required to restrain cars and ensure the use of small, quiet lorries for necessary commercial functions, while working to reduce the demand for transport through integrated land use.

In most respects, using a car is, and should be seen as, a fundamentally anti-social activity, rather than a means of freedom. The benefits of car use are those of accessibility to experiences and facilities, not mobility. Increasingly, such accessibility should not have to depend on personal motorised transport. Much of the problem is related to image: the image of the car is promoted as exciting and opportunistic; the image of public transport as inconvenient, dirty and 'second-class'. In other countries, public transport provides, and is seen to provide, a fast, clean and cheap service. Similarly, cycling is accepted as a healthy, enjoyable, safe and unpolluting means of travel. Use of the car in some countries is restrained through pricing mechanisms and through wide installation of area-wide traffic calming schemes. These could be UK priorities too.

The car industry's propaganda is a myth: they are in fact driving us toward a dirty, dangerous and fume-filled greenhouse.

References

1. Robertson, T., 'Changing transport policy to combat air pollution from vehicles' in proceedings of Seminar F of the Planning and Transportation Research Consultancy (PTRC) European Planning and Transport 17th *Summer Annual Meeting*, PTRC Education and Research Services, London, 1989. Also Warren Spring Laboratory data which show transport to be the fastest growing source of CO_2 in the UK.
2. Hillman, M., 'Road Transport: What Next? policy options for the future', paper delivered to the annual conference of the Institute of Road Transport Engineers, 1988a.
3. Department of Transport, *Roads for Prosperity*, HMSO, London., 1989.
4. May, T., 'Getting about in towns: solutions', presentation to the Town and Country Planning Association conference *British Towns and the Quality of Life*, London, 1989.
5. Hillman, M., 'Social Goals for Transport Policy' in Institution of Civil Engineers, *Transport for Society*, ICE, London, 1976.

6. Plowden, S., *Transport reform, Changing the rules*, Policy Studies Institute, London, 1985.
7. Society of Motor Manufacturers and Traders, *The Motor Manifesto*, SMMT, London, 1985, p12.
8. Department of Transport, *Trunk Roads, England, Into the 1990s*, HMSO, London, 1990.
9. Adams, J., 'Car Ownership Forecasting: pull the ladder up or climb back down?', *Traffic Engineering and Control*, March 1990.
10. Adams, J., 'On the juggernaut route to disaster', *The Independent*, 7 June, 1989a.
11. Adams, J., *London's Green Spaces: What are They Worth?*, Friends of the Earth, London, 1989b.
12. Hillman, M., 'Neglect of Walking in UK Transport and Planning Policy', paper delivered to *Feet First* Symposium, 19 May, 1989.
13. Hillman, 1976, *op. cit.*
14. Department of Transport, *Road Accidents in Great Britain 1986*, HMSO, London, 1987.
15. Hillman, 1989, *op. cit.*
16. *Ibid.*
17. Appleyard, D. and Lintell, M., 'The environmental quality of city streets: the resident's viewpoint', *American Institute of Planners' Journal*, March 1972, pp. 84-101.
18. Hillman, 1976, *op. cit.*
19. *Ibid.*
20. Adams, 1989b, *op. cit.*
21. Whitelegg, J., *What good reasons are there for expecting an increase in the amount of goods carried by road vehicles after 1992?*, Working Paper of the Institut für Landes-und Stadtentwicklungsforschung des Landes Nordrhein Westfalen, 1989.
22. CBI, *The Capital at Risk*, CBI, London, 1989a.
23. Shankleman, J., 'Policy Approaches to extending use of low-noise commercial vehicles – experience in OECD countries' in proceedings of Seminar F of the PTRC European Planning and Transport 17th *Summer Annual Meeting*, PTRC Education and Research Services, London, 1990.
24. House of Commons, *Hansard*, Vol. 165, No. 36, 1990, Col. 735.

25. Teufel, D., *The social costs of road transport of goods*, UPI Report No. 14, Heidelberg, 1989.
26. Hillman, M., *Interview transcript*, July 1989.
27. Adams, J., 'Road Pricing for London', unpublished paper, 1989c.
28. Lester, N., *Interview transcript*, November 1989.
29. *Ibid.*
30. OECD, *Cities and Transport*, OECD, Paris, 1988.
31. Transport and Environmental Studies, *The company car factor*, London Amenity and Transport Association, London, 1984.
32. Hillman, M., 'Foul Play for Children: a price for mobility', *Town and Country Planning*, Vol. 57, No. 12, 1988b.
33. Hillman, M., 'The Wrong Turning: Twenty Years on from Buchanan', *Built Environment*, Vol. 9, No. 2, 1983.
34. Newman, P. and Kenworthy, J., *Cities and Automobile Dependence*, Gower Technical, Aldershot, 1989.
35. Hillman, M., 'Influencing personal travel decisions: the role of public policy' in J.D. Carr (ed.), *Planning for Radical Change*, Gower, Aldershot, 1986.
36. Hillman, M., *Conservation's Contribution to UK Self-Sufficiency*, PSI and RIIA, Joint Energy Programme Paper No 13, Gower, Aldershot, 1984.
37. CBI, 1989a, *op. cit.*
38. Hillman, 1984, *op. cit*, p.19.
39. *Ibid.*
40. Southern California Association of Governments, *Air Quality Management Plan*, SCAG, Los Angeles, 1989.
41. *This Common Inheritance*, CM1200, HMSO, London 1990.
42. Hillman, M., *The role of walking and cycling in transport policy*, Discussion Paper 8, Transport and Society series, Rees Jeffreys Road Fund, Oxford, 1990.
43. Hillman, M., and Whalley, A., *Energy and Personal Travel*, Policy Studies Institute, London, 1983.
44. Hillman, M., 'The Greening of Road Safety Policy', paper delivered to London Centre for Transport Planning, 16 March, 1988c.
45. Krommendijk, E., *A quantification of some environmental effects of a bicycle oriented traffic policy in Groningen*, Prof. H.C. van Hall Instituut, Groningen, 1988.

46. Hillman, 1988c, *op. cit.*
47. *Ibid.*
48. Hass-Klau, C., (ed), 'New Ways of Managing Traffic', *Built Environment*, Vol. 12, Nos. 1/2, 1986; Hass-Klau, C., (ed.), *New Life for City Centres*, Anglo-German Foundation, London, 1988.
49. Keller, H.H., 'Three Generations of Traffic Calming in the Federal Republic' in proceedings of Seminar F of the PTRC European Planning and Transport 17th *Summer Annual Meeting*, PTRC Education and Research Services, London, 1989.
50. OECD, *op. cit.*
51. Hillman, 1988c, *op. cit.*
52. Harrison A., and Gretton, J., (eds), *Transport UK 1987: An Economic, Social and Policy Audit*, Policy Journals, Newbury, 1987.
53. Robertson, *op. cit.*
54. Mogridge, M., *Travel in Towns: Jam yesterday, jam today and jam tomorrow?*, Macmillan, London, 1990.
55. *Ibid.*
56. CBI, *Trade Routes to the Future*, CBI, London, 1989b.
57. Simpson, B., 'Hold-Ups on the Line' *The Surveyor*, 30 June 1988.
58. Simpson, B., 'The True Cost of Keeping on the Rails', *The Surveyor*, 31 December 1987.
59. Taplin, M.R., Haywood, P.G., Jones, R.N.H. and Walker, P.J. *Light Rail Transit Today*, Light Rail Transit Association, Milton Keynes, undated.
60. Hall, P., and Hass-Klau, C., *Can Rail Save the City? The Impacts of Rail Rapid Transit and Pedestrianisation on British and German Cities*, Gower, Aldershot, 1985.
61. Taplin *et al.*, *op. cit.*
62. Mathew, D., 'Have Bike, Will Travel', *Surveyor* Vol. 172, No. 5062, 1989.
63. Renner, M., *Rethinking the Role of the Automobile*, Worldwatch Paper 84, 1988.
64. Hamer, M., *Wheels within Wheels: a study of the road lobby*, Routledge and Kegan Paul, London, 1987.
65. *Ibid.*

Chapter 3: Energy

Introduction

Sustainable urban development must vastly reduce the city's demands for energy, particularly finite fuels, primarily through policies and action to promote conservation. The residual demand should be met efficiently using the cleanest technology available to meet energy needs.

The use of energy is concentrated in urban areas (see Table 3.1 and Figure 3.1), and many urban functions are energy-intensive. Urban transport based on the car is particularly wasteful of energy. The needs of urban residents are often met through energy-intensive solutions. For example, long food supply lines involve refrigerated transport, while high temperatures in the city's buildings are reduced by artificial air conditioning.

The present

The way we use energy at present is inefficient and wasteful, yet the case for a more sustainable approach to energy is not new.[1] The Secretary of State in the Sixth Report of the Energy Select Committee, *Energy Policy Implications of the Greenhouse Effect*, noted that 'these are finite resources we are using up and the more we can conserve them and the less we waste them, the better'.[2]

The ecological costs of energy profligacy are severe. Climatic change in the form of global warming, largely caused by the production of CO_2 from combustion of fossil fuel, is one of the most pressing environmental problems that we face. Energy generation and supply is also linked to acid rain, accumulation of radioactive waste, and increased risk of radiation release or accidents such as oil spills. The fact that we all, by demanding energy, contribute to these problems is not universally recognised, and thus constitutes a major obstacle to progress.

Public policy objectives, on the one hand, seek to promote energy conservation while at the same time they continue to encourage people to adopt increasingly energy-intensive patterns of living:[3]

> The emphasis on improving efficiency appears to stem from the belief that the ownership and use of energy-consuming equipment will inevitably rise in the future as part of the process towards society attaining a higher standard of living.

Energy saving is still a minority concern in Britain, compared with countries such as Sweden. Changes are required in the way we think about energy, and the way we actually design our cities.[4] For example, in the United States, considerable work has been undertaken on the use of energy audits as part of the urban planning process, examining how cities are laid out (concentrated versus dispersed), and the effect of this on energy consumption.

Hillman suggests that the extent to which the potential for energy conservation can be realised depends far less on technological innovation than it does on surmounting political and institutional barriers.[5] He also usefully distinguishes between energy efficiency as a reduction in energy consumption in a particular activity and energy conservation which also includes reducing dependence on energy-consuming activity.

Conservation of energy would improve equity for three groups whose interests are largely overlooked at present. First, the present generation's future needs, secondly, the claims of future generations, and thirdly, the current needs of the people of the less developed countries which represent nearly two-thirds of the world's total population, but account for only one-seventh of its present energy consumption. Thus energy conservation contributes to meeting both the inter-generational and intra-generational equity conditions of sustainable development.[6]

Table 3.1 shows clearly the concentration of energy use in urban areas: agriculture accounts for only a small proportion of energy use, while cities hold the majority of domestic, industrial, public and commercial users. Transport in urban areas accounts for almost 50% of transport CO_2 emissions.[7] Thus even excluding the use of energy for transport *between* cities, over 75% of energy use is urban.

The main sectors identified are transport, industry, and domestic. Within the latter two, the heating of buildings is a major component. Jackson estimates that space heating is responsible for over 25 per cent of the UK's CO_2 emissions.[8] Below we consider ways in which needs in these four sectors can be met, in terms of their resource requirements, ecological and health impacts and economic costs, such that optimum policies can be identified.

Table 3.1: UK energy consumption by sector

Energy consumption by sector (heat supplied basis)

	Million therms		% contribution
	1986	1988	to CO_2
Industry	16,092	16,842	29.5
Transport	16,257	18,002	23.5
Domestic	17,456	16,737	29.1
Public administration	3,545	3,287	]
Agriculture	564	536	] 17.9
Miscellaneous	3,946	4,067	]
Total	57,860	59,471	100.0

Source: Department of Energy, *Digest of Energy Statistics 1989.*

Figure 3.1
Use of energy by sector (UK, 1988)

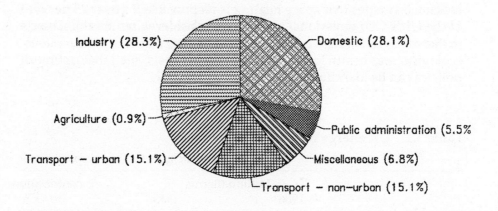

Source: As Table 3.1 above.

Industrial processes

Industrial production is still the base of the urban economy. Although the potential for reducing the energy demands of industrial processes is generally independent of location, the arguments are worth rehearsing as sustainable urban development will be based, at least in part, upon sustainable industrial development. Table 3.2 illustrates the increasing consumption of energy as differentiated between industrial sectors in the UK for the period 1984-8 during which UK gross domestic product grew by 11.6%. This 'growth' varied between sectors. Taking into account changes in the production levels of the industries, the chemicals, vehicles and paper, printing and publication sectors improved their efficiency of energy use relative to the average for all secondary industry, while efficiency in the textiles, leather and clothing and non-ferrous metals sectors showed an absolute decline.

At a national level, the energy efficiency of UK production in 1986 (measured per unit of Gross National Product) had shown one of the lowest rates of improvement of any industrialised country since 1970. The UK had achieved a reduction in energy use of just 14% per unit of GNP while Sweden, for instance, had not only cut energy use per unit by 33%, but had also achieved an absolute level 40% lower. The USA, on the other hand, was still at a much higher level, but had achieved a 35% cut since 1970.[9]

Table 3.2: **Energy consumption by main industrial sectors (heat supplied basis)**

	Million therms		Increase
	1984	1988	(%)
Sector			
Non Ferrous Metals	502	604	20
Mineral Products	1,506	1,627	11
Chemicals	3,772	3,339	-11.5
Engineering	1,500	1,531	2
Vehicle manufacture	727	700	-4
Food, Drink and Tobacco	1,602	1,597	-
Textiles, Leather and Clothing	452	519	15
Paper, Printing and Publishing	841	890	6
Other industries	1,540	1,557	-
Construction	423	475	12
Iron and Steel	2,935	3,235	10
Total Industry	16,311	16,842	3

Note: - indicates negligible change
Source: Department of Energy, *Digest of Energy Statistics 1989.*

The efficiency of industrial equipment and processes can often be improved. Existing technologies include systems for recovering waste heat, heat exchange pumps, use of waste products for fuel, improving the thermal insulation of machinery, simplified techniques for drying and evaporation, and increased efficiency of operating motors by such devices as speed control of pumps and fans, and electronic controls. In particular, motors account for the largest single category of electricity use in industry and typical cost-effective savings of at least 25 per cent can be achieved by the use of such controls. Hillman estimates that even improved management practices could lead to an additional 10 per cent reduction in consumption.[10]

Prolonging the life of industrial goods, (including consumer 'durables') which are energy-intensive in terms of production, has a similar effect. Built-in obsolescence in effect increases the amount of energy needed to meet the consumer's demands over a fixed time period.

The government has a stated objective of setting realistically high prices to encourage energy conservation. But there are other government priorities which have set obstacles in the way of this policy. For instance, in the fight against inflation, there is always political pressure against increasing energy prices to reflect their true cost. Pressure by industry to the effect that increased prices would lead to a loss of international competitiveness has also played a part. However, some form of tax-trading (reducing existing taxes, on labour, for example, in order to compensate for higher energy taxes) would reduce the impact on inflation as well as maintaining competitiveness of the economy as a whole.

In the industrial sector, Hillman speculates that price rises have been insufficient to generate much reduction in demand. And the government has failed to give reliable signals to industry about future fuel prices to aid it in its long-term plans for investment in new equipment.[11]

Another problem is that fuel switching can result if price rises are not co-ordinated. This may constitute efficient energy use from the private viewpoint and can produce environmental benefits where users switch, for example, from electricity to direct use of gas, but it does not in itself involve energy conservation. It is, however, the main response to price rises where it is feasible as a short-term response.

The 1982 Armitage Norton Report, commissioned to identify the obstacles to realising energy saving in industry, found that industry's difficulty was simply identifying its consumption of energy; fuel costs tended to be lost in overall costs.[12] A study commissioned by the European Commission in 1987 found that even amongst companies which had implemented some energy-saving measures in the five years previous to the study, only half related energy consumption to other variables. In addition, the study found that senior management often lacked conviction about the value of investment in energy conservation.[13]

One way of solving this problem is used in Japan, where industries consuming more than a specified amount of energy are required by government to employ qualified energy managers. In the UK, however, it is only the largest organisations that are likely to have a resident energy manager. Indeed, it is uncommon for any employee to have sole responsibility for this aspect of management.

Agriculture is also an energy-intensive industry. Leach argues that horse-based intensive rotation agriculture produced a ratio of food energy gained to energy input of around 100 or even 200:1. In the 1970s the ratio had climbed to over 1000:1, but if the hidden subsidy of fuel, electricity and petrochemicals is taken into account, the profit of 1000:1 turned into a net loss of 1:2.[14] However, the overall efficiency of agriculture, including indirect energy inputs in artificial fertilisers, has increased since the 1970s. But reduced use of agrochemicals (production of which is energy-intensive as well as directly consuming petroleum), more efficient machinery, increased labour intensity, use of waste straw as a fuel and an increased emphasis on locally and home-grown food could all produce further savings.

Space heating

Two basic uses of energy in heating have a considerable potential for reducing general energy consumption: raising the thermal efficiency of existing buildings, and when constructing new ones, ensuring that they meet high thermal standards. The great majority of the building stock in the UK was constructed many decades before such standards were recognised as desirable or indeed even considered. Three-quarters of existing dwellings were constructed before 1965, and only a small proportion of the remaining 5-6 million built more recently have been subject to the Department of the Environment's Building Regulations on thermal efficiency.[15]

Since 1973, efforts have been made by government and manufacturers to promote energy-saving products. With regard to space heating, efficiency measures are of three types: improved control, insulation and improved supply. Improved control, certain insulation measures such as cavity wall and loft insulation, and ventilation control by draught-proofing tend to be the most cost-effective measures. Other insulation measures, such as secondary glazing, and improved supply technologies, such as condensing boilers and heat pumps, require longer payback periods.

Table 3.3: **Illustrative costs for space heating efficiency measures, compared with supply side measures**

	Cost (£)	Annual saving	Lifetime (payback) in years	Cost £/GJ (8%)	(10%)
Measure					
Draught-proofing	30-60	15-40	5 (3)	3.8	4.0
Loft insulation	100-250	35-105	30 (3)	1.3	1.6
Cavity wall insulation	250-400	50-125	30 (6)	2.6	3.2
Secondary glazing	300-1500	25-70	25 (6)	2.8	3.3
Improved control	n/a	n/a	25 (3)	1.4	1.7
Supply improvements[b]	n/a	n/a	15 (6)	3.5	3.9

Notes   a: Cost per gigajoule is given at two different discount rates.
            b: Includes use of condensation boilers and heat pumps.
Sources: Columns 1-2 from Hillman, M., *Conservation's Contribution to UK Self-Sufficiency*, 1984. Columns 3-6 from Jackson, T., *The Role of Nuclear Power in Global Warming Abatement Strategies*, 1989.

The cost-effectiveness of these measures is demonstrated in Table 3.3, which details the variation of installed and annuitised costs of the various measures. The range of space-heating efficiency cost lies between about £1/giga-joule (GJ) and £4/GJ. *[16] Although these costs are marginal with respect to existing heat supply technology and plant, they are not marginal with respect to the need for new electricity generating capacity or heat supply technology.

In spite of the considerable benefits in energy saving to householders, Table 3.4 shows that in 1982 much of the existing stock of dwellings in the country still lacked many of these measures.[17] The most recent information available indicates that the proportion of dwellings with loft insulation in England had increased by about 5 per cent, that with double glazing by about 11 per cent and that with wall insulation by about 5 per cent in the period between 1982 and 1986.[18] A proportion of the increase is accounted for by new construction, so the absolute numbers lacking such measures fell by a smaller amount.

There is, also, a significant difference between the levels of energy savings that can be achieved with a payback of 3-4 years and those which are technically achievable, of around 8 per cent of current use. In new construction the gap between economically viable and best technical savings is 12 per cent, with an energy saving of 65 per cent of current average use being currently technically achievable.[19] These gaps indicate that regulation or market manipulation is necessary.

Recent research has indicated that government efforts in improving the energy efficiency of existing stock are largely misguided:[20]

> decentralised programmes [achieve] considerably greater successes in terms of mobilization of consumers' energy savings and cost effectiveness than the traditional centrally administered information campaigns and loans and grants schemes directed to 'consumers at large'.

* 1GJ = 1 thousand million joule – a joule being a measure of energy equivalent to just under one quarter of a calorie.

Table 3.4: Lack of various energy conservation measures in existing dwellings, 1982

	Unnecessary heat loss due to lack (%)	Proportion of of dwellings lacking measure[a]
Proportion		
Draught stripping to doors & windows	10	60 [b]
Insulation to hot water cylinder	10	15
Roof insulation	25	25 [c]
Cavity wall insulation	35	91
or solid wall insulation	35	N/A
Floor insulation	5	N/A
Double glazing	15	77 [d]

Notes: a: Of dwellings known to have the possibility of applying the measures.

b: A further 25% have less than half draught-stripped

c: A further 30% have only 1-2" of insulation.

d: A further 8% have less than half their windows double glazed.

Source: Hillman, M., *Conservation's Contribution to UK Self-Sufficiency*, 1984.

Greater investment by the government in promoting energy efficiency directly, and via the energy supply companies, is necessary. To encourage the installation of energy-saving equipment in homes, such materials and equipment should be placed in the lowest band of VAT, thus providing a tax differential to favour conservation. It should be noted that, unlike the rest of the EEC, the UK levies no VAT on domestic fuel.

Recent housing developments have shown that it is already possible at little additional cost to reduce heating costs to two-thirds to one-half of those in otherwise equivalent houses by incorporating higher insulation standards than are currently required, and to one-third by conscientiously adopting an energy-saving approach to design, entailing additional building costs which will be covered by savings on energy bills within five to seven years. Higher standards of insulation, efficiency of heating systems, and sophistication of control devices can all be incorporated in new buildings more economically than in the existing stock. Hillman points to further savings:[21]

> judicious location and massing of building ... [can] ... minimise exposure to cooling winds and ... maximise the benefits of 'huddling together' without overshadowing. The most efficient high-density developments can reduce energy consumption by 25 per cent.

New buildings can also use design techniques for reducing energy demand. Passive solar design involves various techniques for maximising solar gain; by having large areas of glazing on the south side (with insulation blinds to retain heat at night); a south-facing conservatory to collect warmed air for internal circulation; glazed walls to absorb and radiate heat into the building. Felmore housing at Basildon New Town illustrates what might be called 'resource-sensitive design'. The scheme, for 430 units, exploits the natural features and micro-climate of the site. All houses, in three groups of parallel terraces, face south, with the larger windows on the south side. Careful spacing avoids overshadowing; prevailing winds blow along the terraces and are reduced by shelter planting between groups. A group heating scheme, based on three coal-fired boilers, allows fuel substitution, while the tenants' handbook shows how to derive most benefit with a minimum energy consumption.[22]

Adaptability in fuel use is a factor in energy saving. It is one of the advantages of buildings that the low temperature heat energy they use can be provided by several options; coal, gas, oil, electricity, district heating and solar. Building designs which allow for the use of different fuels help to keep energy options open.

Although new building regulations have recently been introduced in the UK, increasing required levels of energy efficiency in new buildings by 20 per cent, these will still be 'below those used elsewhere, particularly in Scandinavia. For example, the UK's new regulations will not provide for mandatory double or triple glazing in new properties'.[23] Indeed, the new regulations will take the UK to the position Sweden was in in 1935! Other countries with stricter regulations include West Germany and Japan.

In the UK building regulations do not reflect a 'technology-forcing standard' but rather a political compromise – not the most advanced standard from a technical viewpoint, but the most acceptable given the attitudes of the building industry and politicians. Standards should be significantly tightened and extended to all new buildings, with appropriate standards set for existing buildings. In Denmark building regulations standards are made applicable to existing property when ownership changes, through the medium of a mandatory energy audit.

Energy use in the construction of new buildings has to be taken into account in the decision whether to improve existing stock or rebuild to increase energy efficiency. Although the construction sector accounts for just 0.8 per cent of total energy use, the production and transport of construction materials increase this figure several fold. The additional energy cost of making new-build more energy-efficient is virtually insignificant in this context. However, where refurbishment is an option, it is likely that the energy savings may be significant in comparison with new-build.

In the existing stock the changes needed are technologically practicable, as long as the extensive programmes needed for refurbishment of housing pay adequate attention to the issue of energy conservation. In the UK, a case study based in Glasgow found that for an investment of £4,600 per dwelling the homes of households suffering from fuel poverty in the deprived Easterhouse area (where very major works were required) could be upgraded to 1990 Building Regulations insulation standards and efficient heating systems installed. The investment would bring financial savings over a seven-year period in comparison with the cost of increasing social security payments or pensions to provide the same benefits. The expected average cost of improvements to this standard elsewhere in the UK is £2,500 per dwelling.[24]

In the Netherlands effective retrofit insulation has been developed which involves fitting expanded foam sheets, or concrete containing foam balls to the outside of dwellings. For new stock, energy demands as low as one-tenth of conventional designs have been achieved through the combination of effective insulation with block heating in Schiedam.

The total annual gas requirement is reported to be 300m^3 per dwelling. This is equivalent to the amount needed to keep a pilot light burning constantly![25]

Energy rating of all housing would raise public awareness of these issues and could be carried out as part of the standard surveyor's valuation. To support this, the energy supply companies must be encouraged to offer to domestic consumers the considerable technical advice on energy management and financing that they offer to industrial and commercial consumers.

Milton Keynes has been dubbed the UK's 'Energy Efficient City'. As a 'New Town' it has been in a position to control the energy efficiency of its building stock. It has developed its own Energy Conservation Index, setting a minimum standard of efficiency which every new building must meet before building permission is given. This minimum standard is higher than the new Building Regulations in the UK. So far nearly 1,000 buildings have been erected to the Milton Keynes standard, using thicker insulation, high-efficiency gas condensing boilers, heating controls and passive solar heating in windows and conservatories. Construction costs for houses to this standard are less than 1 per cent higher than for conventional houses, and heating bills are 30-40 per cent lower.[26]

Table 3.5: Energy use[a] in buildings at previous and current buildings regulation U-values and at Milton Keynes conservation index U-values.

| | Energy Use (giga joules) | | |
	1989 Regs.	1990 Regs.	MK Index
Detached House (114 m^2)	90	78	56
Semi-Detached House (80 m^2)	56	49	36
2 bedroom flat on intermediate floor (60 m^2)	32	29	26

Note a: Energy use for space and water heating only.
Source: Building Research Establishment

Table 3.5 illustrates the large energy savings achievable by adopting stricter standards. But it must be noted that even the Milton Keynes standards are below those applied in Scandinavian countries. Table 3.5 also demonstrates the potential energy savings from changing the mix of the building stock away from detached and semi-detached properties. The energy use per square metre of floor area in a flat is two-thirds that in a detached house.

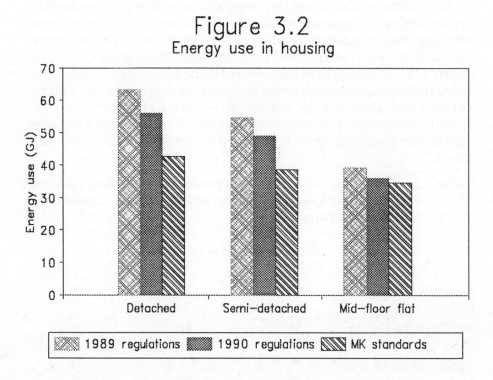

Figure 3.2
Energy use in housing

Source: Data from Building Research Establishment.

In addition to improving the thermal efficiency of the fabric of existing buildings, substantial energy costs can also be avoided by switching to more efficient heating systems, such as the use of gas condensing boilers and heating controls.[27] Methods to spread the peak demand for energy, in particular electricity, do in theory, carry efficiency benefits at the generating plant scale.* However, use of electricity for heating (even off-peak) is inefficient in relation to alternative fuels. Indeed new demand for 'Economy 7' off-peak heating, based on fossil fuel generation of electricity, will produce three to four times more CO_2 per unit of delivered heat than gas central heating. Encouraging householders to take an interest in their energy costs by monitoring their consumption, aided by meters recording this in a more explicit way than at present, could lead to savings in the order of 15 per cent from the more sensible use of space and water heating equipment and 9 per cent from that of electrical appliances.[28]

Domestic use

Considerable reductions in consumption are now possible with many electrical appliances[29] (see Table 3.6). Savings in this sphere are particularly worthwhile because of the high conversion costs: a saving of electricity leads on average to three times higher savings of primary energy.[30]

Legal standards should be set to raise consumer awareness and force rapid shifts to the best available technology. Appliance efficiency standards would complement a labelling scheme by ensuring that a minimum level of efficiency is achieved by all manufacturers. The 1987 National Energy Conservation (Appliances) Act in the US laid down strict minimum energy efficiency standards for a wide range of products, and required design changes to between an estimated 70 and 90 per cent of goods on sale in that country in 1987.[31] Such regulations

---

* The European Colloquium on the urban environment in 1989 even suggested that systems should be introduced to allow power station operators to remotely switch off domestic appliances such as dishwashers and washing machines at times of peak demand.

might be complemented by taxation differentials favouring more efficient appliances.

Table 3.6: Energy efficiency in electrical appliances

Electricity consumption (KWh/yr)

	UK stock	Best available technology
Appliance		
Refrigerator/freezer (0.5 m^3)^a	1,100	75-180
Freezer (0.25 m^3)^{a,b}	1,000	80-180
Refrigerator (frost-free, 0.2 m^3)^a	450	30-80
Washing Machine	400	40-210
Dishwasher	500	50-240
Clothes Dryer	520	10-90
Colour TV	340	70

Notes: a. These volumes are used for illustration only. The stock includes a wide mixture of sizes. The refrigerators discussed have no frozen food compartment.

b. Freezers are manual defrost except where noted.

Source: Friends of the Earth, *Memorandum: Efficiency of Electricity Use*, 1989.

In addition, reductions in demand can be made by changing the way in which we meet our needs. For instance, traditional larders keep most fresh foods adequately cool. Thus a much smaller fridge is all that is required.

Transport

Energy can be used more efficiently by improving the efficiency of motors, but much more can be achieved by changing patterns of use, and in particular switching from use of finite fuels to human energy as a power source. As Table 3.7 illustrates, bicycles consume less energy per passenger mile than any other form of transport, including walking.

Table 3.7: Energy intensity of selected transport modes, United States 1984

	Calories per Passenger Mile
Mode	
Automobile, 1 occupant	1,860
Transit Bus	920
Transit Rail	885
Walking	100
Bicycling	35

Source: Lowe, M., 1989, *The Bicycle: Vehicle for a Small Planet*, Worldwatch Paper 90.

The city is the ideal form for non-motorised transport: it is relatively compact and can be decentralised internally in 'decentralised concentration'. Chapter 2 discussed these land-use issues more fully.

Mass transit is the most energy-efficient of the motorised forms of travel. Provision for use of the car should be limited and cars should also be made more energy-efficient. The present generation of cars are designed for optimum performance at 56 mph. But in terms of energy efficiency, a much lower speed is required to minimise fuel consumption. Hillman comments:[32]

The stage is being reached at which 100 mpg is an attainable objective. If these trends continue and are combined with the typical renewal of the stock every 10 years, a 50 per cent reduction in the fuel consumption of the average car can be anticipated by the end of the century. And even more impressive reductions could be achieved were the government to pursue the policy of restricting manufacturers to designing vehicles incapable of [significantly] exceeding the national speed limit ...

Optimising the fuel/speed relationship for the engine design of lower performance cars would lead to significant fuel economies.

Unfortunately, Department of Transport attitudes to energy saving leave much to be desired, as noted by the Energy Select Committee:[33]

we are no means convinced that energy efficiency is a major concern of the Department of Transport ... (this is) graphically illustrated by the recent Roads White Paper which proposes new road works costing around £6,600 million to cater for a forecast percentage increase in vehicle miles by 2025 of between 83 and 142 per cent without mentioning energy efficiency.

However, the Committee do not go on to embrace the necessary policy of reducing motorised travel. While recognising that curbs on vehicle carbon dioxide emissions are most 'likely to be achieved by reducing the amount of fuel burnt', they state misleadingly that 'the most obvious way to do this is by increasing engine efficiency'. At the same time, they note that the trend has not been encouraging; that is, while cars individually have become more efficient, there are more on the road, they are on average more powerful and travel faster. Here there is potential for the introduction of tax differentials to favour efficient models.

Hillman notes the specific potential for energy conservation in transferring journeys to work, particularly in urban areas, from the car. Such journeys[34]

account for over a quarter of all car mileage, when car occupancy is at its lowest, roads most congested and, therefore, energy costs per passenger kilometre at their highest; ... there is considerable scope for bringing about a transfer to public transport on those commuter journeys for which it is particularly well suited ... Such a policy, however, needs to include traffic management measures, such as bus lanes and parking restrictions, which must be properly enforced.

Traffic management measures have been considered in detail in Chapter 2.

The separation of fixed and marginal costs in the operation of private cars encourages increased mileage. Car users pay various annual costs (licence, insurance, etc.) for unlimited travel, the only other expense being the marginal cost of fuel. Mass transit, in contrast, does not operate in this way: the operators do not charge a fixed fee per year to travel by mass transit, and then just a penny or two a mile. They relate the cost of travel to the use of the system. Thus increasing the marginal to fixed cost ratio of car use would allow users to compare it more directly with mass transit and could be expected to discourage car use, and thereby reduce energy consumption.

Planning is even more important in terms of freight than in regard to personal travel. Increasing regional and local economic self-reliance would significantly reduce freight mileage. Moreover, within existing patterns of production, the increased use of railways, with lower unit energy consumption, for distribution could provide significant benefits. The model of decentralised concentration allows for rail distribution to points of concentration, with transfer to road only thereafter.

To encourage less space-extensive patterns of activity, whether personal or freight transport, new rules are required which will oblige people to relate their consumption of energy to the impact of that consumption on finite reserves. As a first step an increase in the direct tax on road transport fuels should be introduced.

Planning policies and energy conservation

The Department of the Environment has no policy relating to the land-use planning issues affecting energy use, so they are not considered in the policy notes on the myriad of locational issues which influence travel. The energy costs of proposals, policies or practices are not calculated when land-use or transport alternatives are being assessed, or during the processes of development control.

In the absence of such guidance local authorities have not been made aware of the potential for, or are simply unable to encourage, energy saving through land-use planning and the application of development control policies. Owens identifies the most important constraints acting against energy awareness in built development:[35]

> [These] appear to be the small scale of anticipated development, the fact that energy conservation was perceived to be unimportant, either in absolute or (more frequently) in relative terms, and the doubt about the legitimacy of energy as a strategic planning issue.

The latter point is particularly interesting, because these doubts are clearly encouraged by an ambiguous and unhelpful attitude on the part of central government. Owens comments:[36]

> It is the more negative attitude, however, which seems to have the prevailing influence. One of the prerequisites for effective integration of energy considerations into the planning process must be a broadly favourable policy framework; lack of such a framework in the UK contrasts starkly with the national policies of Denmark and the state policies of Oregon.

Indeed energy implications should be an issue the local planning authorities are not simply encouraged but required by law to consider. Adequately empowered local authorities can complement planning policies with transport policies. They could encourage a shift away from the use of cars by maintaining efficient and cheap mass transit services, introducing a range of traffic restraint and improved enforcement methods and creating safe and attractive environments for walking and cycling.[37]

Energy supply

The maximum benefit of an inherently efficient land-use pattern can only be achieved if it is considered as part of a total community energy system. Thus, we need to consider the impact of land use on both energy demand and also on energy supply because the pattern of land use can influence the efficiency of the supply system. A diversified supply system is important in reducing dependence on particular finite resources. All Scandinavian countries have moved to decentralised energy systems. In the city of Malmö, Sweden, 'waste' industrial heat goes into the district heating system.

Combined heat and power (CHP), although dependent on favourable land-use patterns, like district heating, is an opportunity which does not require particularly dense urban development. This is demonstrated by schemes in Denmark and Sweden. Once the primary network for CHP is laid, it becomes economic to integrate quite low-density development, even suburbs. In gauging the size of a CHP scheme, towns with a dense core and a CHP site close to the centre are desirable, with industry as a supplementary supplier or consumer. Hospitals and educational institutions are also potential clients. In the UK, towns like Swansea, Dundee and Luton, with populations of about 200,000, are likely to have sufficiently large and concentrated heat loads to make CHP a viable proposition. Helsinki has found that it has improved air quality after going over to a CHP system, as have several German cities. In the UK official recognition of the economic viability of CHP and district heating (DH) systems came in the early 1980s, but the recent report of the Select Committee on Energy has repeated its earlier exhortations to the government to take effective action to encourage their wider use and recognised the 'distinct environmental as well as economic advantages' of such proven technologies as CHP.[38]

In fact, a variety of decentralised schemes are possible: ranging from CHP, energy-from-waste (either by anaerobic digestion to produce methane, or by non-pollutive direct incineration), through to passive solar systems in individual houses.[39] In Berlin it has been estimated that 30 per cent of the city's electricity could be generated from solar power using photo-voltaic panels. More widely, a study by Friends of the Earth outlined a strategy of investment in renewables and conservation

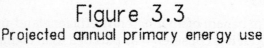

Figure 3.3
Projected annual primary energy use

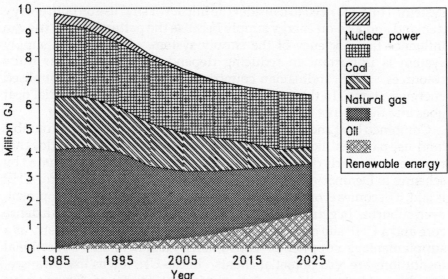

Source: Boyle, S., *An Alternative Energy Path for the UK*, Friends of the Earth, London, 1988.

which conservatively concluded that a 20 per cent contribution from renewables was feasible by the year 2025, assuming a 30 per cent reduction in primary energy demand achieved through energy efficiency and conservation (Figure 3.3).[40] The UK Government's target for renewable energy, restated in the Environment White Paper of September 1990 is just 1000MW* by the year 2000. Yet this constitutes only a fraction of the potential and equates to less than one tenth of the capacity implied by the targets suggested above.

* The target of 1000 MW 'nameplate' capacity is, in fact, no increase over the previously existing target of 600 MW 'declared net' capacity, as the latter figure takes into account the intermittency of renewable energy sources such as wind power.

The potential contribution of renewables is summarised in Table 3.8. Complementary work has revealed the extent to which overall environmental impact, particularly in relation to SO_2, NOx, CO_2 and nuclear waste, can be reduced by utilising energy conservation measures.[41] Increased research and investment into these options is vital.

Table 3.8: **Summary of possible target renewable contributions by 2025.**

	Heat supplied or fuel saved (PJ)	% projected primary
Wind	650	10.7
Biofuels	200	3.3
Geothermal	200	3.3
Solar	60	1.0
Tidal[a]	70	1.1
Hydro	55	0.9
Wave	5	0.1
Total	1240	20.4

Notes: Rounded to nearest 5 PJ; 1PJ = 37,600 tonnes of coal.
        a: This figure does not include the Severn Barrage.
Source: Based on Flood, M., *Energy Without End*, Friends of the Earth, London, 1986.

Denmark has recognised the relationship between energy and the layout of urban areas and is attempting to plan simultaneously for their future development. The most significant policy in this context is the regionalisation of energy supply for heating, described by Owens.[42] Land-use planners have been closely involved in the division of the country into areas where combined heat and power/district heating (CHP/DH) can be introduced or extended, areas which would be better served by natural gas and areas where space heating must be provided in some other way. This exercise also involved examining the availability of waste heat from industry and of heat from refuse disposal. A 'bottom-up' approach is adopted in which present and future energy needs are mapped at district level, and county councils draw up heating plans for ministerial approval; councils then have the power to control the type of heating in new buildings within specified geographical areas, in line with the approved plan.

Owens uses the plan for Århus as a typical example:[43]

> Based on the concept of 'decentralised concentration' it is in many respects a model of energy consciousness. Policies include the strengthening of small to medium sized local centres, integration of land uses, high densities and direction of growth to centres where there are DH networks. CHP schemes are planned for Århus and Randers.

In the UK, the introduction of district heating could be achieved more cost-effectively by installing heat mains at the same time as sewers and water mains are repaired or replaced.

Energy policy and energy saving

There is no evidence to suggest that the UK government has even considered the use of land-use planning policies to reduce energy consumption. Furthermore, energy efficiency is not even considered to need encouragement: the budget of the Energy Efficiency Office was cut in the late 1980s; the increased funding announced in the Environment White Paper of September 1990 relates almost entirely to the redirection of existing grants into a new Home Energy Efficiency Scheme; and its future level of funding is still uncertain in the face of government expenditure restraints.

In evidence to the Select Committee, Baroness Hooper, Parliamentary Under-Secretary of State in the Department of Energy, said that 'the advantages of energy efficiency are so real and manifest that a programme to encourage voluntary compliance is the most effective'. The Select Committee disagreed:[44]

> if the Government is to respond swiftly and effectively to the threat of global warming, it will have to review most carefully its strategy towards the encouragement and promotion of energy efficiency, in both the public and private sectors of the economy, and will have to adopt a much higher profile and pro-active stance.

Improved energy efficiency and conservation have not resulted from the existing levels of economic incentives. The Select Committee noted that:[45]

> serious market imperfections persist in the energy efficiency field and, as a consequence, widespread opportunities to invest profitably in cost-effective measures to improve the efficiency of energy conversion and use are being ignored.

The failure to take advantage of cost-effective efficiency measures was reduced to four generalisations:

- it requires a very large number of small and disaggregated actions;
- these are peripheral to the (main) perceived interests of most consumers;
- the most cost-effective opportunities are limited because of the slow turnover in equipment, and especially in buildings;
- a number of market imperfections exacerbate the above, such as the lack of specific and unbiased information for users.

Together these present a pressing argument for legal standards, combined with an adequately resourced and empowered Energy Efficiency Office. Indeed the Select Committee called for 'a mixture of regulation, penalties, and incentives, all designed to ensure a rising level of energy efficiency in the UK'. In several areas of energy use, new regulations or standards are seen 'as the only means whereby further energy savings might be captured with reasonable certainty'.

One reason for the government's complacency may be the fact that, except in the transport sector, energy consumption has decreased. However, this is explained more by the impact of the recession on the demand for goods whose manufacture requires a significant input of energy, and by structural changes in the economy away from many energy-intensive manufacturing industries, than by the effects of higher fuel prices or improvements in energy efficiency. In Western Europe as a whole these trends produced a 18.9 per cent reduction in energy consumption between 1973 and 1983.[46]

The Select Committee highlighted 'the persistent misallocation of capital resources in favour of more energy supply and to the neglect of demand management and constraints'. An obligation on the supply industries to pursue least-cost planning would require them to promote efficiency and conservation as ways of meeting energy demands. US utilities regard least-cost planning as central to energy management:[47]

> With substantial community involvement in sound local leadership this planning process has proven very successful in balancing both public and private objectives to encourage economic growth, to maintain a stable low-cost electricity supply and to do both in an environmentally responsible manner.

Yet a statutory duty to adopt least-cost planning or to pay full regard to the desirability of conservation, has not been placed in the licences of the UK electricity supply companies. This failure should be corrected. In Rottweil in West Germany, the electricity supply company gives advice on energy conservation alongside investment in decentralised supply.[48]

The price tariffs and charging practices of the energy supply companies form a further important institutional obstacle to energy conservation. The standing charge system means that the unit price decreases as consumers use more energy and in fact standing charges have been rising at a faster rate than the unit costs of gas and electricity. Industrial users of energy get lower rates the higher their energy consumption; thus the more they use, the lower the rate per unit.

A system designed to encourage conservation would charge consumers as they use and ensure that the units recorded on meters relate as directly as possible to costs. Indeed, the utilities should charge the lowest rate for consumers who use the least energy. The utilities question this approach, pointing out that consumers with a choice of more than one fuel could balance them off against each other, keeping the use of all low and getting the lower tariff. The answer is simple: the utilities need to get together on a common billing system, which again would lead to a proper perception of the situation on the part of the consumer.

The biggest obstacle, perhaps, is the vested interests of those in the business of catering for demand (the supply companies and fuel companies), who benefit from promoting demand rather than persuading consumers to reduce consumption. In the US and in Scandinavia, on the other hand, many utilities explicitly consider energy-efficiency investments as well as investments to increase supply, in order to determine how to meet the needs of customers for energy services at the lowest cost. The Association for the Conservation of Energy (ACE) points out that:[49]

> overseas utilities which have taken into account the possibilities for improved end-use efficiency in their planning, have as a result instigated a wide range of programmes to improve energy surveys for all consumers, to rebates for the purchase of energy efficient lights or motors.

Indeed, some even find that it saves them money to *give* customers energy-efficient light-bulbs to reduce demand! In the UK the profit levels allowed by the regulatory regime that controls the privatised energy supply companies are currently linked simply to supply. The link should be made to overall performance, which could make demand reduction commercially attractive.

It is also crucial to ensure that the costs which consumers are asked to meet are true costs which include the external costs involved in energy use, such as global warming.

Energy taxation

A strong signal is needed from government to public institutions, industry and commerce, and domestic consumers, to the effect that energy saving is paramount in all activities. Such a signal can be effectively provided through the price mechanism. Guido Brunner, a former European Commission Energy Commissioner, proposed that all members of the Community should act in concert in instituting an energy tax which could be used to promote energy-saving practices.

In Denmark taxation is used as an important element of energy policy: the government has a policy of maintaining a stable level of delivered energy prices in order to provide consumers with the correct price signals.

The currently popular concept is a 'carbon tax'. The report of the Energy Select Committee suggests that this 'might be a 10 or 15 per cent discriminatory tax placed on those forms of primary energy that emit greenhouse gases, in part to mirror their external costs'. Such a tax would have to be paralleled by a nuclear tax, so as to reflect its external costs also.

Yet the UK Government only suggests increases in the relative prices of energy and fuel as long term measures, rejecting them in the short term as counter to the 'overriding importance' of reducing inflation, despite recognising the possibility of complementary reductions in other taxes.[50]

Hillman suggests that such taxes should be introduced progressively, accompanied by advice on energy conservation. The revenue raised could be invested in encouraging adequate supply alternatives.[51] The implications would be far-reaching. For example, in the transport sector, Hillman notes:[52]

> Raising the cost of petrol markedly would have implications for other spheres of energy-related public policy: price increases could act as a further incentive for industry to produce, and the consumer to demand, more energy efficient vehicles. They are likely to lead in time to a reduction in the distance that people travel. They would also be likely to encourage greater use of public transport,

fares would hardly have to be increased as fuel costs represent a very small percentage of the total costs of providing services.

It is open to speculation how severely fuel has to be taxed to achieve a sufficient change in behaviour. Some researchers have found the price elasticity of energy to be high, so that people will be prepared to pay more to maintain consumption.[53] If this is so, a general fuel tax will prove less effective in the short term than a regulatory approach. Hillman and Whalley, on the other hand, discovered a close correlation between petrol prices and petrol consumption: as one went up the other went down, even for relatively small price rises.[54] The exact form of a general fuel tax, and the compensatory mechanisms needed to prevent inequity, need careful examination. A study by the Institute of Fiscal Studies found that a 15 per cent tax on electricity would reduce demand by 4 per cent and its undesirable effects on the poor and elderly could be compensated for through the benefits system.[55] On the other hand, the London Business School estimate that in the longer term a 20 per cent reduction in demand would result from an average tax on fossil fuel of 19 per cent.[56]

Conclusion

Urban development is currently energy-intensive, and wasteful of energy resources. But potential for conservation of energy can be seen in all sectors of the economy, most notably in industry, transport and buildings. The biggest obstacle to realising this potential is the vested interests of the energy utilities and fuel companies who benefit from promoting energy demand rather than energy conservation.

Strong guidance is needed from government to public institutions, industry, commerce and domestic consumers to the effect that energy saving is paramount in all activities.

By the very nature of their concentrated land-use activities, cities are conducive to energy saving. Planning policies to shape the pattern of development should complement more specific government investment, regulation and economic incentives to conservation, while supply efficiencies should be increased as a direct consequence of the density of urban areas.

References

1. Lovins, A., *Soft Energy Paths*, Penguin, Harmondsworth, 1977; Leach, G., *A low energy strategy for the UK*, International Institute for Environment and Development, London, 1979.
2. Select Committee on Energy, Sixth Report, *Energy Policy Implications of the Greenhouse Effect*, Vol. 1, HMSO, London, 1989.
3. Hillman, M., *Conservation's Contribution to UK Self-Sufficiency*, PSI and RIIA Joint Energy Programme Paper No. 13, Gower, Aldershot, 1984.
4. See for example Greater London Council, 1980, *Energy Policy and London*, GLC, London, 1980; Owens, S. and Rickaby, P., 'Energy and the Pattern of Human Settlements' in *Built Environment*, Vol. 9, 1983, pp.150-9; Cope, D., Hills, R. and James, P., *Energy Policy and Land-Use Planning*, Pergamon, Oxford, 1984; Owens, S., *Energy Planning and Urban Form*, Pion, London, 1986.
5. Hillman, *op. cit.*, p.75.
6. Pearce, D,, Markandya, A. and Barbier, E., *Blueprint for a Green Economy*, Earthscan, London, 1989.
7. Commission of the European Communities, *Green Paper on the Urban Environment*, COM(90) 218 final, Brussels, 1990.
8. Jackson, T., *The Role of Nuclear Power in Global Warming Abatement Strategies*, Friends of the Earth, London, 1989, p.21.
9. World Resources Institute and International Institute for Environment and Development, *World Resources 1988-89*, Basic Books, New York, 1989.
10. Hillman, *op. cit.*, p.27.
11. *Ibid*, p.61.
12. Department of Energy, *Energy conservation investment in industry*, Energy Paper No. 50, HMSO, London, 1982.
13. March Consulting Group, *Energy Study of the North-West Region of the UK*, March Consulting Limited, Manchester, 1987.
14. Leach, *op. cit.*

15. Hillman, *op. cit.*, p.20.
16. Several studies confirm these figures; for example, Olivier, D. and Miall, H., *Energy Efficient Futures: Opening the Solar Option*, Earth Resources Research, London, 1983; Mathews, G., *An Energy Analysis of Cornwall's Housing Stock*, Earth Resources Research, London, 1988; Hillman, M. and Bollard, A., *Less Fuel More Jobs*, Policy Studies Institute, London, 1985.
17. Hillman, *op. cit.*, p.22.
18. Department of the Environment, *English House Condition Survey 1986*, HMSO, London, 1988.
19. Danskin, H., 'Potential for improvement in UK housing stock', *Energy Management*, Apr/May, 1990.
20. Gaskell, G. and Joerges, B., 'Household Expenditure and Energy Efficiency', proceedings of OECD International Conference on *Urban Environmental Improvement and Economic Development*, Berlin, 1989.
21. Hillman, *op. cit.*, p.23
22. Kasabor, G., (ed.), *Buildings: the key to energy conservation*, Royal Institution of Chartered Surveyors, 1979.
23. Select Committee on Energy, *op. cit.*, para 114.
24. Boardman, B., *Fuel Poverty and the Greenhouse Effect*, Heatwise Glasgow, Friends of the Earth, Neighbourhood Energy Action and National Right to Fuel Campaign, Glasgow, London, Newcastle and Birmingham, 1990.
25. Zijdeveld, C., presentation to SEEDS *Green Plan Environment Conference*, Brighton, 20 October 1989.
26. Milton Keynes Development Corporation, *Energy Park News*, Issue 3, 1987, p.3.
27. For a discussion of energy efficiency technology, see Association for the Conservation of Energy, *Solving the greenhouse dilemma*, ACE, London, 1989; and Hillman and Bollard, *op. cit.*
28. Hillman, *op. cit.*, p.26.
29. Friends of the Earth, *Memorandum: Efficiency of Electricity Use*, FoE, London, 1989.
30. Hillman, *op. cit.*, p.25.
31. Friends of the Earth, *op. cit.*
32. Hillman, *op. cit.*, p.13.

33. Energy Select Committee, *op. cit.*, para.121.
34. Hillman, *op. cit.*, p.16
35. Owens, S., 'Energy Demand: Links to Land-Use and Forward Planning', in *Built Environment*, Vol. 11, No. 1, 1985.
36. *Ibid.*
37. Hillman, M., and Whalley, A., *Energy and Personal Travel*, Policy Studies Institute, London, 1983.
38. Select Committee on Energy, *Energy Conservation in Buildings*, Vol. 1, HMSO, London, 1982; Select Committee on Energy, *Combined Heat and Power*, Vol 1, HMSO, London, 1983; Select Committee on Energy, 1989, *op. cit.*, para 129.
39. Leach, *op. cit.*; Olivier and Miall, 1983, *op. cit.*; Flood, M., *Energy Without End, The Case for Renewable Energy*, Friends of the Earth, London, 1986.
40. Boyle, S., *An Alternative Energy Path for the UK*, Friends of the Earth, London, 1988.
41. Skea, J., *Electricity for Life? Choices for the Environment*, Friends of the Earth and Council for the Protection of Rural England, London, 1988.
42. Owens, 1986, *op. cit.*
43. *Ibid.*
44. Select Committee on Energy, 1989, *op. cit.*, para 111-113.
45. *Ibid.*, para 107.
46. Odell, P., 'Energy and Regional Development: A European Perspective', *Built Environment*, Vol. 11, No.1, 1985.
47. Rice, N., 'Least Cost Electric Utility Planning in the Pacific Northwest United States', OECD International Conference on *Urban Environmental Improvement and Economic Development*, Berlin, 1989, p.120.
48. European Colloquium, *Discussion Paper: Urban Resource Management*, Ministry of Urban Development and Environmental Protection, Berlin, 1989.
49. Association for the Conservation of Energy, *op. cit.*
50 *This Common Inheritance*, CM1200, HMSO, London, 1990
51. Hillman, M., *Interview transcript*, July 1989.
52. Hillman, 1984, *op. cit.*, p.66.
53. Owens, 1986, *op. cit.*
54. Hillman, and Whalley, *op. cit.*

55. Johnson, P., McKay, S. and Smith, S., *The distributional consequences of environmental taxes*, (Interim report, May), Institute for Fiscal Studies, London, 1990.
56. Barrett, F.S., 'Pricing the environment', *Economic Outlook*, February 1990.

Chapter 4: Green Space and Wildlife

Introduction

Sustainable urban development must embrace nature as integral to the city itself. Cities must become much less disruptive of the workings of the natural ecosystem: its climate, its hydrology and its ecology.

In practice, an important issue is bringing nature (insofar as it exists in densely populated countries) into the life of city dwellers through a diversity of open landscapes: formal parks in the Victorian tradition, playing fields, extensive informal parks, public gardens, adventure playgrounds, shared streets (such as the Dutch *woonerven*), walkways and cycle ways, small greens, copses and thickets, meadows, and rough wild areas. In this way urban dwellers can experience nature without always having to visit rural areas.

The present

Cities in Britain today show little sign of a relationship with nature. Open space is generally uniform, fragmented and increasingly threatened by development. Air, water and soil are often polluted, and watercourses are usually channelised to deal with run-off from the impermeable surfaces.

As Goode laments:[1]

By building cities in the way we have we are divorcing ourselves from nature. What contact is there with the seasons in a modern air-conditioned shopping mall with its built-in trees? Sadly we have banished nature from most of our townscapes and the resulting environment reflects only too well the assumption that we can exist entirely in isolation of the natural world.

Indeed, most urban open space in the UK has become a landscape of mown chemically-retarded grass, with a few scattered trees and a standard set of play equipment. The quality of the landscape is poor, both aesthetically and ecologically. This has resulted in part from misguided health and safety concerns about 'untidy' environments, and in part from short-term responses to financial constraints. The product is our present landscape which creates social costs because it fails to stimulate our senses and simultaneously costs, in financial terms, more to manage than is necessary.

These parks were never intended to be just mown grass and a few trees but for many years prior to 1987 managers of parks had not been planting trees. As a result, there is no age structure in the tree populations, which often consist of vulnerable trees up to 300 years old. In many cases new planting has occurred recently, prompted by widespread storm losses. However, unless such planting continues on a regular basis the age structure of the UK's urban tree population will remain distorted. Very little money has been made available for rehabilitation and maintenance of most British municipal parks. The natural urban landscape has received much less money and attention than the built environment, although even support for our built heritage has been inadequate.

Urban parks have lost many of their more interesting features as far as many urban users are concerned. Handley and Bulmer record the cases of two post-war parks in Knowsley, an urban area of Merseyside in the UK.[2] Between 1974 and 1986, 45 ornamental flower beds, twelve tennis courts, four bowling greens, two paddling pools and seven other features of recreational or ornamental interest were lost. It is hardly surprising that almost 99 per cent of the managed green space in Knowsley is mown grass, over half of which is cut sixteen or more times each year.[3] As well as creating a landscape of less interest to humans, such frequent cutting, although conducive to tidiness, leaves no opportunity for most wild species.

The urban nature conservation movement

In reaction to these developing problems, an enthusiastic voluntary sector urban nature conservation movement has emerged in the UK (as in many other countries). This has centred on the importance of providing urban people with the opportunity to experience nature and on providing educational programmes for children. Attempts have been made to improve awareness amongst land-use decision-makers of the nature conservation value of their land and of the benefits to be had from adopting conservation principles in its management. Central among them is the contribution to sustainability of the urban system as a whole that results.

Goode suggests that urban nature conservation differs from other more traditional approaches to conservation in that it does not place priority on rare or endangered species or habitats, but gives considerable weight to the values and benefits of urban wildlife to local people and aims to be a grass-roots movement.[4] But there is a need to do much more to demonstrate that in reality urban nature conservation does not conflict with the needs and aspirations of less wealthy communities, particularly ethnic minorities, for developments that will provide affordable housing and accessible employment.[5]

Arguments for the conservation of totally artificial habitats, such as disused railway land or neglected cemeteries, have established new precedents in the case law of planning and are now reflected in many local plans.[6] But the 'greenspace' movement is not concerned only with nature reserves and includes all aspects of greening from city farms to window boxes.[7]

Conservation of 'natural' habitat

The obvious alternatives to planned open space can be seen in the many so-called 'natural' open spaces to be found in cities. The key characteristics of such places, which include disused railway lines, abandoned quarries, woods, subsidence flashes and river valleys, is that they are virtually, if not totally, unmanaged. In a social sense, these open spaces are 'uncommitted' and people can experiment with how they use them. Conservationists have often found that those places that had been left to nature are rich in wildlife and present visitors with the opportunity to observe the natural world close to their home rather than in the countryside (Table 4.1).

Table 4.1: Wildlife habitat in the city: the example of Leicester

	Area (ha)	% of High Ecological Value
Formal open space	1429	23
Agricultural land	805	10
Grassland	336	24
Arable	332	0
Allotments	137	2
Land left to nature	392	53
Woodlands	80	77
Unmanaged land	308	46
Wetlands	4	95
Total land	7337	8
Total undeveloped land	2627	22

Source: Leicester City Council, *Leicester Ecology Strategy*, 1989, Appendix 3.

St James's Park in London is a good example of what can be achieved in ornithological terms in the centre of a city through good design, in this case by providing an important buffer between birds and people. However, this park has many exotic species. Other examples in the UK where native species predominate are Walthamstow Reservoir in London and Radipole Lake in Weymouth. Figure 4.1 shows the distribution of sites of metropolitan importance for nature conservation in London.

Yet existing habitats are not adequately protected. The current system of habitat protection in the UK is largely based upon voluntary conservation and compensation, rather than upon statutory protection for designated sites. The network of some 5,000 Sites of Special Scientific Interest, considered by the Nature Conservancy Council to be the

**Figure 4.1: Map showing sites of metropolitan importance for nature
conservation in London**

KEY

.   0.5 - 10 ha

•   10.5 - 100 ha

●   > 100 ha

△   Sites originally designated of Metropolitan Importance, but
which have subsequently lost this status.

Source: London Ecology Unit, 1988.

minimum area that must be protected, is being eroded. Better protection and more vigorous designation of sites is needed, particularly in or near urban areas where the pressures for development or change of use are most severe.

Much effort in urban nature conservation is devoted to protecting existing habitats which are increasingly under pressure for development. A major objective must be to ensure that green space is available to people within a city environment. Currently, there is no statutory guidance for provision of open space in relation to population.* For example, there are no minimum standards for wildlife within cities. The London Ecology Unit has established a new category: 'an area of deficiency of natural vegetation' and is producing maps showing the distribution of such areas in each borough. This term has been accepted at public inquiry and means that the need for some kind of habitat to be created has been accepted.

Creation of naturalistic habitats

To complement protection of habitats, creation of new ones is necessary to rectify 'deficiencies of natural vegetation'. Holland has had a major influence on urban landscape design, pioneering what has become known as the ecological approach. Central to the philosophy of this approach is an appreciation of how the consumers of landscape view and use it, from which it follows that the consumers should be involved in the design of landscapes. By the early 1970s, there emerged from Holland:[8]

a stream of experimental landscapes designed to be played in, walked through, touched and smelled, to provide freedom and excitement. At Utrecht a reed-fringed wetland was laid out round an office block. At Delft the courtyards of high-rise flats became woodland glades ... [in] inner areas of the Hague old buildings were knocked down to make

* The National Playing Fields Association is actively campaigning for standards for formal and informal recreational space.

way for parks. Fresh types of green space were invented: cuddle gardens for children, and *heemparks*, where native flowers ... grew in their natural Dutch habitat of dyke, dune and polder.

Much of the Dutch experience has grown from concern for the social consequences of urbanisation. The social goals, which British environmental planners have often ignored, included attempts to mitigate the tower block excesses of the early 1960s, most notably the gaunt 260-feet high Bijlmermeer estate in Amsterdam. The estate, like most of its contempories in Britain, was plagued with appalling social problems. The whole approach is to help people feel that they are in touch with nature despite the fact that their home is a huge tower block. A similar approach is being followed in Helsingborg in Sweden. Planners thus recognise that such positive initiatives help people psychologically.[9]

In *A Green Renaissance*, Goode discusses the place of ecology in landscape design:[10]

But planning only goes so far, and much of the urban [natural] environment is determined by landscape designers ... Until recently ecology had no place in landscape design. Naturalistic planting is becoming more widely accepted.

In those parts of cities where all vestiges of nature have been eradicated, habitat creation must now take priority. Examples like Camley Street Natural Park in London, currently under threat from development, have a vital role as demonstration areas. The potential for creation of more extensive wildlife habitats in urban areas is already well illustrated by examples such as Tift Farm wetland nature reserve created on a disused hazardous waste dump on the outskirts of Buffalo in the USA or the Leslie Street Spit offshore from Toronto which, though totally artificial, has been colonised by a great variety of plant and animal species and now has considerable value as a prime wildlife resource in close proximity to this major city.

Landscape designers, ecologists and horticulturists have the skills to create new habitats. As Goode points out, 'we cannot recreate ancient woodlands, ... but many other kinds of naturalistic vegetation can be created very effectively'.[11] In particular, he highlights the possibilities for wetland habitat creation:[12]

> Derelict docks and sewage farms offer possibilities for wetland wildlife that could be very popular in urban areas. Future plans for the vast acreage of Beddington Sewage Farm near Croydon include an extensive nature reserve with lakes reedbeds and lagoons for marshland birds. It will be a most attractive landscape for people as well as waterfowl.

More generally the habitats which have developed so successfully on derelict or vacant land demonstrate what is possible.[13] They provide a particularly good guide since most of the species involved are already closely adapted to the artificial conditions of towns and cities. We should look at our remaining bomb sites, examine their natural history and use the plants as the basis for design work in the urban situation, because these are the plants already adapted to the city. These sites can have a wide variety of plants and insects associated with them. Such areas can be created throughout the city without dropping bombs!

In most cases natural areas are substantially cheaper to manage than a traditional park. Research has been carried out on the costs of producing natural areas and the costs of their after-care/management. Dawe estimates that a traditional Victorian park costs three times as much to establish as one based on natural habitat, and that the cost of after-care of the natural park is, at most, half.[14] Nicholson-Lord also provides some estimates:[15]

> The new landscapes advocated by the small-scale city greeners had the inestimable benefit of cheapness ... Native semi-natural planting can cost less than a tenth of orthodox

grass with trees and, somewhat surprisingly, a fifth, in both laying and maintenance cost, of concrete on hardcore. At Warrington new town, ecological planting costs, even without voluntary labour, are put at between a tenth and a quarter of conventional methods.

Recent work on land reclamation on Merseyside indicates that native landscaping (using largely self-sown native vegetation) is cheaper to establish and maintain than conventional contemporary amenity landscaping (largely mown grass), while naturalistic landscaping (creating new habitats to simulate native vegetation), although more expensive to establish, is substantially cheaper to maintain (see Table 4.2).

Table 4.2: The aftercare costs of land reclamation schemes in St Helens and Knowsley (£/ha/yr)

	Establishment Cost (Years 0-5)		Maintenance Cost (Years 6-10)	
	Average	Range	Average	Range
Type of scheme				
Native	£353	£104-774	£168	£60-432
Naturalistic	£2120	£512-3144	£716	£348-1190
Amenity	£1498	£290-4188	£1103	£290-3518

Source: Handley, J. and Bulmer, P., 'The Design and Management of Cost-effective Landscapes', (typescript, St Helens Groundwork Trust).

However, Dawe cautions against justifying naturalistic landscaping on economic grounds alone:[16]

> ... arguing for the introduction of nature to areas of cities purely on the basis of cost savings is an ideologically bankrupt approach which may further discredit the movement for nature in cities. There are much more important arguments concerning the relevance of nature in

improving social conditions, the quality of life for urban residents, the tourism potential of certain cities and even the attractiveness of urban centres for industry and commerce... Why else, for example, have so many Dutch, German and Swedish cities placed such great emphasis on both the quantity of their green open spaces, and their *quality*?

Interestingly, the Department of the Environment's own commissioned research reinforces this viewpoint in its implicit analysis of the benefits of improving the 'natural environment' in urban areas.[17]

In Warrington New Town an ecological approach was used in the design of landscapes for housing on a former factory site.[18] The result is a wooded landscape within which the new town has developed. The belts of trees linked to the surrounding countryside can be seen as continuous threads of nature through the residential environment. A similar effect has been attempted with Russia Dock Wood, a newly created park within the Rotherhithe Docklands in South-East London. Naturalistic planting, together with a series of pools and weirs, has created a remarkably natural landscape in close proximity to housing.[19]

There have been some social problems with the Warrington approach, with people wishing to be less enclosed by woodlands. Now, new ideas are being implemented which are more sensitive to locating woodlands close to housing. In a similar way, Milton Keynes' original woodland structure planting was acclaimed initially, but was later found to be unsatisfactory in respect to corridor routes, such as cycle tracks and pathways. People felt insecure closed in by trees. The woodlands are now being managed so that views open up from the paths.

Goode describes other (at least partially) successful initiatives:[20]

So far most habitat creation schemes in urban areas of Britain have been at the modest scale of ecology parks. The William Curtis Ecological Park, which existed near Tower Bridge from 1978 to 1985, was a fine example of what is possible on an inner-city site. It was remarkably successful, not only in the range of habitats and species it supported, but also in catering for local school-children who would

otherwise have had little or no contact with nature ...
Recently a number of ecology parks intended to be
permanent have been created in London including Camley
Street Natural Park at King's Cross, Tump 53 Nature Park
in Thamesmead, and Lavender Pond and Rotherhithe Park
in the Surrey Docks. They all have dual roles, providing for
education, and enjoyment by local residents. Those
developed within housing schemes at Rotherhithe and
Thamesmead demonstrate that by careful design a variety
of wildlife can be accommodated despite the close
proximity of people.

However, the partial acceptance of the value of ecology by the London
Docklands Development Corporation is not reflected elsewhere. The
Kings Cross development proposals suggest attempting to move the
Camley Street park (although the developers have had an ecological
strategy for the site prepared and are offering some potential ecological
gains), while in Cardiff the Urban Development Corporation is
proposing the destruction of a valuable Site of Special Scientific Interest
(SSSI).

Effective management must follow habitat creation. Dawe
comments:[21]

> Greater training is required for [park managers]. The
> London Ecology Unit has been involved in changing park
> mowing regimes, with mowers being trained to have a
> wider view of the natural environment in parks.

However, vested interests, notably those of the chemical industry,
combine with the commitment to 'modern methods' demonstrated by
both the media and the horticulture industry to influence the
management of land. Not only are public open spaces subjected to
chemical-based management but the public is encouraged to treat wild
plants as something to be got rid of, using chemicals in the process. Thus
private gardens also rarely contribute their full potential to the natural
environment of the city.

Overall, the target of creation and protection should be to provide a network of habitats, not only to provide corridors for the movement of wildlife, but also to improve the urban climate.

Working within the natural ecosystem

Increased urban temperature and lowered humidity result from the dominance of artificial surfaces in the city and generate demands for controlled environments dependent on air conditioning in buildings. Yet vegetated zones linking the centre with the periphery can improve air circulation and counter these local climatic changes. More localised greening, in open spaces, on roofs, walls and in courtyards, can trap particulate pollution, as well as increasing humidity and limiting extremes of temperature within the buildings.[22]

Natural areas have an important role in the hydrological cycle in cities as well as serving wildlife. In the USA storm water basins and retention basins are of recognised importance for wildlife conservation. Naturalistic open space, being permeable, is of benefit to the city's hydrology in slowing the speed of run-off of rainfall. We should be using natural ecological systems to the best advantage, saving the financial costs of unnecessary engineering works. Increasing the area of permeable land will reduce run-off and the need to culvert all water courses in the city to contain great fluctuations in water levels. That technological fix is necessary because of the impermeability of developed city land. The London Borough of Sutton has such a policy. New materials are now available which provide a surface which is load bearing, but also permeable. This is particularly useful for car parks and commonly used in Holland.

Designing with nature is beginning to happen on a number of fronts, for example using the floodplain areas of a river as a golf course and accepting that it will flood now and again, or designing two-level storage areas within parks. In Köln virtually the entire floodplain downstream of the city centre takes the form of public open space. More extensive urban fringe land uses can also be of value for nature conservation, notably woodlands and reservoirs.

Another example of the important function of nature in cities is in indirect pollution control. Natural areas work to reduce pollution. There is plenty of evidence that forests in urban areas filter the air and help enormously to keep down aerial (particulate) pollution. Water pollution can also be ameliorated. In Fife in Scotland reed beds are being used for sewage effluent filtration.

Vegetation in various urban areas in Britain is badly affected by certain emissions. For example Merseyside suffers considerable sulphur dioxide pollution, while the effect of traffic emissions in central London is such that in the worst affected areas very few tree species can tolerate the conditions, all of them hybrids or alien species which support relatively few insect and bird species.[23]

Working within natural ecosystems can provide benefits for society as a whole, and also for the individual developer. Certainly, it is accepted in some quarters, particularly in the house-building sector, that 'ecology pays', that the investment potential of an area will be increased by an ecologically more sustainable environment, attractive to housebuyers, industry and commerce. A good environment is not an extra but provides the basis for sustainable development, particularly with regard to quality of life and general well-being.

Goode argues that we must go further than merely creating green space, we must look for green development:[24]

> If we can create ecology parks to compensate for areas with a deficiency of nature why should we not create more varied habitats on and around buildings? Green rooftops are becoming accepted in West Germany where the technology is now well developed, and there are clear advantages for river engineering in having reduced run-off from such rooftops during spate conditions. On the Odham's Walk building in London's Covent Garden, a series of small gardens has been constructed at different levels within open courtyards, creating the impression that the building is covered in trees and shrubs. The scheme was not designed to promote wildlife, but has resulted in a variey of birds breeding in a part of London where they would not normally occur.

Indeed many species of wild flora and fauna can be accommodated in the city; all that is required is to provide slightly different habitats and accept their existence.

It is also important to look at green space from a wider psychological point of view, people's perception of their need for green space. A recent study by Mostyn and Millward shows that being with and amongst nature is good for people; that people enjoy the 'feel of the countryside' within the city.[25] Nicholson-Lord argues strongly that emotional commitment must be channelled creatively:[26]

> As practised in schools and local authorities, [environmental education's] underlying theme is care for surroundings, the prevention of vandalism in the widest sense of the word.

> In Edinburgh the Environmental Resource Centre has since 1976 done outstanding work in fostering the message that community development and environmental conservation go hand in hand.

Every city offers some opportunity for creating ecosystems that will be productive, for example by producing a crop or acting as a filter for water supply. One example is the cropping of grasslands for hay; in Leicester semi-natural grasslands are being created in the parks and the hay produced is sold to stables. The fact is that wide-ranging cropping opportunities exist, and, as in this case, only require such practical measures as the local authority changing its grass equipment in order to be able to cut agricultural-length grass.

Urban forestry

Another example is provided by urban forestry. One option is the rotational growing of trees on wasteland and interim derelict sites. All clearance sites can be used temporarily to grow trees and the wood can be chipped for use as fuel for greenhouses or sold as chopped wood mulch.

If a more permanent forest is created it will pay for itself (mainly in avoided costs) within a reasonable time period. It may be more expensive initially to plant trees in a forest regime than it is to establish and mow grass. But after a few years management is minimal and the ecosystem is relatively self-sustaining. In the longer term, the costs are even less. Near Schiedam in Holland, land acquired by the city for housing has been planted with trees. By the time the site is needed for development an economic crop should have been produced.[27] More generally, if costing were done in 10-year terms instead of annual budgets, it would pay to create much more diverse landscapes in cities.

Research in 1976 indicated that grass cost £200 per hectare to establish and £93 in annual maintenance. Establishment of semi-natural woodland cost £700 per hectare but annual maintenance was only £12.[28] This indicates that the forestry scheme should pay back the investment (even without cropping) after eight years.*

Good management practice is demonstrated by Bristol which initiated its woodland advisory panel in 1977. Foresters and conservationists sit alongside local amenity and wildlife representatives. In 1980 its first woodland officer was appointed and in 1981 a forestry grant was applied for. The city meanwhile produced a new woodland estate working plan.

Under the management guidelines laid down in this ambitious document, the 'outline' of the woodland canopy should be retained and trees kept beyond economic maturity. Rotation forestry, the routine clear-felling of large tracts of woodland, is prohibited. Treatment is of 'small, random irregular' areas, aiming at a multi-storeyed woodland and greater wildlife diversity. Native species, notably the old English sessile and pedunculate oaks, figure prominently in planting. Equal stress is laid on traditional woodcraft skills: pruning, hand weeding of young trees, and 'brashing', or removing lower dead branches. Operations are labour-intensive, and avoid chemical sprays. Public access and safety is not used as an excuse for overtidiness. 'As well as

---

*   Assuming future benefits (costs forgone) are discounted at a rate of 10 per cent. At a lower discount rate the project should appear even more favourable.

harvesting and marketing woodland products', the plan notes, 'we are marketing a recreational facility.'

Urban forestry sees trees as a croppable resource in economic terms. As an urban forestry initiative for the EEC, Chambers looked at the feasibility of urban forestry in Tower Hamlets.[29] She identified three main problems:

i) Councillors perceived the whole initiative as 'eco-freakish';
ii) Five different departments in the authority dealt with trees, and communication between them was practically non-existent;
iii) The cropping/pruning of trees would provide wood chips for sale, but the money would never acrue to the department carrying out the work, instead going to the central budget. This administrative arrangement would provide little financial incentive to the department to crop its own products. (Meanwhile, the authority was buying in chips at £4 per tonne from suppliers who were maintaining its trees, chipping the wood and selling it back to the authority.)

However, an initiative was begun in 1985, with the planting of ten derelict sites as part of the borough's forestry management plan, designed to provide wood for local timber companies and craft industries.

A recent study by the London Borough of Hounslow recommends the planting of hardwoods 'as they are more versatile, hardier than conifers in an urban situation, have a wider range of uses and can potentially achieve as high yields and higher financial returns'.[30] The study suggests that markets exist for veneer wood, sawlogs, fuel wood and energy cropping.

The urban forest may be a large-scale exercise in afforestation on the urban fringe, as in Bos Park, Amsterdam, or West Forest Park in Copenhagen, the latter begun in 1967 and planned to cover 3,200 acres. A minimum size is often involved. Sweden's urban forests, for example, used largely for timber production, cover at least 125 to 250 acres and also serve a recreational function, being accessible on foot, bicycle, ski or public transport from the city.

Figure 4.2: Map showing location of proposed community forests.

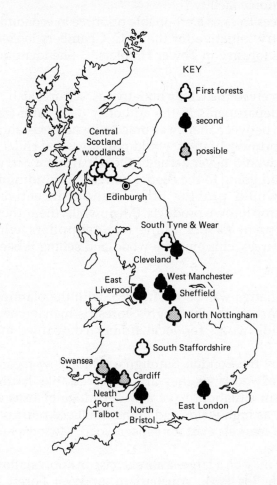

KEY

First forests

second

possible

Central
Scotland
woodlands

Edinburgh

South Tyne & Wear

Cleveland

East
Liverpool

West Manchester

Sheffield

North Nottingham

South Staffordshire

Swansea

Cardiff

Neath
Port
Talbot

North
Bristol

East London

F.O.E. FIG 4·2

Source: Countryside Commission.

In the UK the Countryside Commission and Forestry Commission are promoting the development of urban fringe 'community forests' of around 15,000 hectares with a mix of recreational and productive uses (see Figure 4.2). Planting has already begun in South Staffordshire and South Tyne and Wear. The Forestry Commission has recently published its *Urban Forestry Handbook*. Estimates suggest that major urban fringe forests of this scale will cost between £20 and £25 million to establish, but that such large-scale initiatives can attract private sponsorship, as well as providing for commercial as well as amenity use.[31] A specialist Urban Forestry Unit is being established in the Black Country, funded by the local authorities, the Development Corporation, the Forestry Commission, the Countryside Commission (via the Black Country Groundwork Trust), and private sponsors.

The benefits of urban forestry span several of those outlined above: they can provide experience of the natural environment and a recreational resource, they can benefit the urban climate and to some extent reduce the effects of pollution, and in addition can provide raw materials to meet local needs. However, urban forestry only provides certain types of wildlife interest and should not be promoted on sites where it might damage existing wildlife value (even if the sites are derelict).

Planning for the natural environment

The financial benefits of naturalistic landscaping and urban forestry will not alone generate an adequate strategy for the urban natural environment. In the UK, in parallel with voluntary organisations, some local authorities have taken a lead in developing policies for protecting urban wildlife. London, Manchester and the West Midlands all developed strategies for conservation as part of strategic planning prior to abolition of the Metropolitan County Councils.[32] Goode describes the process in Greater London:[33]

> this involved a comprehensive survey and evaluation of 2000 sites of potential value for wildlife, representing one fifth of the land area of the capital. Sites were graded

according to their value in London as a whole, within individual boroughs and even at the local level. This evaluation took account of people's needs for nature as well as the intrinsic wildlife quality of individual sites. [See Figure 4.1 which shows those sites graded as 'of metropolitan importance'.]

The West Midlands was the first local authority to produce a nature conservation strategy in 1984. Nicholson-Lord comments:[34]

> The content of this remarkable document – its designation of inner-city wildlife action areas, of green reservoirs, corridors, stepping stones, its plans for hedges, flower meadows, 'wild areas', in parks and on road verges – is in a sense less important than the vision it expresses.

> Conservation, said the strategy, was not merely about the survival of wildlife but 'the survival of the physical and mental well-being of the human species'. People needed woods, heaths, pools and meadows, but they needed them near at hand – within a thousand metres of where they lived. A greener inner city might even persuade people to resist the lure of the suburbs and the shires, might come to be regarded as part of their 'standard of living'.

Goode describes the development of such initiatives:[35]

> we are witnessing new values being established in many cities in Europe and North America. Perhaps the most impressive application of an ecological approach to planning is that of West Berlin, where a complete inventory has been made of ecological factors throughout the city. All vegetation has been mapped and many ecological variables measured. This data provides the basis for a rigorous process of ecological planning.

Planning authorities are beginning to provide frameworks for nature conservation in regional or local planning based on comprehensive surveys. These frameworks inform policies, while new criteria which take account of social values are being developed for evaluation of wildlife resources. Such policies can form a firm basis for the protection of wildlife habitats.

It is important to enable the local community to participate in site decisions. They are the ones who will use and care for the site on a day-to-day basis. If they prefer allotments, or bedding plants, or alien species, then they should not have naturalistic landscaping forced upon them.[36] Children in particular should be involved more widely because they are major users of the landscape. However, with a few praiseworthy exceptions, such as the London Borough of Lambeth's work on (for example) Tulse Hill nature garden in Brixton, it is only adults who define the landscapes that we have in UK cities. In Helsingborg in Sweden the Rosengorden scheme is a child's play area which contains natural woodland integrated with formal play structures. Children seem to play more in the natural areas.

Strategic planning policies need to accept new, naturally-oriented values which the existing planning guidance from the Department of the Environment, including the recent London Strategic Planning Guidance, fails to do. The interests of conservation are in fact the same as those of development if improved welfare or quality of life is seen as the aim of development. But the necessary planning controls are not in place because conservation is regarded as a real constraint to development. It is important to introduce ecological thinking into strategic planning to ensure that a good environment is created and maintained, rather than destroyed by piecemeal built development. This could be achieved, at least in part, by making it a statutory requirement for development plans to include nature conservation strategies based on comprehensive surveys.

Increasing the natural area in the city calls into question the balance between extensive versus intensive land use in cities, which is considered at length in Chapter 1 on the built environment. In any large city, it is possible to accommodate a vast number of people in relatively small areas and still maintain an extraordinary amount of greenery. With good design it is possible to have natural areas in a city, which add to the quality of life, as long as the pattern of land use does not encourage extra travel. Thus the model of decentralised concentration along with an understanding of the functioning of the urban ecosystem should guide the provision of intensive and extensive open spaces.

Obstacles to change

First and foremost, the greatest obstacle to sustainable urban development is the overwhelming pressure of the development machine in which land prices reflect investment potential; and the dynamic of the process determines what happens in cities. Ecology is secondary to financial gain, and those involved rarely accept that a high-quality environment provides economic benefits.

Speculative investment has different priorities from those of local residents. The local community is prepared to put environmental improvements before financial return. Unfortunately new development is rarely designed for the local population but normally for the profit of the investment company, and often gives rise to development which is not required locally.

In today's investment climate, pressure for development is so great that land which has lain fallow for a long period, such as railway edges and embankments, is being gobbled up very quickly. Open land which has been relatively wild for 100-150 years is being developed piecemeal for housing, along the embankments of all London's railway lines. This pressure is not being guided by a strategic planning framework. The statutory undertakers are under pressure to sell off all land surplus to perceived requirements, whether or not there is a likelihood of it being needed for strategic reasons in the future.* There will thus be pressure on remaining open space to replace, for example, the railway lines and railheads that are being lost now.[37]

* In 1980, the government established the Public Land Register, on which all land held unused by public bodies such as British Rail and local authorities is listed and is thereby made available for purchase by developers.

136

The problem is two-fold: the attitudes as a whole within the development machine and the heavy weighting of the political and economic incentives in favour of the development process. In environmental terms, on a global scale, the odds are astronomically in favour of development and exploitation, explaining why we have lost between 50 and 80 per cent of semi-natural habitats in Britain's countryside, post-war.[38] In the cities we are in danger of doing the same thing again, losing options for the future, instead of protecting existing natural areas and examining what more can be done.

At the time of writing, Rainham Marsh in London, at 1,166 acres, one of the largest urban SSSIs, is under threat of development. Even created sites are not safe: the William Curtis ecological park at Tower Bridge was lost to development and 'replaced' with a paved area and 'lollipop' trees. As stated above, statutory protection for the best sites is vital, but more generally, mechanisms for balancing the natural value of a site against its value for development or as a transport route must be improved. Currently mechanisms in cost benefit analysis of roads fail to take into account the environmental value of open space[39] and virtually all development grants from government are awarded without consideration of the actual or potential environmental value of the site.

Conclusion

Cities are becoming increasingly out of touch with nature to the detriment of city dwellers. What open space does exist in the city is relatively uniform, fragmented and increasingly threatened by development. The mown grass and scattered trees experienced in parks offer little psychological benefit.

To bring nature back into the city, naturalistic landscaping should be introduced at every level in the built environment, in buildings, streets and all public open space. Working with nature in this way has economic and social as well as ecological advantages. Natural areas provide wildlife habitats and also work to reduce pollution and improve urban hydrology, while urban forestry can provide both recreation and a croppable resource.

References

1. Goode, D., 'A Green Renaissance', Introduction in Gordon, D.(ed.), *Green Cities: Ecologically sound approaches to urban space*, Black Rose Books, Montreal, 1990.
2. Handley, J. and Bulmer, P., 'The Design and Management of Cost-effective Landscapes', typescript, St Helens Groundwork Trust, 1989.
3. *Ibid.*
4. Goode, D., 'Nature in the City', *Urban Design Quarterly*, Vol. 24, 1987a, pp. 12-14.
5. Agyeman, J., 'A Pressing Question for the Green Organisations', *Town and Country Planning* February 1988, pp.50-51; Agyeman, J., 'Where is our place?', *New Statesman and Society*, 3 February 1989.
6. Several examples of these precedents are discussed in Goode, D., 'Creative Conservation for Public Enjoyment', in Talbot-Ponsonby, H. (ed.), *Recreation and Wildlife: working in partnership*, Countryside Recreation Research Advisory Group, Bristol, 1987b.
7. See Goode, D., 'Green Vision', *Architects Journal*, February, 1986a, pp.44-46.
8. Nicholson-Lord, D., *The Greening of the Cities*, Routledge and Kegan Paul, London, 1987, pp. 111-12; see also Ruff, A., 'Holland and the ecological landscapes 1973-1987', in Deelstra, T., (ed.), *Urban and Regional Studies*, 1, Delft University Press, Delft, 1987; many examples of ecological approaches to urban landscape design are described in A. Ruff and R. Tregay, (eds), *An Ecological Approach to Landscape Design*, Department of Town and Country Planning, University of Manchester, 1982.
9. Dawe, G., *Interview transcript*, May 1989a.
10. Goode, 1990, *op.cit.*
11. Goode, 1987a, *op. cit.* For a good practical handbook, see Emery, M., *Promoting Nature in Cities and Towns: a practical guide*, Croom Helm, London, 1986.
12. Goode, 1990, *op. cit.*
13. Burton, J.A., *The Naturalist in London*, David & Charles, Newton Abbot, 1974; Goode, 1987a, *op. cit.*

14. Dawe, 1989a, *op. cit;* also see Corder, M. and Brooker, R., *Natural Economy: an ecological approach to planning and management techniques in urban areas,* Kirklees Metropolitan Council, 1981.
15. Nicholson-Lord, *op. cit.,* p.182.
16. Dawe, G., *Introduction to Habitat Creation - the use of native plants,* Packard Publishing, Chichester, 1989b.
17. Ecotec, *Greening City Sites: Good Practice in Urban Regeneration,* Department of the Environment, London, 1987.
18. Scott, D., *et al.,* 'Warrington New Town: An Ecological Approach to Landscape Design and Management' in Bradshaw, A., Goode D. and Thorp E., (eds), *Ecology and Design in Landscape,* Symposium of the British Ecological Society 24, Blackwell Scientific Publications, Oxford, 1986, pp. 143-60.
19. Goode, 1987a, *op. cit.*
20. *Ibid.* For further discussion, see Goode, D. and Smart, P., 'Designing for Wildlife' in Bradshaw et al., *op. cit.,* pp. 219-35.
21. Dawe, 1989a, *op. cit.*
22. European Colloquium, *Discussion Paper "Nature in Towns and Cities",* Proceedings, Technical University of Berlin, 1989.
23. Southwood, T.R.E., 'The number of species of insect associated with various trees', *Journal of Animal Ecology,* Vol. 30, 1961, pp. 1-8; Kennedy, C.E.J. and Southwood, T.R.E., 'The number of species of insect associated with British trees: a re-analysis', *Journal of Animal Ecology,* Vol. 53, 1984, pp. 455-78.
24. Goode, 1990, *op. cit.*
25. Millward, A. and Mostyn, B., *People and Nature in Cities,* Urban Wildlife Now **2,** Nature Conservancy Council, Peterborough, 1989; Mostyn, B., *Personal benefits and satisfactions derived from participation in urban wildlife projects: a qualitative evaluation,* NCC, London, 1979; Harrison, C., Limb M. and Burgess, J., 'Popular values for a living world', *Journal of Environmental Management,* Vol. 25, 1987, pp. 347-62.
26. Nicholson-Lord, *op. cit.,* pp. 132 and 136.
27. Zijdeveld, C., presentation to SEEDS *Green Plan Environment Conference,* Brighton, 20 October 1989.
28. Dawe, 1989b, *op. cit.*

29. Chambers, K., 'Urban Forestry in the London Borough of Tower Hamlets', *Arboricultural Journal*, February 1987.
30. Northern Planners, *Timber Production in the London Borough of Hounslow*, An Urban Forestry Economic Feasibility Study for the London Borough of Hounslow Planning Department, 1989.
31. Forestry Commision, *Urban forestry handbook*, Forestry Commission, 1989; *Urban Forests* Journal, No. 1, Autumn 1989.
32. Goode, D., 'Urban Nature Conservation in Britain' in *Journal of Applied Ecology*, Vol.26, pp.859-73, 1989.
33. Goode, 1987a, *op. cit.*
34. Nicholson-Lord, *op. cit*, p.86.
35. Goode, 1987a, *op. cit.*
36. Dawe, 1989a, *op. cit.*
37. Goode, D., *Interview Transcript*, July 1989.
38. Nature Conservancy Council, *Nature Conservation in Great Britain*, NCC, Peterborough, 1984.
39. Adams, J., *London's Green Spaces*, Friends of the Earth, London, 1989.

Chapter 5: Food – Production and Supply

Introduction

Urban development cannot be sustainable unless the production of food for its inhabitants is sustainable. Globally the food production system must be able to continually feed the urban population. However, in 'developed' countries the nature of the production system is the current priority. An ecologically sustainable agricultural system in the hinterland of the city is of great importance. Sustainable urban development must increase rather than reduce the integration of the city with the surrounding countryside as a hinterland which produces food for it, particularly through increased nutrient recycling. If at the same time the production of unwanted surpluses can be halted then the agricultural production bases of 'less-developed countries' will be less threatened by depressed world market prices and food dumping.

The production of food within the city can be increased, but this cannot be expected to supply all its needs. Thus remaining food supply lines must also be shortened through orienting production in the immediate hinterland to the city's needs, obtaining temperate foodstuffs from within the UK and non-temperate foodstuffs from nearer sources where possible. The net effect would be an increasing level of local self-reliance.

In the UK the results of these processes would be a more diverse mixed farming economy with less specialisation, a greater variety of local food available to the city and an environmentally sound, public-health-oriented diet which was still convenient. Easy access to fresh foods is imperative (and an excellent model exists in Holland's vegetable markets), while processing of food should take place within the urban system where the food will be consumed.

The present

Urban demand for food is a major cause of environmental degradation in rural areas in that agricultural practices are responsible for habitat loss and chemical pollution. The present system of agriculture is environmentally unsustainable. There are diverse problems which include the high degree of specialisation, leading to a polarisation between arable monocultures and intensive livestock 'factory' farming. One consequence of this is that animal wastes, in particular, but also straw and human excrement are not fully utilised as valuable resources able to help maintain the fertility and structure of the soil. Yields have instead been increased by the use of synthetic fertilisers, combined with plant varieties dependent on high inputs of chemicals. Soil erosion is an increasing problem. Pesticides have also been used increasingly, often to excess, thus destroying the balanced relationship between insect 'pests' and predators. Feedstocks for livestock are imported from 'less-developed' countries where land for local food production is increasingly scarce.

Food is a key determinant of public health, and health concerns about the food provided by contemporary agriculture are plentiful. Coronary heart disease, the fats, salt, fibre and sugar debate, additives, irradiation, pesticide residues, hormones and anti-biotics are all immediate concerns. Urban diets are often less healthy, especially in deprived groups.

Agricultural practices have been responsible for the contamination of groundwater with nitrate and certain pesticides, while intensification and farm 'modernisation' have had significant negative impacts on wildlife. At the same time public concern has risen because of over-production and thus increasing public costs in the storage and even destruction of surplus agricultural produce. Improving public health in cities (a major aim of development) can be achieved by intervention in the agricultural system.

Internal production in the city

Land can be used within the city to produce food. Some commercial production can be maintained. As long as strong planning controls keep land values down, urban areas are the ideal location for market gardening: they are close to the market, they experience higher ambient temperatures because of the urban heat island, there is more carbon dioxide in the atmosphere (enhancing plant productivity) and greater potential for linking into district heating and sewage composting.

Brown and Jacobsen record some cases from East Asia where internal production is high, but which still have scope for improvements in animal welfare and for the reduction of other environmental impacts:[1]

> Hong Kong, a city of 5 million occupying an area of just over 1,000 square kilometers, has a highly sophisticated urban agriculture which grows 45% of its fresh vegetables. Fifteen percent of its pork needs are satisfied by pigs fed with indigenous food wastes, including some 130,000 tons per year from restaurants and food-processing plants. Relying on imported feed, the city also produces 60% of its live poultry supply. Some 31% of Hong Kong's agricultural land produces vegetables. Fish ponds, occupying 18% of the agricultural land, are commonly fertilized with pig and poultry manure and yield 25-74 tons of fish per hectare [per annum]...

> Shanghai, a city of 11 million, extended its boundaries into the surrounding countryside, increasing the city area to some 6,000 square kilometers ... As of 1986 Shanghai was self-sufficient in vegetables and produced most of its grain and a good part of its pork and poultry.

However, the precondition for growing food in many cities must be a reduction in pollution, so that the food that is grown is uncontaminated. Currently, such food is potentially dangerous because of the level of pollution, notably from lead. The Campaign for Lead Free Air (CLEAR) produced information in 1983 which suggested that no one in London should eat vegetables that were grown in their own gardens.[2] A repeated examination of the lead content of London allotment soil and vegetables grown there, conducted by the Association of London Chief Environmental Health Officers (ALCEHO), has confirmed several conclusions of the earlier CLEAR survey.[3] The ALCEHO survey found that approximately 50 per cent of their samples would be classed as 'contaminated' by lead when compared to limit values given by the various authorities on this subject (Table 5.1).

Environmental health implications result in recommendations concerning the washing of leaf produce, the unsuitability of growing lettuce and blackberries in inner London, and the screening of land proposed for allotments. Clearly land that has been in industrial use is highly likely to be contaminated. However, the balance of sources of contamination in food from air and from soil is not generally clear. A study in Brooklyn, New York found evidence that airborne lead was of greater concern than soilborne.* The same study found no difference in cadmium levels between the urban and suburban test sites although levels were below those in other reported studies.[4] Thus strict air pollution controls to reduce lead contamination may permit food growing on most sites within cities although in the longer term controls to prevent further contamination of soil and groundwater by pollutants such as cadmium are vital.

In general, city dwellers can grow some food on the limited area of land available to them. This should be encouraged, not for self-sufficiency, but because it creates a link in the minds of urban dwellers to the fact that they are dependent on the countryside for food. It is well known that the countryside is dependent on the city, but urbanites tend to forget that they are also dependent on the countryside. Therefore, educationally, urban growing of food is important in helping demonstrate this interdependence, and can thereby provide improved understanding of what sustainability might mean. It is also important

---

* The lead concentrations were not considered to be a health concern, but it must be noted that US regulations on vehicle emissions forced reductions in lead emissions well before the date of the study.

Table 5.1:   Lead in soil: results of 1988 ALCEHO survey

	Total lead (mg/kg)
Survey results	
Upper 95%	1200
Mean	378

Upper limits for uncontaminated soil[a]

	Total lead (mg/kg)
Origin	
CLEAR	169
EEC Directive (86/278/EEC)	300
ICRCL and GLC	500

Note a: There is no statutory or other formal standard for lead contamination
to use as a guide in interpreting the survey results. The standard used
in the CLEAR survey was derived from a literature search of academic
work on soil contamination and was expressed in terms of EDTA
extractable lead. Other informal published standards are those laid
down by the Department of the Environment's Interdepartmental
Committee on the Redevelopment of Contaminated Land (ICRCL) and
by the former Greater London Council (GLC) Scientific Services
Branch in its Guidelines for Contaminated Soils. The 1986 EC Directive
(86/278/EEC) on sewage sludge application to land, not yet
implemented in the UK, sets out a range of limit values for heavy
metals in soil. The relevance of their criteria here is that they broadly
indicate the upper limits of lead concentration in uncontaminated soil
and thus provide a yardstick against which the ALCEHO soil survey
results can be measured.

Source: *Lead in London Soils and Vegetables*, London Environmental Supplement
No. 16 Spring 1988

because of the relationship between city dwellers and their gardens. In
the garden it is easier for the individual to perceive the potential dangers
of overuse of chemicals. Such perception can be translated into
increased and more widespread demand from the urban population for
changed practices in agriculture and in the agro-chemical industry.

There should also be coherent plans for the city's hinterland. Today much of the hinterland may be no more than agricultural land waiting to be turned into housing land, with the hope of high values. As such it can be found in a derelict state. Yet the hinterland is a logical location not only for intensive commercial production in market gardening, but also for non-commercial food production in allotments. This is the case in Copenhagen in Denmark where large areas outside the city are available for allotment gardening. This means of growing its own food is part of the city's history, a way of life for many of its residents who travel out and live on their allotments at week-ends. However, allotments are of very limited habitat value and land allocated to food production should not be at the expense of valuable wildlife habitats.

Allotments provide for both efficient food production and recreation. Leach has estimated that production on allotments yields up to 2.2 times as much as the commercial production of vegetables.[5]

Local authorities need to be encouraged to promote the use of existing allotments and then to consider setting up more, mainly on the fringes of the city. Very few authorities actually do this, although Oxford's pro-active allotments strategy, designed to encourage the use of allotments by disadvantaged groups in particular, is a valuable exception. Historically, allotments were provided for the rural population who had recently arrived in the city. Now we are several generations removed from contact with the land. Local authorities could employ specialist educational advisers responsible for setting up allotment areas and helping people with gardening, and facilitating the whole educational process based around allotments. If take-up is poor, school garden schemes could be implemented, as in The Hague, which has hundreds of plots where schoolchildren grow vegetables and provide their own food. All children should regularly visit farms to understand how food is produced.

Increasingly, the opportunity to visit a farm can take place within the city itself. Urban greening increasingly involves the use of wasteland to produce food, in city farms and community gardens, such as Windmill Hill in Bristol.[6] Windmill Hill was one of the earliest city farms and is still in production after a decade which has seen the movement grow from two farms in 1976 to nearly 60 in 1987. The National Federation of City Farms, a national co-ordinating body, has a widening membership of farms and community gardens and is busy helping them not only to extend their role as social and education centres, but to develop small businesses based on food production, horticulture and crafts. In practice this has meant that a city farm is not only a park, garden, allotment and nature reserve. It can also be a school, workshop, playground and social club.

The worsening social and environmental conditions of many inner- and outer-city housing estates has stimulated some communities to renovate their neighbourhoods in ways which combine work on land and buildings. In the words of Nicholson-Lord:[7]

> City farms are attempts to bandage up the wounds of inner-urban dereliction ... [but are] merely the most visible of a wide range of earthworking initiatives in the cities, from bottle banks and neighbourhood schemes to municipal recycling projects, from bee-keeping and timber growing to co-operative food production.

Such initiatives have often been local, spontaneous, and unco-ordinated, and their significance has been unnoticed. In Sparkbrook, Birmingham, for example, weed-choked gardens have been joined together to form Ashram Acres, an exercise in small-scale land reclamation, animal husbandry and horticulture undertaken by local Asian residents, many of them small farmers by origin.[8] In Toronto, Canada there are examples of working-class, low-income areas setting up their own shops and allotment systems.

From Australia has come 'permaculture', the 'perennial agriculture of human settlements': a reaction to the unsustainability of conventional agriculture. It is described as a design system which can be applied at any scale and whose basic principles are diversity, maintaining ground cover, retaining moisture and minimising the energy inputs required for food production. In practice it is based on the growing of a highly diverse mix of perennial and non-perennial food plants, especially trees. Permaculture systems include animals, such as poultry and pigs, as part of the system and rely on biological pest control.[9]

Protection for existing agricultural and horticultural land within and on the fringes of the city is currently inadequate and must be improved.

However, the process of food importation is inevitable. There is no way that the back gardens of London, for example, even if every park were made productive, could feed 6.7 million people. It is important, therefore, that food production systems in the wider urban hinterlands reflect the progression towards sustainability. For urban dwellers, that means, perhaps above all else, that they are provided with high-quality healthy food.

Food quality

The quality of our food is no longer maintained by independent scientifically-based protection. In the post-war period independent food science has become almost non-existent and today the vast majority of food scientists work in or for the food industry. For example, the British Nutrition Foundation is financed by the food industry. At the same time, the recent avalanche of new products, ingredients and processes, sold more aggressively and extensively in urban markets to match urban consumerist lifestyles, has stretched public food law enforcement agencies such as Environmental Health Officers, Trading Standards Officers and Public Analysts. The capacity of the law to pre-empt food-related problems rather than just react to them has weakened. Recently, cuts in local authority finances have limited the scope of enforcement officers even further.

However, Lang argues that people have become much more aware in the last 4-5 years of the food adulteration that has been going on in their name, and they are increasingly unhappy about it. Through public education these consumers can be encouraged to take positive action. They can demand labelling which tells them what is in or on a product, and can also try to anticipate new problems, including those caused by the food industry on their behalf.[10] Irradiation is an example. The government and the nuclear industry argue that irradiation is necessary to tackle food poisoning. This argument is dismissed by most independent observers.[11]

Additives in food are of similar concern. Even where they are considered safe in the diet at present levels, there is some evidence that employees in the food processing industries, who are chronically exposed to these chemicals, exhibit symptoms of ill health as a result.[12]

The marketing strategies of the food industry are also a root cause of problems with food quality. For instance, the marketing of out-of-season food not only involves high expenditure and extended supply lines but can also create health risks. Consumer expectations have changed to demand unseasonal food. However, it is healthier to eat food seasonally: food tends to concentrate chemical residues to a greater extent if force-grown outside its season. Nitrate levels may be as much as twelve times higher than usual when lettuce is grown in winter under glass with poor light conditions, regardless of the fertiliser used.[13] The Elm Farm Research Centre has shown that whether organic or inorganic methods are used to grow summer vegetables, if they are grown in winter, under glass, the nitrate levels can go up dramatically, particularly in those that concentrate nitrate such as lettuce and spinach.[14]

Food can also contain pesticide residues. The Ministry of Agriculture Fisheries and Food (MAFF) Working Party on Pesticide Residues in Food (WPPR) reported in 1989 that 58 per cent of 223 bread samples analysed had detectable residues of organophosphorus pesticides.[15]

Since the 1980s there has been worldwide debate over pesticides and their impact on health. A global campaign to ban or control a so-called 'dirty dozen' pesticides (13 particularly persistent and hazardous chemicals) has been run by environmental groups including Friends of the Earth, 'Third World' groups and consumer bodies. Table 5.2 shows some pesticides in use in the UK but banned in other countries. Consumers have become concerned about the risks to children from the effects of residues, and the increased risks of cancer. A report in 1987 for the National Research Council noted in the USA that 30 per cent (by volume applied) of insecticides, 60 per cent of herbicides and 90 per cent of fungicides were agents presumed by the Environmental Protection Agency to be oncogenic (tumour inducing) or for which positive oncogenicity data were under review.[17] Most of these pesticides are approved by the Ministry of Agriculture for use in the UK and many are widely used.

So as the sales of fruit and vegetables continue to rise, in line with nutritional advice, the consumer faces possible harm from an increased

Table 5.2: Pesticides other countries ban

Pesticide	WHO classification[a]	Use in UK	Banned
Amitrole (herbicide)	Acute hazard unlikely (possible carcinogen)	119,000 kg/yr (orchards)	Sweden, Norway Finland
Azinophos-methyl (insecticide)	Highly hazardous	7,500 kg/yr (fruit & veg.)	India
Carbaryl (insecticide)	Moderately hazardous	16,000 kg/yr (orchards)	W. Germany
Chlordane (molluscicide)	Moderately hazardous	Unknown (grassland)	Finland, Turkey, Portugal
Demeton-s-methyl (insecticide)	Highly hazardous	102,000 kg/yr (fruit & veg.)	USSR
DNOC (insecticide)	Highly hazardous	3,600 kg/yr (soft fruits)	Sweden
Endosulfan (insecticide)	Moderately hazardous	13,000 kg/yr (soft fruits)	Bulgaria
Fonofos (insecticide)	Extremely hazardous	8,500 kg/yr (cereal)	Malaysia
Methomyl (insecticide)	Highly hazardous	1,500 kg/yr (cereal/hops)	Malaysia
Paraquat (herbicide)	Moderately hazardous	270,000 kg/yr (veg, fruit & cereal)	Sweden, W. Germany Finland
Pentachlorophenol (insecticide & herbicide)	Highly hazardous	Unknown	Sweden
Phenylmercury acetate (fungicide)	Extremely hazardous	Unknown (seeds)	Turkey, New Zealand
2,4,5-T (herbicide)	Moderately hazardous	87,000 kg/yr (grazing pasture)	Sweden, Finland
Thiophanatemethyl (fungicide)	Acute hazard unlikely (possible carcinogen)	113,000 kg/yr (cereal, fruit)	Finland

Note a: This is a classification by the World Health Organisation based on the danger of using the chemicals. The risk is assessed only for the acute danger not for the longer-term risks. Where the susbstance may be carcinogenic, this has also been indicated.

Source: New Statesman and Society, *This Food Business*, 1989.

intake of pesticides. In addition, these pesticides can be polluting, a threat to wildlife and a hazard to farm workers. Residues are not only found in fruit and vegetables; the 1987 study conducted by the US National Research Council estimated oncogenic risks (from pesticide residues) for different foodstuffs. It found that the three foodstuffs with the highest such risk were tomatoes, beef and potatoes. Pork and chicken also featured in the top fifteen.[18]

In the UK, the poverty of the official testing systems and cuts in food safety research, despite the creation of a new Food Protection Agency, have encouraged retailers to take a much more active role in controlling residue levels in food sold in their outlets. Major retailers, including Tesco, Safeway, Marks & Spencer and Waitrose have implemented their own testing programmes. These should be linked to a commitment not to sell food with residue levels in excess of the Maximum Residue Level (MRL). The London Food Commission comments:[19]

> So inadequate are current British controls over pesticide residues in foods that moves by the EEC to harmonise regulations governing food trade have tended to improve public protection in Britain. ... Eventually it will probably be forced to introduce legally enforceable limits on the residues permitted on foodstuffs sold in the home market.

In September 1990 the UK Government announced proposals to make use of the results of retailers' tests, along with those carried out by manufacturers and local authoriites, but only to improve the data underpinning the pesticide approval process rather than to set residue standards or to improve the information to the public.

Yet the conflicting responsibilities, for promoting agricultural output and protecting the health of those at risk from pesticide residues, lie with only one ministry, the Ministry of Agriculture, Fisheries and Food (MAFF). The latter function could be far more effectively carried out if responsibility lay with an independent Environmental Protection Executive.

Agrochemicals and sustainable farming methods

The rapid rise in food production since the Second World War has been largely dependent on low-cost inputs of artificial nitrogen fertiliser. Consumer concern over excess fertiliser use takes three main forms: the tax costs of supporting a wasteful farming system, the potential health risks linked to rising levels of nitrate in food and water, and the ecological effects of fertiliser use.

The spectacular growth of fertiliser use in the UK since 1940 has been cut off by the same Common Agricultural Policy (CAP) mechanism which fostered it so effectively over the last four decades. Table 5.3 and Figure 5.1 show that average application rates in England and Wales have risen to 150 to 200 kilograms of nitrogen per hectare (kgN/ha).

Table 5.3: **Average amounts of fertiliser nitrogen used on winter wheat and potatoes in England and Wales (KgN/ha).**

	Winter wheat	Potatoes
Year		
1950	33	117
1962	74	157
1970	90	166
1979	135	193
1983	188	

Sources: Fertiliser Manufacturers' Association (wheat); Cooke, G., 'Changes in Fertiliser Use in the UK from 1950 to 1980', paper presented to the Fertiliser Society of London, April 1980, (potatoes).

These figures apply to most crops, but may exceed 200 kgN/ha for grassland.

A turning point in total fertiliser use came with the introduction of milk quotas in May 1984, which had a significant impact on demand for nitrate fertilisers. Demand did not fall, but stopped rising after years of annual growth of around 6 per cent.[20]

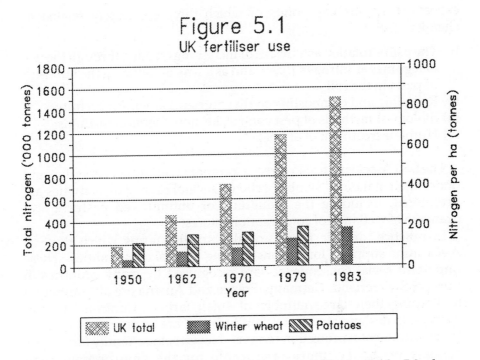

Figure 5.1
UK fertiliser use

Sources: Fertiliser Manufacturers' Association (total). As Table 5.3 above
(wheat and potatoes).

However, the quantities currently used offer little or no hope for
reducing water pollution, even disregarding the potential historic
backlog of nitrate still to enter groundwater. Nor are the implications
for resource conservation good. The production of agrochemicals is
energy-intensive and directly depletes scarce petroleum resources.
Thus the sustainable agriculture required as a contribution to
sustainable urban development must reduce its dependence on them.

Organic agriculture is more sustainable in many respects, although it
is only one alternative system. The Soil Association's concept of organic
farming, which defines the standards for British organic farmers, can be

expressed in four key points of which three are closely related to chemical use:

i)   The use of rotation as a means of increasing fertility, through the use of legumes as nitrogen fixers, and as a way of reducing the build-up of pests in the soil.
ii) Recycling and composting so that nutrients are used carefully.
iii) Biological methods of pest control, i.e. non-chemical methods.
iv) Humane treatment of animals.[21]

The Soil Association also directly promote wildlife conservation and under their standard 'symbol' scheme several damaging activities are prohibited, including the ploughing of unimproved pastures and drainage of wetlands of conservation interest.[22]

In practice, organic farms are also smaller farms which the Soil Association supports for reasons relating to rural communities. These important social consequences are recognised by many countries in Europe; Switzerland, Germany, France and Austria are all committed to keeping their large number of small farms. Controls on land ownership designed to favour 'family farms' are by no means adopted for environmental protection reasons. Nevertheless, 'family farms' are, at least in theory, more favourable for the environment than 'commercial' holdings. The family should regard the land holding as its home and the costs of family labour are normally discounted, thus providing the time to protect or enhance the landscape and wildlife of the farm. In addition, modernisation is often linked to farm amalgamation and as a result smaller farms are more likely to retain wildlife features such as wet patches.[23]

There is little point in having a small area of more sustainable agriculture, within or outside the city, surrounded by areas of conventional farming. That situation can result in the production of 'organically grown' foods which may contain pesticide residues.[24] Thus growers in much of Britain's most fertile farmland, such as the Vale of Evesham, may be unable to farm organically because, even if they use organic methods, chemicals may drift on to their crops from adjacent land. Herbicides used to control weeds in wheat have on several occasions destroyed broad-leaved food plants such as tomatoes in adjacent fields, leading to a number of legal actions for damages.

New integrated programmes have recently been developed in Sweden and Denmark to address this widespread pollution. Initially, both governments set a firm policy target to reduce national pesticide use to a specified level and subsequently developed programmes to achieve this target. In 1985 the Swedish government announced that it would introduce measures to reduce the use of pesticides in agriculture by 50 per cent over 5 years. Denmark has set a longer period for the same reduction, and Holland too is introducing similar measures.[25]

Table 5.4: Food nitrate regulations in European countries (mg/kg)

	Switzerland		Austria		W.Germany
	Guide value	MAC	Guide value (organic)	MAC	Guide value
Babyfood		40			
Babyfood with vegetables		250		250	
Cabbage	875		800		
Beetroot	3,000		800	3,500[a]	3,000
Spinach (raw)	3,500		1,200	3,500	2,000
Lettuce	3,500	4,000	2,000	3,500[a]	3,000

Notes: MAC: maximum admissible concentration
a: Winter values at 4,500
b: West Germany does not set MACs, merely guide values.
Source: London Food Commission, *Food Adulteration and How to Beat It..*

In a similar fashion, a number of countries have set strict controls on the use of nitrogenous fertilisers in agriculture,[26] and Switzerland, Austria, West Germany and Holland impose nitrate limits on some foods, including baby products and green vegetables (Table 5.4). The UK does neither of these things, relying instead on a voluntary scheme of Nitrate Sensitive Areas. In these areas, free advice and subsidies are available to farmers to promote changes in farming practices which will

Figure 5.2: Nitrate concentrations found in UK studies compared with some European standards

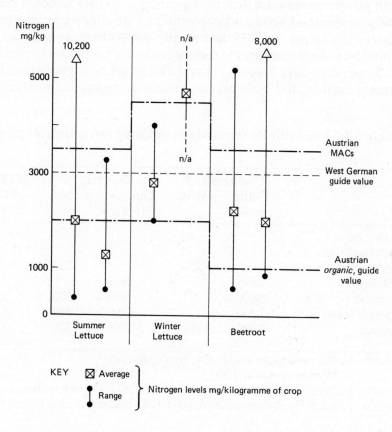

KEY ⊠ Average
     ● Range } Nitrogen levels mg/kilogramme of crop

F.O.E. FIG 5-2

Source for data: As Tables 5.4 and 5.5

reduce nitrate leaching. This scheme is considered inadequate even by the official water protection body, the National Rivers Authority. [27]

No systematic monitoring of nitrate concentration in individual crops has taken place in the UK to date. Some figures representative of the scientific literature are shown in Table 5.5. Figure 5.2 compares these UK levels with the West German and Austrian maximum admissible concentrations and guide values.

There should be direct support for more sustainable and less chemical-intensive production methods, coupled with clear regulations as to the standards of 'organic' and 'conservation' grade food, which would then be able to command premium prices and help maintain farm incomes. The European Community is developing regulations for the monitoring, production, and labelling of organically grown products. Austria has issued a set of guidelines defining which products may be sold as organically or biologically produced. These include restrictions on production locations relative to roads; prohibit the use of mineral fertilisers, pesticides or sewage sludge; and limit animal densities.[28] Recognised standards have recently been agreed in the UK: the United Kingdom Register of Organic Food Standards (UKROFS).

The base of support for food production should be adequate funding for research into more sustainable agriculture. The current lack of research into organic techniques demonstrates the problem. Until recently this was researched almost entirely by a single charitable trust, the Elm Farm Research Centre in Reading. Of MAFF spending on research only 0.25 per cent supports organic research. In 1989 this amounted to £400,000 out of a total research budget of £200m,[29] while an additional £25,000 is spent on the national organic certification scheme. This can be contrasted with Sweden where the total budget is much smaller but £1.5m. has been spent on organic research over the past two years and £400,000 a year is given to the Swedish Organic Advisory Service.[30] In the UK the development of Integrated Pest Management systems (designed to make use of natural pest-predator relationships and substitute improved management and biological control techniques for much of the use of chemical pesticides) has been slowed by the closure of the leading research establishment at

Littlehampton and its merger with the National Vegetable Research Station at Wellesbourne.

Table 5.5: Reported nitrate levels in commercially grown fresh vegetables and salads (mg/kg fresh weight)

	Range	Weighted average
Vegetable		
Foliage Crop		
lettuce	145-10200	1880
" (summer)	160-3100	1100
" (winter)	2000-3850	2700
" (winter)		4820
Root Crop		
beetroot	100-4700	2200
	495-8060	1950
	630-6800	
Legume		
green bean	45-840	490

Note: The table includes the results of several different surveys.
Source: As Table 5.4 above.

More sustainable agriculture could be further encouraged by financial support: the introduction of subsidies for the conversion period, particularly for farms with a large debt. In the case of organic production, once a farm is producing to recognised standards, the produce commands a considerable premium, currently around 20-30 per cent. This is reflected in the value of organically farmed land: anecdotal evidence suggests a premium of up to 150 per cent for land farmed organically for over 20 years.

But when food has such influence on health it is surely inequitable if access to safe food is restricted to those who can afford it. The organic premium would be reduced if the true costs of intensive chemical farming practices were reflected in food costs. In the shorter term increasing sales volumes may allow producers using more sustainable alternative production systems to share some of the economies of large-scale distribution currently enjoyed by conventional producers. In the longer term increasing transport costs will give advantages to localised distributors.

Table 5.6: Costs of conventional and alternative crop rotations

Costs/acre[a]

	Conventional[b]	Alternative[b]
Inputs		
Fertilisers & pesticides (including application)	72.52	15.00
Field operation (tillage, planting & harvest)	45.44	35.00
Overheads & insurance	11.44	6.82
Total	129.40	56.82
Average yield of winter wheat (bushels/acre)	60.3	62.6

Notes   a. Costs in US dollars per acre of rotation per year.
        b. The conventional system was a four-year wheat-barley-wheat-pea rotation with use of fertiliser and pesticide inputs every year. The alternative was a low-input system with a three-year pea plus a medic-medic-wheat rotation, with pesticide used only on the peas. In three of four scenarios the alternative system was equal or more profitable than the conventional. Where government price support was excluded the alternative system proved consistently more profitable.

Source: National Research Council, *Alternative Agriculture,* National Academy Press, Washington DC, 1989.

Although current production surpluses mean that increasingly there are grants available from the government for converting to alternative farming systems, neither more sustainable systems in general nor organic farming in particular are major targets. Only under the most recent EC 'extensification' Directive is organic production even a recognised option. Pilot extensification schemes were consulted on by MAFF in 1989, yet only in the Environment White Paper of September 1990 was consultation on a grant scheme to assist conversion to organic farming announced. Yet a survey carried out by Elm Farm in 1988 found out that over 75 per cent of people wanted better access to organic food.[31] A similar survey by Gallup, for *The Daily Telegraph*, showed that 75 per cent preferred the introduction of organic methods instead of 'set-aside' as a means of reducing production surpluses.*

However, conversion to full organic production in the short term is not an option for the majority of UK agriculture. But there are alternative systems available which can reduce the environmental damage caused by agriculture and thus increase the sustainability of the urban system as a whole. What is necessary is action at the national and European levels to encourage wide-scale adoption of more sustainable agricultural techniques through the existing mechanisms.

Recent work in the USA has identified some principles of alternative systems which would form a useful foundation for more sustainable agriculture generally. These include crop rotations that mitigate pest problems, increase available soil nitrogen and reduce soil erosion; integrated pest management, utilising crop rotations, biological controls and other techniques to minimise the use of pesticides; improved management systems; soil- and water-conserving tillage; and animal production systems that emphasise disease prevention through health maintenance. The study found that:[32]

> Farmers successfully adopting these systems generally derive significant sustained economic and environmental benefits. Wider adoption of proven alternative systems would result in even greater economic benefits to farmers and environmental gains for the nation.

Table 5.6 shows the potential economic advantages of one of these systems.

---

*   Set-aside is a European Commission policy which pays farmers to take land out of arable production.

Return of waste materials

In the longer term one of the highest priorities in developing sustainable agriculture is increasing the recycling of nutrients from urban waste. Most urban organic waste is currently disposed of through solid and sewage waste disposal systems, while agriculture depends on vast inputs of artificial nutrients. Although some 40 per cent of sewage sludge is spread on farmland, this does not provide nutrients to crops in the most effective manner.[34]

Anaerobic digestion, producing biogas, could be a valuable tool for dealing with both urban and agricultural organic wastes. Although the digestate which remains contains nutrients in such a concentrated form that it can 'scorch' crops, it can be composted with other organic waste. Composting works by mixing animal manure and plant matter with a balance of carbon and nitrogen, producing a system from which nitrogen is released more slowly. Compost also acts as a soil conditioner, improving its structure. There is potential for composting both sewage and other organic waste, including straw,[34] but further research is still needed to maximise the safety and hygiene of the system.

Food producers are currently wary of sewage sludge from many sources because of its contamination by heavy metals, caused by mixing human and industrial waste. Although research is being carried out into composting of existing sewage, with a successful scheme operating at Canterbury, wider use depends on the elimination of contamination from industrial effluent. Britain's nineteenth century sewers are in poor repair, while a proposed European Commission Directive on the discharge of untreated sewage to sea will require significant changes in UK practice, particularly regarding coastal urban sewage waste, much of which is discharged to sea after only mechanical treatment. Sewage planning is therefore an important issue in sustainable urban development and it is considered in more detail in the following chapter.

Composting of other organic wastes can be used to improve soil quality in city gardens: organics can be separated in the home, composted by the local authority, and sold as horticultural compost in local shops. Composting kitchen waste for home use is an immediate possibility for all households with gardens or allotments. Municipal composting of the organic component in domestic refuse also has great potential. In Britain, Cardiff City Council are setting up such a system of composting as part of the Friends of the Earth 'Recycling City' initiative.

Composting has another environmental benefit: compost is an effective substitute for peat in horticulture and gardening. Peat is obtained by large-scale commercial 'mining' of peat bogs and moors, thus destroying valuable wetland habitats and releasing stored carbon dioxide to add to global warming.

Food processing and distribution

The discussion of food provision for urban areas cannot be complete without consideration of food processing, which is largely an urban function. Its relationship to food quality was discussed briefly earlier in the chapter. Food packaging, on the other hand, is the source of an apparent conflict between environment and public health. It uses scarce resources but is considered important for hygiene. Research is needed into ways of eliminating unnecessary packaging and ensuring that the maximum proportion of necessary packaging is recyclable.

However, there are other implications of policies promoting sustainability for both food processing companies and distributors of fresh food. Whatever the system of agricultural production, sustainable urban development can be promoted by shortening the supply lines to the city. Long-distance transport of food damages the environment, increases the need for artificial maintenance of food freshness, and also restricts significantly the potential for recycling of urban waste nutrients into the agricultural system.

The current distribution system in the UK encourages the lengthening of supply lines as individual companies control ever more suppliers. In fact a mere six companies control 70 per cent of the imported food market (Figure 5.3). Most of them have also pursued policies of developing ever larger out-of-town retail stores dependent upon the car-borne shopper, with severe environmental impacts in comparison to the maintenance of high street shopping. The issue of suburban development was considered in more detail in Chapter 1. The

Figure 5.3
UK grocers' market share (1987/8)

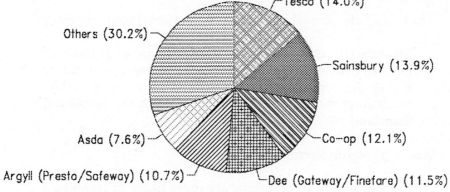

Tesco (14.0%)

Others (30.2%)

Sainsbury (13.9%)

Asda (7.6%)

Co-op (12.1%)

Argyll (Presto/Safeway) (10.7%)

Dee (Gateway/Finefare) (11.5%)

Source: New Statesman and Society, *This Food Business*, 1989.

protection of such land for agriculture is particularly important in that it is often of the highest quality.

European figures suggest that North European food retailing markets are equally concentrated and it is of concern that the implementation of the Single European Market may further encourage concentration.[35] Increasing the direct costs of transport, as proposed in Chapter 2 on transport, would provide a strong incentive to increased localisation of marketing, even within a small number of companies.

This would also discourage the current importation of foodstuffs necessary to maintain high livestock populations in inhumane intensive production units. Although a sustainable farming system would involve livestock, it would be at a much lower intensity. Less livestock in total would be one way of increasing total agricultural efficiency in Britain, in that more food would be grown directly for human consumption.

Agricultural policy

The current framework set by the Common Agricultural Policy means that sustainable farming systems are not competing on a fair basis, because almost all subsidies are geared toward maximisation of production.

The OECD identifies the specific problem of set-aside schemes:[36]

> Measures to curtail excessive production by withdrawal of land may not be the best solution to the problem of surpluses if they are combined with continued price support, thus motivating more intensive production on the remaining farm land.

And suggests an alternative approach:[37]

> Policies which, in principle, are more likely to combine a reduction of surpluses with an improvement of the environment include levies on excessive use of fertilisers and pesticides ... Finland, Sweden and Austria have taxed fertiliser and pesticides for a number of years. In the case of nitrogen and phosphorus the Swedish levy amounts to 25 per cent.

But policies designed to reduce chemical use are only one strand. They need to be combined with better incentives for dis-intensification, and with support for landscape and habitat conservation measures by farmers, for instance, through extension of the Environmentally Sensitive Areas principle or co-ordinated through, and tied to, preparation of a comprehensive farm management plan. Fertiliser management plans are already required by law in Denmark, combined with regulations on cover crops in an effort to reduce fertiliser pollution.[39] This principle should be extended to cover the use of other chemicals and land management proposals. Initially non-transferrable nitrogen quotas or nitrogen taxes should be introduced throughout the Community.

Conclusion

We must move on from the green vision of the 1970s, with its notion of city back gardens as mini-farms, to tackle directly the relationship between the city and the countryside. The countryside must revive its role as an urban hinterland for the city around which it lies. National policies must seek to regain a rural-urban balance. The city should serve the countryside through its government functions and its role as the location of land-owning and food processing, distributing and retailing companies. These indirect functions have more influence over the sustainability of agriculture than do farmers themselves. Incentives and regulations therefore need to extend to their operations too.

The current food production system is wasteful of resources. City dwellers are dependent on an unsustainable agricultural and processing system for their food supply. The situation must change at a number of levels. The opportunities should be provided for more food to be grown in cities, raising the consciousness of city dwellers to their interdependence with the countryside, as well as providing them with recreation and a supply of fresh food. Resources must be provided to tackle toxic pollution of land in urban areas.

Government control of inputs to the existing agricultural system should ensure healthier foods. At the same time, support for alternative systems should provide for sustainable agriculture in close proximity to the city. Nutrients from urban waste can be recycled for use in production, to replace the wasteful and polluting artificial inputs in contemporary agriculture.

References

1. Brown, L.R. and Jacobsen, J.L., *The future of urbanization: facing the ecological and economic constraints*, Worldwatch Paper 77, New York, 1987, pp. 28-9.
2. Davies, B., *Lead in Food – a CLEAR special survey*, CLEAR, London, 1983.
3. Denton, D., *Lead in London Soils and Vegetables* London Environmental Supplement No.16, ALCEHO, London, 1988.

4. Hibben, C.R., Hagar, S.S. and Mazza, C.P., 'A comparison of lead and cadmium content of vegetable crops in urban and sub-urban gardens', *Environmental Pollution (series B)*, Vol. 7, 1984, pp. 71-80.
5. Leach, G., *Energy and Food Production*, IIED, London, 1976.
6. Davidson, J., *How Green Is Your City?*, Bedford Square Press, London, 1988.
7. Nicholson-Lord, D., *The Greening of the Cities*, Routledge and Kegan Paul, London, 1987, p. 151.
8. Davidson, *op. cit.*
9. Mollison, W., *Permaculture One*, Tagari, Tyalgum, NSW, 1978.
10. Lang, T., *Interview transcript*, June 1989.
11. Webb, A. and Lang, T., *Food Irradiation: Myth and Reality*, Thorsons, London, 1990.
12. Clutterbuck, C., *The TUC Food Education pack*, Trade Union Congress, London, 1990.
13. London Food Commission, *Food Adulteration and how to beat it*, Unwin Hyman, London, 1988; also see Vogtmann, H. and Biederman, R., 'The Nitrate Story: No End in Sight', *Nutrition and Health*, Vol. 3, 1985, pp. 217-39.
14. Elm Farm Research Centre, *Nitrate in Vegetables*, Research Note No. 5, 1988.
15. Ministry of Agriculture, Fisheries and Food, *Report of the working party on pesticide residues 1985-88*, HMSO, London, 1989.
17. National Research Council (Committee on Scientific and Regulatory Issues Underlying Pesticide Use Patterns and Agricultural Innovation), *Regulating Pesticides In Food*, National Academy Press, Washington DC, 1987.
18. *Ibid.*
19. London Food Commission, *op. cit.*, p. 102.
20. *Ibid.*
21. Soil Association, *Soil Association Standards for Organic Agriculture*, Soil Association, Bristol, 1989.
22. Soil Association, *Guidelines for Conservation*, Soil Association, Bristol, 1990.
23. Munton, R., Eldon, J. and Marsden, T., 'Farmer's responses to an uncertain policy future' in Baldock, D. and Conder, D., (eds), *Removing Land from Agriculture: The implications for farming and the*

environment, Council for the Protection of Rural England and International Institute for Environment and Development, London, 1987.

24. Ministry of Agriculture, Fisheries and Food, *Report of the Working Party On Pesticide Residues (1982 to 1985)*, Food Surveillance Paper No.16, HMSO, London, 1986.

25. OECD, *Agricultural and Environmental Policies: Opportunities for Integration*, OECD, Paris, 1989, pp. 105-7.

26. *Ibid.*

27. National Rivers Authority, Response to Ministry of Agriculture, Fisheries and Food consultation on Nitrate Sensitive Areas, NRA, May 1989.

28. OECD, *op. cit*, p. 113.

29. MAFF figure given in letter to the pressure group 'Parents for Safe Food'.

30. New Statesman and Society, *This Food Business*, New Statesman and Society, London, 1989.

31. Stopes, C. and Woodward, L., *Consumer demand and the market for organic food*, Elm Farm Research Centre, 1988.

32. National Research Council, *Alternative Agriculture*, National Academy Press, Washington DC, 1989, pp. 5-6.

33. Brown and Jacobsen, *op. cit.*

34. Border, D., Coombes, C., and Shellens, S., 'Composting straw with untreated liquid sludge' *Biocycle*, July 1988.

35. London Food Commission, *Grasp the Nettle*, LFC, London, 1989.

36. OECD, *op. cit*, p. 141.

37. *Ibid.*

38. *Ibid.*

Chapter 6: Waste and Pollution

Introduction

Sustainable urban development should minimise the generation of waste, and treat waste as a resource. It should involve the efficient use of resources and recycling of materials, thereby contributing to the minimisation or elimination of environmental contamination. This will require the use of improved product and process technology.

It will also require efficient planning. Of the waste generated, a large percentage can be reclaimed and recycled, thus conserving resources, and minimising the amount of residual waste for disposal. The residual waste should be disposed of in the most environmentally-benign method possible. Reducing wastes and using more recyclable materials will cut the need for imported resources, and reduce energy consumption and habitat destruction as well as land, water and air pollution.

The present

The concentration of industry and traffic means that pollution of water, air and land is often most severe in and around urban areas (particularly downstream or downwind). For example, a study in Budapest showed levels of six heavy metals in tree leaves to be 2-9 times higher in the urban-industrial environment compared with a rural area.[1] Another example from Australia showed that particulate pollution of the atmosphere was not only greater over urban areas, but was directly related to the population size of the urban area.[2] Unfortunately statistics are not normally disaggregated so that such concentration is clear. Similarly cities contribute disproportionately to national and global pollution problems.

Waste also raises particular problems and opportunities in urban areas. Waste is not coincidental to economic activity, but is an integral part of it. Total waste generation (and per capita waste generation) expands as a city swells in size, as consumers earning more money increase their spending on food, beverages, and so-called 'durable' goods, and as growing demands for greater convenience encourage the marketing of more heavily packaged products. The waste of cities is concentrated geographically, causing problems in traditional disposal methods: there does not even normally *appear* to be an 'away' to which waste can be thrown!

Waste generation

Table 6.1 shows the estimated annual waste arising in the UK. Agricultural waste is the largest component, but most of this is returned to the land as slurry, or straw ploughed in. Mineral waste, the second largest component, tends to be disposed of on site. Solid sewage waste is returned to the land or dumped at sea (see below) while the effluent (included in the figures in Table 6.1) is discharged to the rivers and watercourses, often without adequate treatment (see Table 6.9 below).

Most industrial waste is directly disposed of or collected and disposed of within the private sector. The amounts disposed of in different ways are unknown. However, some 3.7 million tonnes of hazardous waste, including 1.6 million tonnes of special waste (wastes containing specified substances and of danger to life because of corrosivity, toxicity or flammability) were generated in 1986.[3] Most of this was disposed of to landfill and small amounts were dumped at sea, treated or incinerated. Most hazardous waste is generated by industry, but it does include an amount of medical waste. The majority of sites generating hazardous wastes are located in urban areas. We return to industrial waste and pollution later in the chapter.

Around 20 per cent of waste collected by local authorities (municipal waste) is commercial and industrial; the rest is from households.[4]

Table 6.1: Estimated total annual waste[a] arising in the UK

	Million tonnes
Waste arising	
Agricultural	250
Mines and quarries	130
Industrial[b]	80
Sewage[b]	20
Household	18
Commercial	12
Total[c]	500

Notes   a: excludes liquid industrial effluent of approximately 2,000 million tonnes

               b: sewage sluge landfilled or incinerated is included under industrial waste and not under sewage.

               c: the total is rounded down in the original source to 'reflect the uncertainty of the estimates'.

Source: Department of the Environment, *Digest of Environmental Protection and Water Statistics*, HMSO, London, 1989.

Figure 6.1 shows the approximate composition of domestic waste by weight.

Whilst the total waste collected by local authorities continues to increase (Table 6.2), the methods of treatment and disposal of waste (Table 6.3) largely remain the same.

Urban areas depend on the surrounding hinterland for landfill disposal, sites for which are increasingly limited. In the UK this is most pronounced in the South-East. Even without pressure to develop sites for more lucrative retail and leisure developments, and to protect semi-natural areas, many parts of the South-East will have inadequate landfill capacity by the end of the century. Surrey, Berkshire and Kent have indicated that they have too little space for their own long-term needs and are trying to restrict waste coming from London. In Hampshire, a county notoriously short of landfill sites, a landfill operator is sorting waste to reduce the flow and extend the landfill's life.

Figure 6.1
Composition of domestic waste by weight

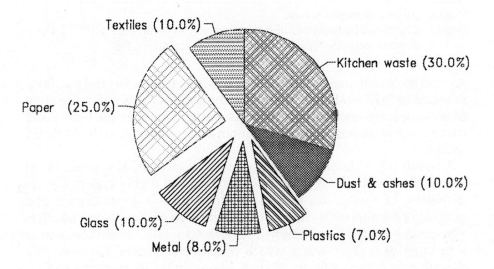

Source: Hay, A, and Wright, G., *Once is not enough*, Friends of the Earth, London, 1989.

Table 6.2:   Waste arising, England and Wales 1981/2 - 1987/8

000's tonnes

	1981/2	1983/4	1985/6	1987/8
Source of waste received				
by disposal authorities				
Collection authorities[a]	19,206	18,950	15,451	14,824
Commerce & industry	6,182	6,187	7,089	7,116
Civic amenity sites	n/a	n/a	3,718	4,461
Other waste	2,077	2,612	1,805	1,843
Total waste arising	27,465	27,749	28,063	28,244

Note a: mainly domestic waste.
Source: Chartered Institute of Public Finance and Accountancy (CIPFA), *Waste disposal statistics 1982/3 to 1986/7*, CIPFA, London, 1988.

As sites have been used up, there is increasing pressure to produce 'hills' of waste, or to fill in such sites as low-lying marshy areas which are often of ecological significance. These pressures are shown in the higher and rising costs of disposal for metropolitan authorities shown in Table 6.5 (p.234).

Landfill still ultimately takes the vast majority of UK wastes. What was at first seen as an easy, low-tech, and relatively cheap way of disposing of waste, has turned out to require a sophisticated and expensive monitoring system for the explosive gas, methane, which is a by-product of the breakdown of household waste. In fact methane is a product of organic waste which could be separated for anaerobic digestion or composting to produce easily utilisable methane and/or compost. Methane generated by landfill sites is often simply vented to the atmosphere: this produces over 20 per cent of the UK's atmospheric emissions of methane.[5] Methane is a greenhouse gas with an impact per unit thirty times greater than CO_2: the contribution of landfill methane to global warming should not be ignored.

Fly-tipping of trade and construction waste is often carried out on derelict sites, exacerbating problems of land reclamation, by operators keen to avoid the costs of legal disposal. It involves significant expenditures by many urban authorities, particularly to deal with

Table 6.3: Methods of treatment or disposal of waste (England and Wales, 1979/80 - 1987/8)

	1979/80 %	1983/4 %	1987/8 %
Method			
Compacting, shredding & baling	2	10	13
Incineration processes	8	9	8
Reclamation by other methods	2	3	4
Disposal to landfill (untreated)	88	65	61
Civic amenity sites	n/a	13	14

Note: A proportion of compacting, shredding and baling waste together with elements of this waste which arises at Civic Amenity Sites is ultimately taken to landfill for final disposal. The balance is either reclaimed, recycled or incinerated.

Source: As Table 6.2 above.

construction wastes. For example, London's authorities spend over £5m. per year clearing up fly-tipped waste. Yet new construction materials are mined by opencast methods, with all their problems in terms of noise, disturbance, traffic generation, dust, damage to habitats and other pollution. Like landfills, these quarries are often located close to conurbations, competing with other valuable land uses. Construction wastes could be recycled for use as aggregate, while road-building materials could be directly recycled. Construction materials could also be derived to a much greater extent from secondary sources such as colliery spoil, pulverised fuel ash, gypsum produced by flue gas desulphurisation and china clay sand, all of which currently add to the size of our waste tips as they are seen as uneconomical in comparison with the costs of virgin materials (which do not reflect their full environmental costs).

Current methods of waste disposal are extremely wasteful of energy as well as other resources, particularly in comparison to recycling. Aluminium recycling uses only 5 per cent of the energy needed to refine the metal in the first place, paper just over 50 per cent and glass 75 per cent[7] (see Table 6.4 and Figure 6.2). Plastics recycling can use as little as 20 per cent, according to American figures. Saving energy can also save money for these industries.

Table 6.4: Environmental benefits derived from substituting secondary materials for virgin resources

	Aluminium	Steel	Paper	Glass
Environmental benefit				
Reduction of:				
Energy use	90-97	47-74	23-74	4-32
Air pollution	95	85	74	20
Water pollution	97	76	35	-
Mining wastes	-	97	-	80
Water use	-	40	58	50

Source: Pollock, C., *Mining Urban Wastes: The Potential for Recycling.*

Recycling also reduces the degradation of the environment caused by the extraction of raw materials such as sand, oil and metal ores.

Waste management options

Waste management options can be ranked in terms of priority. This is likely to underpin the forthcoming European Community Directive on waste management, but is already applied in the state of Oregon in the USA:[8]

> The most desirable goal is to reduce the amount of waste generated, then to reuse the material for the purpose for which it was originally intended. Next comes recycling of the nonreusable material, followed by energy recovery from waste that cannot be reused or recycled, so long as the energy recovery facility preserves the quality of air, water

and land resources. The last step is to dispose of the remainder by landfilling or other approved method.

By reducing the amount of waste they produce and recycling a large share of their discards, individuals can contribute to the solution of the waste problem. But consumers cannot effect widespread changes on their own; they need the assistance of industries willing to manufacture recyclable products and governments willing to legislate to alter waste disposal practices.

Incineration

Only 6 per cent of domestic refuse in the UK is currently disposed of in high temperature furnaces. Hay and Wright suggest that the investment required, some £40-£50m., to build new incinerators has proved unattractive to most local authorities. Very few incinerators are designed to use the waste to generate heat or electricity. Hay and Wright comment:[9]

> Burning waste, is, for most local authorities, simply a matter of disposing of the rubbish and not a question of recycling energy. The economic viability of incineration (and indeed other forms of reclamation) will start to increase when landfill costs increase to a more realistic level.

However, this process has begun. In London a consortium of local authorities are planning a waste incineration plant that will generate electricity and provide heat for industrial and district heating.

Yet incineration is not the least environmentally damaging option, and in Denmark incinerators are being phased out because of concerns over toxic pollution, particularly dioxins from the incineration of plastics and other materials containing chlorine. Indeed such concerns are greater where energy recovery is involved, as burning temperatures are lower and thus toxic pollution greater. In the UK many local authority incinerators have closed in recent years because they cannot meet existing standards on emissions to the atmosphere of smoke, particulates and chemicals from their chimneys. Of those remaining, 80-90 per cent are expected to be put under pressure by further tightening of EC standards.[10] Incinerators used for industrial waste disposal are also under pressure.

Incineration also acts as a disincentive to reclamation as the removal of high calorific value wastes such as paper, from incinerator inputs reduces their efficiency.

Recycling

In January 1989 Hay and Wright estimated that UK household sector waste could be reduced by one third by the year 2000 if a serious recycling programme was set in motion. Later in the year the government set a target of recycling 50 per cent of the recyclable proportion of domestic waste by the end of the century. This target is equivalent to around 30 per cent of the total, as 50-60 per cent of domestic waste is directly recyclable given current technology.

More of the products used should be made from recycled materials, and more recyclable materials should be fed back into the production processes. Cooper's vision is of a self-sustaining materials economy:[11]

> The amount of materials we use per capita has reached a peak. From now on we could perhaps be using less. At the same time, we have a huge store of capital locked up in goods produced to date which can be fed back for reprocessing. In the future, therefore, we could require no new raw materials, merely reusing those already extracted over and over again. However, to achieve this we must change the throwaway mentality that is part of our recent heritage.

The full environmental costs of conventional disposal methods must be accounted for. In such accounting, reclamation and recycling normally become the most economic form. Yet one of the greatest costs of not taking a more responsible attitude is simply the loss of the opportunity to use the material or product again. Table 6.5 shows the

Table 6.5: Costs of waste collection and disposal by type of authority (England and Wales)

| | Gross revenue expenditure | | | | | |
| | £ per person | | £ per tonnne | | Total (£m.) | |
	1983/4	1986/7	1983/4	1986/7	1983/4	1986/7
Collection						
London boroughs	13.0	14.2	34.7	38.4	87.7	99.4
Metropolitan districts	9.6	10.8	30.1	31.5	107.7	120.3
Non-metropolitan districts	8.5	9.3	26.4	27.8	244.4	271.3
Wales	8.9	9.5	18.1	19.3	25.0	26.8
England & Wales	9.4	10.2	27.9	28.7	464.8	514.9
Disposal						
Greater London Council	8.1	n/a	n/a	n/a	55.3	n/a
Metropolitan counties	6.0	n/a	n/a	n/a	67.6	n/a
Non-metropolitan counties	3.8	4.3	n/a	n/a	109.7	125.7
Wales	2.8	4.3	n/a	n/a	8.0	12.0
England & Wales	4.8	n/a	n/a	n/a	240.7	n/a

Source: Chartered Institute of Public Finance and Accountancy, *Waste collection statistics 1982/3 to 1986/7* and *Waste disposal statistics 1982/3 to 1986/7*, CIPFA, London, 1988.

increasing money costs of waste collection and disposal, excluding environmental costs.

Table 6.6 shows the comparison for a city in the US. Recycling is found to be the least expensive strategy. Collection costs are higher for landfills because of the transportation distances involved. These costs are likely to increase as landfills become scarcer.

Thus it should be clear that a realistic price per tonne must be charged for the disposal of waste received at disposal sites. This would encourage waste reduction. Hay and Wright report that some areas of the UK claim their current disposal costs are as low as £1.50 per tonne.

Yet the Department of the Environment estimated in 1986 that the absolute minimum was £9.00 per tonne, and in 1989 a departmental civil servant estimated that a minimum gate fee of £13.45 was necessary if the costs of preventing greater pollution and of monitoring methane are taken into account. Transport costs of around £7.00 per tonne for a twenty-mile journey bring the total cost of collection and disposal to over £50.00 per tonne.[12] More recent estimates indicate that in the medium term, the marginal costs saved per tonne recycled range (depending on material) from £39.00 to £60.00. This includes an element for collection costs saved of £17.00 to £31.00 assuming that a 10 per cent fall in weight collected would lead to a 5 per cent fall in cost after adjustments in vehicle size and collection route scheduling had been made.[13]

Table 6.6: Comparison of waste management costs (USA)

dollars per ton

	Collection	Processing	Total
Method[1]			
Recycling[1]	-	-	30
Composting	50	15	65
Current landfill	70	20	90
Incineration	50	$40-60^{2}$	90-110
Future landfill	70	25-30	95-100

Notes [1] = Collection + processing - revenues.
         [2] = Includes revenues from electricity sales.
Source: Pollock, C., *Mining Urban Wastes: The Potential for Recycling.*

Increasing costs of waste disposal, as well as encouraging direct waste reduction, will also enhance the economics of recycling. However, these also depend on the markets for the recovered products. This may seem obvious, but government policy has yet to introduce co-ordinated approaches to both recycling and sale of recycled products. For years, recycling has been hampered by the belief that it should make money directly. But recycling is a cost-effective 'disposal' option as long as it requires fewer government subsidies than landfilling or incineration.

Lower costs and therefore lower local taxes, energy savings, and a cleaner environment are the true advantages. As landfill costs continue to rise because of space constraints and stricter environmental regulations, and as the high capital costs of incinerators and their pollution control technologies cut into local authority budgets, the appeal of recycling will inevitably grow. Pollock gives the example of the densely populated northeastern section of the USA:[14]

> the average cost of running a weekly curbside refuse collection and recycling programme is $20 to $30 a tonne; an amount rarely recouped by selling the recovered materials. But it costs some $40 to $60 a tonne to haul refuse to the landfill, and $70 to $120 a tonne to burn it. ... [In fact] virtually all materials except aluminium are worth more when recycled as a cost-avoidance mechanism than for their value on the open market.

The failure to recognise this means that the funds allocated to recycling are rarely commensurate with the goal. The assumption that start-up costs and collection and processing expenses will be fully and immediately covered by revenues dooms recycling programmes to failure. In Ontario, Canada, however, the provincial government provided 'seed' funding for three years to establish recycling initiatives in a number of the province's cities, with the target being to reduce waste going to landfill by at least 10 per cent. In fact some cities reduced their waste stream by over 15 per cent within the period.[15]

Pollock reports that the Portland, Oregon metropolitan area has determined that up to 52 per cent of its waste stream is potentially available for reduction, re-use, or recycling and that the remainder can be dumped in landfills designed to recover methane gas or burned to generate electricity. Communities within the metropolitan area are able to devise their own strategies for meeting these targets. If they are not achieved, waste loads containing a high percentage of recyclable materials are not accepted at disposal facilities that do not process waste for recovery. The residents of the region already recycle 22 per cent of their wastes.[16]

In West Germany a number of innovative schemes are in operation. In Munich a pilot scheme is evaluating the possibility of introducing wide-ranging packaging deposits to encourage return of packaging to stores. In Hesse separate collection of paper, glass, metal, certain plastics, drugs, batteries and some organic wastes has been introduced, with a target reduction in volume of waste landfilled of 50 per cent in just three to four years.[17] A similar scheme has been set in progress in Cardiff as part of the Friends of the Earth 'Recycling City' initiative which launched an innovative multi-material kerbside collection in Sheffield in November 1989, and in Cardiff in May 1990.

There are two key barriers to successful recycling programmes: non-participation by individuals and the lack of effective markets for recovered materials. The purchase-consume-dispose habit is well entrenched in all of us. Increasing the householder's responsibility for his or her own waste to the extent that they have to separate it provides an educational link between the generation of waste and its disposal. This has two potential advantages. First, the householder is encouraged to think about waste as a resource, to be re-used and recycled; and secondly, to question his or her own consumption patterns and habits with a view to avoiding generating waste.

Hay and Wright found that the most effective recycling technique in terms of resource recovery is one where the householder separates waste into a number of bins for each material and places it on the kerb for routine collection.[18] This is the fastest growing type of recycling programme in industrial countries and is already widely used in Canada. In Oregon, USA, residential kerbside pick-up of recyclables is required at least once per month in settlements of 4,000 or more people; in smaller communities, recycling depots must be established at disposal sites.[19] In Britain progress is slow. Although the London Borough of Richmond has managed to reduce its waste stream by 8 per cent, 2 or 3 per cent is the UK norm.

However, separated collection of waste without markets for the materials does not constitute recycling. If no market exists, the material will not be recycled, merely (temporarily) diverted from the waste stream. Demand for recycled materials must be generated at both consumer and business levels. Business demand can be enhanced by support for local industry utilising the recovered materials as local source of supply. More generally, economic incentives such as tax credits for investment can be offered to waste processors and companies that use recycled materials as product inputs. Raw materials that could be replaced by recycled materials could be subjected to a 'resource tax'. Recycled products could be zero-rated for VAT and this would boost consumer demand. Public bodies could be required to operate procurement policies that favour (or at least do not discriminate against) goods made with recycled materials.

Low and volatile prices are the bane of secondary materials markets. Without a dependable floor price, or ample storage space to maintain price-stabilising buffer stocks, programme planning is impaired. Economically sustainable recycling requires high consumer participation rates and the involvement of either a public or private facility willing to hold and process large volumes of materials despite market swings. In Holland, buffer stocks enable collectors of waste paper to sell to a government-established fund when prices drop below a pre-determined level. The stock is sold when prices rise.

Businesses in each industry need to work together to offer stable prices to voluntary groups for the materials they collect. This has been done successfully by the glass industry and partly in the aluminium industry. But some metals and paper merchants continue to offer cut-throat prices which are prejudicial to a developing industry, and are themselves the result of the fluctuating prices offered by the steel industry and paper mills. Medium- and long-term planning is important. The infrastructure implications of increased recycling are significant, particularly in terms of modified production and distribution systems, with associated decentralisation. Short-term changes should be considered with the long-term vision in mind.

It is industry which dictates the markets for recyclable materials. To date those markets have been slow to appear because it has been too easy for primary industries not to take responsibility for their products. In the UK the Conservative government has been unwilling to intervene because of its commitment to the 'free market'. This inertia, together with the lack of commitment at a local level, has resulted in Britain having one of the worst recycling records in Europe, certainly when compared to countries like Switzerland, Holland, West Germany, Denmark and Sweden. For example, it recycles only 16 per cent of its

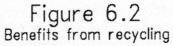

Figure 6.2
Benefits from recycling

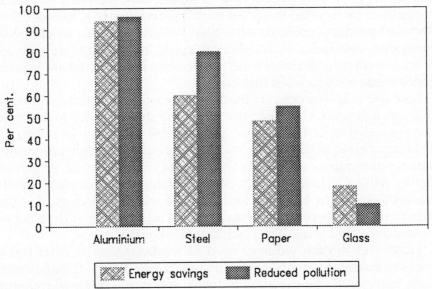

Source: As Table 6.4 above.

glass, less than a third of its paper, only 8 per cent of its cans and virtually none of its plastics. In contrast, Holland collects more than half its aluminium, paper and glass for recycling. In effect, Holland requires no raw materials for making its paper and glass one year out of two.[20]

To date in the UK, only the glass manufacturers have set up realistic national programmes for recycling, guaranteeing to take up all cullet at guaranteed minimum prices, thus creating the requisite stable framework. The market in the UK is wide open; there is no technical limit to the amount of glass that can be recycled. The problem lies in the derisory collection facilities, with only one bottle bank per 14,000 population and a target of just 1:5,600 by 1995. This compares with figures for 1985 of 1:1,400 in the Netherlands and 1:2,000 in West Germany.[21] Local authorities are as much to blame for the shortage as the industry.

Sadly, the situation in the paper industry is not as optimistic. There are limits on the amount that can be recycled, imposed by paper producers and the buyers themselves who dictate how much paper they will re-use when producing newsprint, or any other type of paper. Britain fulfils only about 30 per cent of its requirements for paper and board. As a result, it imports much of its writing and printing paper and huge amounts of newsprint; 1.46 million tonnes in 1988, equivalent to 77 per cent of the newspaper produced in the country.[22] To change this situation four things are needed:

i) to adapt existing production processes to use a greater percentage of secondary material;

ii) to invest in new production processes, to utilise waste fibre as raw material;

iii) to greatly improve collection facilities, keeping different grades of fibre separate; and

iv) to establish a market for the paper, if necessary by regulating for minimum levels of recycled inputs.

The market for metals, such as ferrous metals and aluminium is constrained by industrial inertia. Currently, Britain exports nearly 4 million tonnes of reclaimed ferrous metal each year because the steel industry in its present form requires large quantities of imported iron ore. Again, several things are needed to improve metal reclamation: adaptation of existing production processes; wider investment in new plant,* notably the electric iron furnace for ferrous metal recovery; and improvement of collection facilities, especially for tin-plated and aluminium cans. The present facilities are very limited and, as a result, although all cans can be recycled, only 8 per cent of the 12 billion steel containers and 3-5 per cent of the 3 billion aluminium beverage cans produced in Britain each year are recovered, less than half the European average.[23] The situation is complicated by the existence of both

---

* Although a new plant for reclaiming aluminium at Warrington was recently opened, there is a need for much more such investment.

aluminium and tin-plate drink cans, each of which has about 50 per cent of the market.

The situation is different in regard to plastics. There are currently only very limited recycling facilities, particularly in the UK, for post-consumer plastics, even though the technology exists. This is worrying because the plastics share of municipal waste has increased dramatically so that it is now 20 per cent or more of the total volume.[24] A major obstacle is that combinations in which the plastic is commonly used are expensive to separate and, because no identification system exists (such as the one currently in use in the US), it is impossible to distinguish one plastic resin from another.

The organic component of municipal waste, including paper and vegetable wastes, can be recycled as compost, both on a household and a municipal scale. Organic wastes in landfills can give rise to rapid release of soluble organics, and thus leachate with a high ammonia content and high BOD (Biological Oxygen Demand) as well as methane-rich gas accumulation. However, if the compostable material is not mixed with other wastes and not contaminated by heavy metals, high quality compost suitable for use on agricultural land as a fertiliser and conditioner can be produced. France has over one hundred plants producing some 800,000 tons of compost per year, much of.it used on vineyards. In Sweden one quarter of solid waste is composted, and in some cities, such as Heidelberg in Germany, the proportion is even higher, at one third.[25] Compost provides a substitute both for fertiliser and for peat, which is supplied at high environmental cost because of the destruction of the valuable wildlife habitats of peat bogs. Even the lowest grade compost has useful properties in odour control and can be used, for example as cover material for landfill sites, replacing bought-in soil.

Because of difficulties experienced in the past, for example, in door-to-door collection, centralised sorting and separation, and unstable prices for secondary materials, most local authorities have put recycling on the 'back-burner'. Civil engineers, concerned with engineered solutions to waste disposal, still dominate the hierarchy in both collection and disposal. Local authorities should be required not only to integrate recycling in statutory waste management plans but also to employ or designate recycling officers with adequate powers. Those concerned with economic development of their areas should promote recycling as part of that process. Davidson documents its significance at the grass-roots level of the local economy, where such efforts 'generate jobs and offer opportunities for training in new skills'.[26] The main reason is that, while raw materials are usually imported, many recycled materials can be made available at low transport costs.

Reducing waste

The European Commission is challenging the glass, metal, plastics, and paper industries to take responsibility for their products on the basis of the 'polluter pays' principle. As far as the 1975 Directive [75/442/EEC] is concerned the polluter is 'the producer of the product from which the waste came' and should bear the cost of disposing of (or recycling) the waste. A resource tax would place the responsibility firmly on the shoulders of the 'polluting' industries. However, the primary function of a resource tax is reduction of the consumption of the resource in question, whether aluminium or oil, by providing an incentive to use untaxed recycled sources. It will only be effective in reducing waste volumes if it is combined with regulation preventing substitution of non-recyclable materials for the resource in question.

Regulation is needed as well as fiscal incentives. Labelling is crucial if waste is to be reduced or separated for recycling. Under draft proposals amending the 1985 Directive [85/339/EEC] on containers for liquids for human consumption, by 1993 standard symbols will be displayed on containers or labels, indicating whether the container is refillable and recyclable. For example, a returnable symbol tells the consumer that the used container can be returned to the retailer and should not be treated as refuse. No trader in the Community who sells products in these containers will be able to refuse to accept their return. Stringent recycling targets are also expected.

One major trend has been the disappearance of returnable or at least recyclable glass bottles and their replacement by plastic, which is currently to all intents and purposes unrecyclable. West Germany, which uses one-tenth of the quantity of plastic that is used for bottles in Britain, has now introduced much tougher legislation to encourage recycling. Using a different approach, the Danish government has prohibited non-refillable containers for beer and soft drinks on the grounds that non-returnable bottles are an unnecessary burden on the environment. Holland is taking steps to re-introduce the returnable milk bottle.

In general, waste volumes will not be reduced significantly until products, packages, and materials are designed for durability, re-use, and recycling. Standardised refillable containers that can be interchangeably used by multiple producers, as in the Netherlands, are one example of this approach. Just like traditional wine and beer bottles that differ primarily by their paper label, standardised containers could be developed for fruit juices, milk, spirits, and soft drinks.

Refillable glass bottles are already the most energy-efficient beverage container on the market. If these were also standardised, and their use made interchangeable, great savings in transport, fuel, and goods vehicle emissions could be realised. Computerised inventory and tracking systems would facilitate this network. In the Netherlands, 95 per cent of retail soft drinks, and 90 per cent of retail beer sales, are already in returnable bottles.[27]

Industrial waste and pollution

Currently, much of UK industry's solid waste is landfilled, either in private or public landfill facilities; and its liquid waste is discharged to the public sewage system or directly to watercourses. Industrial hazardous waste is either disposed of on site or transported to special facilities for its treatment or direct disposal. Wastes that are not dumped in landfill tips, rivers or the sea are burned in special incineration plants. Procedures for disposal are regulated by public bodies, notably the waste disposal authorities, the National Rivers Authority which has taken over responsibility for monitoring the condition of the country's watercourses and recording and investigating incidents of water pollution from the Water Authorities, and Her Majesty's Inspectorate of Pollution (HMIP). The Department of the Environment has a network of stations for monitoring air pollution, although these provide far less comprehensive coverage than equivalent networks in several other countries, including the Netherlands and the USA.

Industry has a direct financial incentive to undertake recycling to reduce raw material and energy costs and to save on waste disposal costs for which it pays per unit. However, without regulation this incentive will mean that pollution control and waste reduction are carried out in the cheapest way, rather than by the use of the best available technology.

In the USA, the growing difficulty and cost of complying with ever more complex environmental legislation has been a major factor in a number of companies making major changes in their waste practices. The company 3M is often quoted as a pioneer of the development of systematic efforts. Its 'pollution prevention pays' programme initially focused on measures to reduce wastes at source by means of product reformulation, process modifications, equipment redesign, and recovery of by-products for re-use. One measure adopted by 3M was raising the charges for in-house incineration and disposal of wastes generated at its US plants, by at least a doubling of the existing fees, bringing them close to commercial rates. This was intended to ensure that any current risks and potential future liabilities are fully accounted for in present production costs, providing an added stimulus to waste reduction efforts. However, it neither ensures that those incinerators are actually meeting high environmental standards, nor fully reflects environmental costs.

Overall, 3M's initiatives, over a decade, are calculated to have saved them over $482 million and eliminated an annual 122,000 tonnes of waste pollutants, 16,100 tonnes of water pollutants, 400,000 tonnes of solid wastes, and 1.6 billion gallons of wastewater. 3M estimates that the effective cut in waste streams is about 50 per cent but, due to the company's growth, the actual amounts of waste produced by 3M world-wide are higher today than in 1975. As a result, its environmental programmes have been reappraised and new targets set: to reduce its world-wide hazardous emissions to atmosphere by 90 per cent, and to reduce the generation of all types of hazardous residues by 50 per cent, by the year 2000. The company has set itself the general goal of moving towards 'zero pollution'. The new initiatives are not expected to bring it net savings.[28]

In the UK the strategic approach to pollution control has been largely voluntary and no companies have even devised programmes comparable to the 'pollution prevention pays' scheme. Some companies operating in the UK have taken innovative steps, including forms of integrated pollution control. Rhone-Poulenc have introduced an 'environmental index' of liquid effluent discharges, with a targeted annual reduction of 10 per cent, and computerised waste accounting to separate disposal costs from general overheads.[29]

This voluntary approach is not adequate, even in the perception of industry, with its desire for a 'level playing field'. The problems of uneven standards are enhanced by limited enforcement of even the existing regulations. The poverty of resources provided and the poor staff conditions in HMIP have resulted in infrequent inspection visits and a low ratio of prosecutions to known offences.[30]

The true costs of continued industrial pollution are only beginning to become clear. For example, studies of the Birmingham and Coventry aquifers have revealed that industrial pollution of land with toxic chemicals has led to high concentrations of synthetic organic solvents in groundwater, a problem which may be common to other urban areas.[31]

Overall, the full extent of land contamination in the UK is unknown, although the results of small-scale surveys imply that there may be over 50,000 hectares in as many sites in mainly urban areas contaminated with substances including heavy metals, phenols and cyanides.[32] The main categories of land-use include waste disposal sites, gas-works, petrol stations, power stations, iron and steel works, petroleum refineries, chemical works, textile plants, timber treatment works and manufacturers of integrated circuits and semi-conductors. Effective treatment is vital if recycled land is to be used for future urban building.

The Environmental Protection Act of 1990 introduced a duty on local authorities to maintain registers of land that may be contaminated. However, there is no indication of how (or even if) resources will be made available to compile these. Application of the polluter pays principle, in the form of rigorous planning conditions on potentially polluting land-uses to ensure restoration, and/or the attachment of absolute retrospective polluter liability as a legal 'charge' on the land, and regulation requiring that it cannot be sold without the contamination being disclosed, are ways in which the incidence and effects of contamination may be reduced.

Traffic and other air pollution

Table 6.7 and Figures 6.3 and 6.4 show the sources of air pollution in England and Wales. Most of these are urban, or relate directly to urban demands. Traffic is already the largest source of several of the pollutants shown, and is expected to increase significantly (see Chapter 2 on transport).

That traffic pollutants are reaching levels worthy of serious concern is shown by a recent study by Friends of the Earth which found that nitrogen dioxide levels may be above EC guide values in a wide range

Table 6.7:   Air pollution by source, England and Wales, 1988

	Nitrogen oxides '000 tonnes tonnes		Carbon monoxide '000 tonnes		Carbon dioxide M. tonnes carbon		Volatile organic compounds '000 tonnes	
Domestic	72	(3%)	388	(8)	24	(14)	58	(3)
Commerce & public service	59	(2%)	9	(-)	9	(5)	1	(-)
Power stations	792	(32%)	47	(1)	52	(33)	13	(1)
Industry[a]	331	(13%)	339	(6)	42	(27)	1,098	(59)[b]
Road transport	1,108	(45%)	4,689	(85)	28	(18)	545	(30)
Other	118	(5%)	36	(1)	3	(1)	121	(7)
All sources (ground based)	2,303		5,508		158		1,846	

Notes: a: Excludes power stations, and agriculture.
        b: Includes fuel use, industrial processes and solvent evaporation.
Source: Department of the Environment, *Digest of Environmental Protection and Water Statistics*, HMSO, London, 1989.

Figure 6.3
Sources of VOCs in air

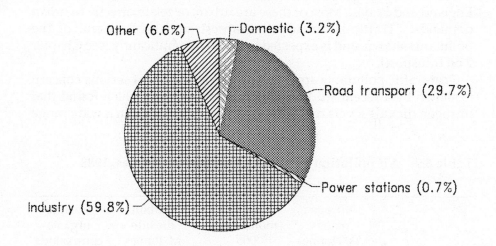

Other (6.6%) ⌐   ⌐Domestic (3.2%)

Road transport (29.7%)

Power stations (0.7%)

Industry (59.8%) ⌐

Source: As Table 6.7 above.

of UK cities, largely as a result of traffic pollution (Table 6.8). The 1985 EC Directive (85/203/EEC) identifies the danger zones for NO_2 as 'canyon streets carrying heavy traffic and major intersections'. Other traffic pollutants are also likely to be found at high levels in urban areas, including carcinogenic polyaromatic hydrocarbons attached to the particulates emitted by diesel engines (particularly when poorly maintained). Diesel fumes are also largely responsible for the estimated £80m. UK building cleaning bill now that other sources of particulates are largely controlled.[33]

Figure 6.4
Sources of NOx in air

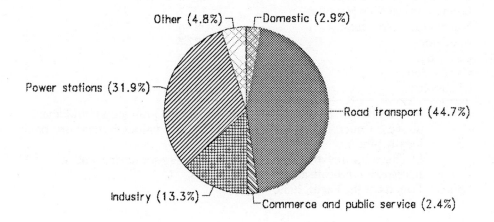

Other (4.8%) — ┌Domestic (2.9%)

Power stations (31.9%) —

Road transport (44.7%)

Industry (13.3%) —

└Commerce and public service (2.4%)

Source: As Table 6.7 above.

Traffic pollution can be reduced in two basic ways: by reducing the unit emissions from each vehicle and by reducing the number of vehicles. These must be pursued simultaneously. Chapter 2 discusses the ways in which vehicle use would be reduced in sustainable urban development. Although EC regulations will soon enforce the fitting of three-way catalytic converters to petrol-driven vehicles, growth in vehicle numbers will eventually counterbalance the likely reductions in carbon monoxide, nitrogen oxides and hydrocarbon emissions, while emissions of carbon dioxide will continue to increase (traffic is the fastest

191

Table 6.8: Nitrogen dioxide levels in UK cities

	Mean NO$_2$ level (micro g/m^3)[a]
Site	
London: High Holborn	115.9
Manchester: City Centre	103.5
London: Royal Free Hospital	100.7
Manchester: Non-central	83.6
Maidstone	77.7
Coventry	70.3
Cambridge	64.9
Cheltenham	57.9

Notes: a: Levels above 84 micrograms/m^3 exceed EC limit values and levels above 56 micrograms/m^3 exceed EC guide values (which are not legally binding).
b: These figures are from a single month's monitoring and do not necessarily indicate actual annual values.
Source: Friends of the Earth, 1989.

growing source of CO_2 in the UK). In addition, greatly improved standards to control particulate and NOx emissions from diesel vehicles are also required.

A shift to electric vehicles cannot offer even a partial solution to these problems given the existing mix and methods of electricity production, as it merely shifts the location of the resultant polluting emissions by increasing the pollution emitted by power stations. Power stations are already the other major source of air pollution. Such pollution reflects largely urban demands for energy but its negative effects are not concentrated in urban areas. Strategies for reducing energy demands are discussed in Chapter 3. Industrial processes, on the other hand, are concentrated in urban areas, and are responsible for significant proportions of some pollutants, notably volatile organic compounds.

Table 6.9:   Water pollution incidents reported by cause (England and Wales)

	1986	1988
Farm	3,495	3,952
Industry	7,729	9,085
Sewage	4,137	4,578
Other	4,286	6,039
Total	19,647	23,654

Source: Department of the Environment, *Digest of Environmental Protection and Water Statistics*, HMSO, London, 1989.

Figure 6.5
Causes of water pollution incidents

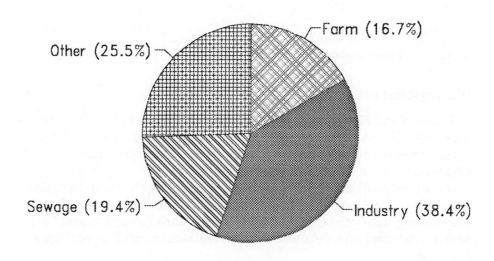

Source: As Table 6.9 above.

Table 6.10: Water quality, England and Wales

Class	1980		1985	
	km	%	km	%
Freshwater rivers and canals				
Good 1A	13,830	34	13,470	33
Good 1B	14,220	35	13,990	34
Fair 2	8,670	21	9,730	24
Poor 3	3,260	8	3,560	9
Bad 4	640	2	650	2
All classes	40,630	100	41,390	100
	1980		1985	
	km	%	km	%
Estuaries				
Good A	1,870	68	1,860	68
Fair B	620	23	650	24
Poor C	140	5	130	5
Bad D	110	4	90	3
All classes	2,730	100	2,730	100

Source: As Table 6.9 above.

Water pollution

Table 6.9 and Figure 6.5 show the causes of reported water pollution incidents. The reduction of pollution as a dimension of the sustainable agricultural system is discussed in Chapter 5. The major urban sources of pollution are industry and sewage treatment.

Industrial pollution of water affects many UK rivers and coastal waters (see Table 6.10). Major sources include the chemical and engineering industries. Many rivers flowing through urban areas are severely affected and thus lose their recreational as well as ecological functions.

Sewage effluents pollute waterways, and mechanically treated but otherwise raw sewage sludge is still dumped at sea. Table 6.11 shows

Table 6.11: Sludge production and disposal in selected industrial countries, 1983

	Annual sludge production	Method of Disposal				
		Farm land	Land-fill[a]	Inciner-ation	Ocean dumping	Unspec-ified[b]
Country						
	('000 tons)	--------------(%) -----------------				
USA	6,200	42	15	27	4	12
FRG	2,200	39	49	8	2	2
Italy	1,200	20	55	-----25-----		0
UK	1,200	41	26	4	29	0
France	840	30	50	20	0	0
Netherlands	230	60	27	2	11	0
Sweden	210	60	---------30------------			10

Note: Figures here are for dry weight of sludge generated and therefore are not comparable to the figure for the UK given in Table 6.1.
a: Includes small amounts for land reclamation and forest application
b: Mostly sludge retained in lagoons

Source: Brown, L. and Jacobsen, J., *The Future of Urbanization*, Worldwatch, 1987.

the routes of sewage sludge disposal currently used in a number of countries. In the UK the often partially treated effluent is discharged into the country's watercourses and coastal waters and the sludge is dumped at sea, landfilled or spread on agricultural land. More widespread agricultural use is precluded by the potentially toxic nature of a proportion of the sludge, resulting from its contamination by industrial waste. Sewage effluent too can be highly polluting, owing to high levels of metals, organic chemicals, micro-organisms and nutrients, all of which can disrupt aquatic ecology.

More generally, sewage treatment works are subject to 'consents' to release certain amounts of pollutants. Many of these consents are not stringent enough to protect the environment, yet, even so, are often breached. In 1988, 17 per cent of those sewage treatment works with numerical consents were found to be in breach of them.[34] However, many consents have recently been relaxed by the UK government to facilitate the privatisation of the industry.

Current sewage treatment practices in the UK are not only polluting but also highly wasteful. Sewage engineers have been asked to 'get rid of waste' rather than to 'recover for the use of agriculture the valuable materials that occur in human sewage'.

In Sweden industrial effluent is kept separate from domestic, and sewage is not mixed with other liquid domestic wastes. The latter (described as 'grey water') is conveyed in separate pipes to a treatment plant, treated and discharged into a river. The treatment required would be significantly reduced if products for domestic use (particularly cleaning materials) were devoid of potential pollutants. Sewage, or 'black water', which contains all the waste of nutrient value comprises only a tiny volume compared with the 'grey water' and after a straightforward treatment process it is used as fertiliser.

However, in the UK such a system would involve high infrastructure costs and thus legislation is necessary to reduce industrial discharges of toxic materials to the sewage system to minimal levels.

Separated sewage can be treated in methane digesters. Methane gas is drawn off as a relatively clean, efficient and, importantly, inexhaustible source of energy. The waste slurry is sterile and after composting can be used as manure. In China there is a methane plant in many villages, with some 70 million of them already in place if planned targets have been met.[35] Such an approach to sewage could be used in some parts of the UK, and particularly merits consideration in areas not connected to mains sewerage.

However, anaerobic digesters do comprise an industrial hazard and are less suitable in urban areas. But sewage sludge could be piped to sites on the outskirts of cities where it could be composted. Such composting of sewage sludge would overcome some of the logistical problems which hinder its use as a fertiliser. These are largely the result of the difficulty of transporting raw sludge, the related odour and the fact that farmers do not need fertiliser all year round. Composting removes the smell, and provides a fertiliser which can be more readily transported and stored until needed.

The effective return of nutrients from urban areas to agriculture could reduce a further major source of water pollution: that of contamination of ground and surface waters by chemical fertilisers. Recycled nutrients in the form of compost can provide a less polluting alternative to chemical fertilisers particularly when combined with appropriate cultivation techniques. Other ways in which pollution from agrochemicals could be reduced (and thus the quality of drinking water in urban as well as rural areas improved) are discussed in Chapter 5.

Reductions in water pollution could also be achieved through water conservation methods, which would also reduce the investment needed in supply infrastructure. In Hamburg, water authority staff advise consumers on how to conserve water, particularly through substituting for potable water, for example using rain water in WCs and washing machines.[36]

Reducing pollution in practice

Even in the long term it is highly unlikely that all the waste products of industry will become economically recyclable. Therefore it is important to act directly to reduce pollution. As in other fields, the measures required are a mix of regulation and incentive. There has been much debate over the ideal mix of these mechanisms, but central to any policy is enhanced monitoring, combined with freedom of information. Pollution controls or taxes can only be enforced if polluters can be identified and their emissions measured.

The adoption of stringent air and water quality standards and the extension of monitoring networks are necessary prerequisites for effective pollution reduction. Currently Japanese standards are the most stringent for most pollutants, in the case of sulphur dioxide being 33 per cent more stringent than that recommended by the World Health Organisation. In general, EC standards do not reflect the best available control technology and in the case of air pollution are generally lower than Japanese, US, Swiss and WHO standards. And even WHO standards for certain air pollutants, such as ozone, incorporate little or no margin of protection. The UK Government's Environment White Paper of September 1990 proposed the establishment of an expert panel to advise on air quality standards, but no timetable for the production or implementation of standards was announced. Increased monitoring and a wider range of standards would also permit publicity of the results in the form of pollution alerts, thus providing a warning to those whose health is at risk.

Current UK regulation measures would need to be extended and improved even after full implementation of the 1990 Environmental Protection Act. The *minimum* targets for reductions in emission levels of non-accumulative pollutants such as sulphur dioxide, need to be set to below local, regional and global ecological *critical loads* or *critical levels*; that is, to levels of pollution which the ecosystems affected can continue to absorb without sustaining long-term damage. Despite the commitment of the UK Government to the critical loads concept in the Environment White Paper of September 1990, experience of policy on sulphur dioxide and oxides of nitrogen indicates that in practice there is no evidence that the UK Government is committed to the cuts needed to reduce acid depositions below critical loads. [37] Where current emission levels do not exceed critical loads, such analysis does not indicate that emissions can be safely allowed to increase, while for persistent, accumulative or dangerous pollutants the application of the precautionary principle indicates that a target of zero emissions must be set. Integrated pollution control (agreeing permitted emission levels in relation to all media – air, water and land – so that pollution is not merely diverted) should be applied to all processes through a unified regulating authority.

In the first instance these standards should be linked, without qualification, to the use of the *best available technology*, and incrementally tightened to force improvements in technology until, at an absolute minimum, ecologically sustainable emission levels are achieved. Even then, the precautionary principle means that further improvement should be required. General adoption of the *best available technology* at present would produce improvements in all polluting sectors, including power generation.[38]

It is also possible to mitigate the effects of pollution through natural methods, but this provides no justification for continuing pollution as it reduces the natural value of the ecosysytems so used and fails to reclaim materials from waste pollutant flows. In effect, vegetation filters airborne particulates from the air, as well as reducing carbon dioxide levels through photosynthesis. In the case of London's Hyde Park, it was found that a green area of 260 hectares reduces effective smoke pollution by 25 per cent. More generally, one hectare of deciduous woodland can filter approximately four tonnes of particulates from the atmosphere each year.[39] In the longer term, however, such filtered materials will leach to ground water, so toxic pollutants must still be reduced at source. The effects of water pollution can also be eased in some cases. Wetlands are effective natural filters capable of reducing phosphorus concentrations, for example, by over 95 per cent.[40]

Conclusion

Waste and pollution are concentrated in urban areas because of the concentration of activity in these areas. Reducing wastes and using recyclable materials are central to a waste management strategy which aims to reduce resource consumption and land, water and air pollution.

The potential for recycling in the UK is enormous. Current levels are very low compared to those in continental Europe, and should be improved through: government action, including fiscal means to improve markets; local authority action, in the provision of improved recycling facilities; and private sector action, in guaranteeing a market for recyclable materials and in the provision of facilities.

The current mixing of industrial and domestic waste in the sewage system prevents the recycling of human sewage, and the minimisation of toxic discharges to the sewers must be of high priority.

Improvement in industrial waste practices could potentially lead to reduced levels of pollution, including hazardous emissions. The charges for public waste disposal facilities should be increased, while information disclosure and pollution control incentives, regulation and enforcement by regulatory bodies must be improved.

References

1. Kovacs, M., Podani, J., Klinsek, P., Dinka, M. and Torok, K., 'Element composition of the leaves of some deciduous trees and the monitoring of heavy metals in an urban-industrial environment', in Bornkamm, R., Lee, J.A., and Seaward, M.R.D. (eds) *Urban Ecology: the second European ecological symposium*, Blackwell Scientific, Oxford, 1982.
2. Ayers, G.P., Bigg, E.K., Turvey, D.E., and Manton, M.J., 'Urban influence on condensation nuclei over a continent', *Atmospheric Environment*, Vol. 16, 1982, pp. 951-4.
3. Department of the Environment, *Digest of environmental protection and water statistics*, HMSO, London, 1988.
4. *Ibid.*
5. Department of the Environment, *Digest of Environmental Protection and Water Statistics*, HMSO, London, 1989.
6. Web, C., 'Moulding a new horizon', *Surveyor*, 14 September 1989.
7. Pollock, C., *Mining Urban Wastes: the potential for recycling*, Worldwatch Institute, Washington DC, 1987.
8. *Ibid.*
9. Hay, A. and Wright, G., *Once Is Not Enough*, Friends of the Earth, London, 1989.
10. *ENDS*, Report 158, 'Emission controls on municipal incinerators spell problems for UK plants', 1988, pp. 22-3.
11. Cooper, J., *Interview transcript*, August 1989.
12. Hay and Wright, *op. cit*; Taylor, R., in *Warmer Bulletin*, Summer 1989; Friends of the Earth, *The true costs of domestic waste*, FoE, London, 1989.
13. Department of the Environment, Recycling: Economics Sub-Group, *Report to the DTI*, unpublished, 1990.
14. Pollock, *op. cit.*
15. Elkin, T.J., *State of the Environment report: Waterloo Region*, University of Waterloo, School of Planning, 1987.
16. Ibid.
17. Hockley, G.C., Walters, J. and Goodall, P., *Generating profit from waste*, Special report No. 1182, The Economist Intelligence Unit, London, 1989.

18. Hay and Wright, *op. cit.*
19. Pollock, *op. cit.*
20. Ibid.
21. House of Commons, *Hansard*, 6 February, written answer from Virginia Bottomley, Parliamentary Under-Secretary of State in the Department of the Environment, 1989.
22. Mockridge, T., *Market barriers to paper recycling*, Friends of the Earth, London, 1990.
23. Bardos, R.P., Barton, J., Burlace, C.J., Derry, R., Ikwue, A., Pendle, W., Prosser, H.J. and Tron, A.R., *Market barriers to materials reclamation and recycling*, Warren Spring Laboratory and Department of Trade and Industry, 1989; Myers, A., *Communication to Friends of the Earth*, British Steel Tinplate, 1990.
24. Chartered Institute of Public Finance and Accountancy, *Waste collection statistics 1982/3 to 1986/7*, CIPFA, London, 1988.
25. Pollock, *op. cit.*
26. Davidson, J., *How Green is Your City*, Bedford Square Press, London, 1988.
27. Netherlands Ministry of Housing, Physical Planning and the Environment, *The environment programme of the Netherlands 1985-89: Concerning Waste Substances*, The Hague, 1986.
28. These initiatives are discussed in *ENDS* Reports 27, pp. 8-10; 70, pp. 8-9 and 174, pp. 9-11.
29. *ENDS*, Report 178, 'Rhone-Poulenc: preparing for the Green Bill', 1989.
30. *ENDS*, Report 178, 'The uncertain road towards integrated pollution control', 1989.
31. Rivett, M., Lerner, D., Lloyd, J.W. and Clark, L., *Organic Contamination of the Birmingham Aquifer*, Report WRC PRS 2064-M, University of Birmingham Water Research Centre, Birmingham, 1989.
32. 'Contaminated land poses new problem', *Planning*, 23 June 1989.
33. Mansfield, T., PhD research at the Centre for Urban Pollution Research, Middlesex Polytechnic, 1988.
34. Department of the Environment, *Digest of Environmental Protection and Water Statistics*, HMSO, London, 1989.
35. Brown, L., *Building a Sustainable Society*, Norton, London, 1981.

36. European Colloquium, *Discussion Paper: Urban Resource Management*, Ministry of Urban Development and Environmental Protection, Berlin, 1989.
37. Friends of the Earth, *Stealing Our Future*, FoE, 1990.
38. Longhurst, J., 'Some Observations on the Environmental Impact of the UK Flue Gas Desulphurisation Programme', *The Environmentalist*, Vol. 8, No.2, 1988, pp. 115-21.
39. Blunden, J., 'Too hot to handle', *New Scientist*, 20 August 1987, p. 54.
40. Dolan, T.J., Bayley, S.E., Zoltek, J, Heraman, J.R and Heraman, A.J., 'Phosphorus dynamics of a Florida freshwater marsh receiving treated waste water', *Journal of Applied Ecology*, Vol. 18, 1981, pp. 205-19.

Chapter 7: Society and Economy

Introduction

It has been argued that cities exist only because of economic activity: the production, marketing and consumption of goods and services. Yet they are also fundamentally social phenomena – places where people interact socially as well as economically. Many of the most widely recognised problems of cities, or at least of inner cities, are social problems irretrievably linked to poverty and powerlessness.

The present study has concentrated so far on six aspects of the urban environment: in economic terms, six 'goods' which urban dwellers require. This chapter considers one further economic 'good', that of employment, alongside the ways in which all these goods are produced and how the resulting well-being is distributed.

Satisfactory urban development requires forms of economic activity in which demands for goods, services and employment are met without leading to environmental degradation or resource depletion: in short sustainable development. But sustainable development involves more than environmental conservation; it embraces the need for equity. Pearce also argues cogently that equity within the existing generation is integral to any form or definition of economic or social 'development'.[1] Both intra-generational equity, providing for the needs of the least advantaged in society, and inter-generational equity, ensuring a fair treatment of future generations, need to be considered.

Inequity is not just a major concern in its own right, it also tends to involve inefficient use of resources, particularly human resources, and can lead to environmental degradation and resource depletion. Thus future urban development must provide for forms of social organisation which prevent inequity from damaging sustainability. Sustainable urban development also requires an economic and social system which looks beyond current political time horizons and hands on to the next generation an amount and quality of wealth, both manufactured and natural, which is at least equal to that inherited by the current generation.

Some problems of cities

The basic environmental problems of economic activity have already been rehearsed in this report. It should be clear that they are concentrated in urban areas, if only because that is where much of the population of the industrialised world lives. Waste and pollution become increasingly visible problems as a result of high concentrations of industry, transport and housing, while urban lifestyles tend to encourage waste of resources, particularly energy. In pursuing economic growth, the decision-making of the current economic system has failed to reflect the values of environmental protection and the needs of future generations which are essential to sustainability, and the values of equity and participation (both in decision-making and in the process of development) which not only contribute to sustainability but are essential to development.

Poverty and serious inequality persist clearly in our cities. In particular, unemployment is concentrated in specific areas and specific social and racial groups, yet socially useful work is left undone. Cadman argues that:[2]

> our culture is dominated by an exclusive economic, consumerist and, in particular, financial ethos, an ethos that pre-determines not only the parameters of the argument but also the language in which the debate can be engaged ... The mechanism of the market, this monologue of prices and cost, this monotone of finance, becomes the message, so that in time it defines the meaning of the city as existing only within its own terms. Thus, the extent to which projects for the redevelopment and renewal of our cities are regarded as viable, and therefore as having reality, is assessed by a

narrow measure of their financial rate of return, supplemented on occasion by their more general contribution to the economic life of the community.

This economic definition of reality has worked to understate and undervalue the damage that has been done to the natural and built environments. The economist's explanation is that many environmental costs are 'external' to, or outside, the markets developed by consumers, governments and enterprises. This is reflected in the pollution of rivers, seas and the atmosphere. It can also be seen in the consumption of renewable resources faster than replacement rates, in the loss of biological diversity and in the depletion of finite resources faster than alternatives can be developed. It is also seen in damage to community life and thus to stocks of human and social 'capital'.

Structural economic changes have impacted unevenly on cities, particularly industrial cities since the mid-1960s, although the effects became especially clear in the late 1970s. The legacy of concentrated unemployment and deprivation in many cities contrasts even more sharply today with the booming financial sector. Regional and sub-regional movements in the locus of industrial development away from traditional industrial inner cities and regions have combined with a more general process of de-industrialisation reflected in a significant fall in the manufacturing share of gross domestic product. Together these trends have caused enormous loss of inner-city employment. Productive, identity-creating employment, so essential to self-esteem, traditionally for men, has often been replaced with unsatisfactory low-paid jobs[3], predominantly in the service sector, but also in the booming informal sector.[4]

Many of the remaining industrial and commercial activities have now moved from the central areas of cities to the periphery, from the rail links to the motorways. Most new manufacturing investment is occurring in scattered peripheral areas, totally divorced from and inaccessible to the poorer inner-city population. Freeman comments:[5]

> ... those who are multiply disadvantaged become ecologically trapped, unable to work because employment has moved to far suburbs or become strung along

motorways, and there is no accessible public transport to take them there.

The trend is epitomised by the development of science parks and industrial parks in pleasant suburban fringe environments, without adequate public transport links to the residential parts of the city.[6]

> The construction of orbital motorways around the outer suburbs of cities has produced a new generation of suburb-to-suburb traffic, attracting industry, business, and even some professional activity out of the central areas. Sold to the public as a solution to urban congestion, these developments tend to create a 'suburban gluepot' of new traffic movements, while accelerating the decline of city centres and making suburb-to-centre public transport uneconomical through loss of passengers.[7]

As a result the impacts are most severe on the carless unemployed and on women with children who need jobs that are local to schools and nurseries.

These problems should not be seen as arguments for a return to some glorious industrial past, but as a demonstration of the increasing economic dependence of communities in cities and as a means of highlighting the waste of human and other resources. Indeed, there has been a continuation of the tendency for manufacturing industry to 'deskill' or decrease its proportion of skilled labour through the increased use of semi-automated technology.[8] This is counter to the meeting of people's needs through employment. Employment is undertaken not only to provide money, but also for some form of self-fulfilment. Later in this chapter we argue that participation is central to achieving such fulfilment.

In most cases, the lack of investment in the inner cities, whether public or private, has fuelled the outflow of those able to leave. Communities have lost their younger, more active, energetic population. On the other hand, where housing in previously depressed inner-city areas has become popular with owner occupiers, prices are bid up, often forcing the existing population out of the market. Housing quality tends to improve, but the beneficiaries are not the original residents of the area and thus economic, social and environmental problems are not redressed, but relocated. One reason for these outcomes is the absence of effective planning guidance within the city and between regions.

Similar problems are evident in many parts of the country. An example can be seen in east Manchester (the industrial heart of Greater Manchester); here there are square miles of empty space but the conurbation pushes out using up agricultural land. This continuing dispersal of population is shown in the enormous pressure to create new housing developments in the counties surrounding London and along the M4 corridor. London's catchment area is now up to a radius of 150 miles.[9]

More recently, investment in the inner cities has failed to replace the jobs of inner-city inhabitants, instead being concerned with the expansion of urban core activities in the financial and administrative sectors, which provide jobs for mobile suburbanites. In the UK, and to a lesser extent the USA, such investment has been directly subsidised by government policy. Under the 'Action for Cities' policies, subsidies have been directed to built development through Urban Development Corporations and City Grant, while investment in the social infrastructure, essential to local economic recovery, has been reduced. Moreover, such built development is reflected in increasing land values which increase housing costs for inner-city residents, who are largely dependent upon the rented sector, and run counter to the provision of support facilities such as local shops and health and community centres for the urban poor, or indeed for any balanced community.[10] The inner-city policies of sustainable urban development must renew the local social infrastructure and local employment base as first priorities if further environmental damage is to be avoided.

The concentration of unemployment in many cities relates to the increasing domination of the economy by high-value tertiary and quaternary services which push land values upwards. The market is unable to make land available for secondary (productive) functions. At the same time, total employment in the secondary sector has fallen, and this, combined with escalating land values, has more recently removed the option of relocation from many of the poorer residents.[11]

Despite this, the phenomenon of dispersal has not been halted, and problems have been generated all along the dispersal line. At its furthest end, the impact of highly mobile incomers on rural communities has increased property prices. This has enhanced the problems of existing rural communities already disadvantaged by declining agricultural employment. At the same time, new suburban communities are often unsatisfactory socially, particularly for those used to the informal support networks of low income urban communities;[12] they offer limited social facilities, still often simply providing isolated housing. They have few social bonds and little social support, with long distances to the nearest services. Different problems are experienced by different social groups, but the elderly, housewives and people with disabilities tend to suffer most. Newman (quoted by Freeman) notes that:[13]

> new suburban communities [are] intentionally designed to be self-contained, and because of the small size of its population, each can support only the most mundane of communal and commercial facilities.

New settlements tend to be better designed in terms of social facilities, but are not immune to the problems created by various degrees of isolation. In both cases, pollution is generated and resources are wasted in travel. Not only are the economically active members of the household required to travel increasing distances to work, but the distances to the shops, to schools, to the cinema, and even to the pub tend to increase.

Wedmore and Freeman argue that:[14]

> Commuting has a directly destructive effect, on the home area, which is not worked in; on the business locale, which is not lived in; and on the places in between, which, used as passage-ways, inevitably cease to be 'places'. 'Public areas which were once intensively used have been reduced to mere arteries, mechanisms to get us from one place to another.'

Large-scale road developments have generally been, and can be expected to continue to be, socially as well as environmentally damaging. The road-building options in the recent Department of Transport assessment studies in London represented a particularly serious threat.* Such road proposals are brought forward with only limited regard given to the social consequences, such as severance of contacts and visual intrusion. The benefits accrue mainly to white male middle-class car-drivers while women, children and people with disabilities are most inconvenienced, often severely.[15] Freeman comments:[16]

> [Community life] would have been much better if grandiose road developments had not been ruthlessly imposed on communities, bringing them few benefits and enormous costs. Ward describes this as 'official vandalism', whose victims are usually well down the social scale. These changes make it much more difficult for pedestrians and cyclists to move around ... whilst previously compact neighbourhoods may become broken up and dispersed.

Economically disadvantaged people are concentrated in the inner cities, suffering the poor quality environments left behind by generations of economic activity. Above-average proportions of these people are from ethnic groups or are single-parent families. Currently they are also forced to be qualitatively more environmentally damaging on certain counts. It is the poor who can least afford to insulate their homes and who can only afford older cars which are less likely to run on unleaded fuel or be fitted with pollution controls. However, this

---

*   The London Assessment Studies began in 1985, and consultants' reports detailing possible options for transport improvements in four areas were published in December 1989. In April 1990, due to pressure from local people and environmental groups, coordinated by Friends of the Earth, the road building options were withdrawn by the Department of Transport.

should not blind us to the fact that the wealthy are quantitatively more damaging: they are more mobile, heat bigger homes, purchase more short-lived consumer goods and so forth.

Life in all cities today is extremely vulnerable to changes beyond the control of the people who live in them. This vulnerability is largely related to past changes in economic patterns which have led to separation, as noted by Morris:[17]

> We separate the producer from the consumer, the farmer from the kitchen, the power plant from the appliance, the dump site from the garbage can, the banker from the borrower and depositer, and inevitably, the government from the citizenry. Development becomes a process by which we separate authority and responsibility, where those who make the decisions are not those affected by the decisions.

For instance, it may mean that decisions affecting the ethnic population of an inner-city area are made, without effective consultation, by white people with no experience of discrimination. Most planners and architects are white, middle-class and male. Overall, the conventional path of development creates dependence. That is one of its essential features. It has made people dependent on organisations and professions to provide for all needs. It also makes localities dependent on outside agencies. This process has resulted in what Robertson refers to as the 'local economy in crisis'.[18] By the middle of the twentieth century local economies throughout the industrialised world had largely become dependent on outside employers to organise their work, on outside suppliers to supply their needs (for food, energy, clothing, shelter, entertainment and so forth), and on outside agencies to provide for their health and welfare.

For the quarter of a century of sustained economic growth and full employment after the Second World War this had a relatively limited impact. But when conventional economic growth and full employment came to an end in the 1970s and 1980s, the economic and social vulnerability of many formerly flourishing industrial cities and regions became all too apparent. Increasingly in today's economic climate cities are competing with each other for a finite 'cultural market' with commodities such as theme shopping, leisure centres and convention centres.[19]

The process of urban dependence is closely linked to environmental degradation. The residents not only lack the power they need to improve their environment, but the environmental capital stock of their locality (clean air, water, soil, green spaces and vegetation) is not under their control. Thus it can be, and has been, exploited and degraded by both the direct actions and the geographic externalities of others. One extreme of the development of external dependence is demonstrated by multinational companies, some of which are responsible both for pollution in many locations, and for the global exploitation of resources, including regional and local reserves of labour, often comprising ethnic groups and women. Frobel, Heinrichs and Kreye note that in the development of a 'new international division of labour' led by transnational companies:[20]

> The dependent and uneven development of plantation agriculture and mining, which has up until now typified the socio-economic development of the under-developed countries, is now, in addition, being reproduced in the industrial sphere as well.

Although economic and social problems are closely linked, we shall first consider the desirable changes in each field separately before examining the integration of these needs.

Economic change

Many of the economic reforms needed have been identified in the preceding topic chapters. Four general areas are paramount to the process of sustainable urban development:

i) that the levels of pollution emitted and the demands made on resources, including energy, in the production of goods and services be reduced;

ii) that the transport required for the distribution of raw materials, goods and services be reduced;

iii) that the waste and pollution resulting from the consumption of products be reduced; and

iv) that economic development which contributes to environmental sustainability be promoted.

There are two sets of mechanisms by which change can be achieved: fiscal and regulatory, the latter including economic and land-use planning mechanisms. It is not necessary here to enter into the debate over whether fiscal means are better or worse than regulatory: neither option can be pursued effectively to the exclusion of the other. The objective is to transform existing economic activities so that they become more sustainable and to penalise those which are particularly damaging. The effective promotion of sustainable forms of economic development requires more positive action. In particular, economic planning policies are needed to direct both public and private investment into sustainable economic activities such as recycling, renewable energy generation, and rail and water transport. Some of these are especially appropriate to urban areas, such as waste recycling, light rapid transit, and co-generation of energy and heat.

The assessment of environmental costs and benefits in project appraisal can build on the social audit concept which compares the financial benefit of a project with its total social benefit; that is, the welfare it provides to society as a whole. This can be used to assess the extent to which a project should be taxed or subsidised for it to provide maximum social benefits within a market exchange economy.[21] The promotion of activities which add to the stock of environmental capital, such as land decontamination, urban greening and such like, are another dimension of economic sustainability, as they add to the capacity of the environment to absorb the damage generated by other projects. Thus many of the schemes outlined in Chapters 4 and 5 on the natural environment and food and agriculture are of relevance in this context.

Future urban development must not follow past trends of top-down development, but should aim to reduce dependence and vulnerability. More specifically, this involves changes in patterns of work and economic activity. Policies need to encourage a change of direction not only towards greater self-reliance, but also to more conserving, as opposed to more wasteful and ecologically damaging, patterns of production and consumption. In fact, the two go together. Conservation involves more efficient use of resources all round, *including actual and potential human resources*. Moves in this direction enable a reduction in dependence at every level, city as well as household and nation, on external employers and suppliers. Such self-reliance can be enhanced by effective democratic participation, in local government and within the workplace.

Self-reliance does not mean complete economic self-sufficiency on the local, regional or even national, scale, but implies 'trade on equal terms', a reduction in dependence and a *greater degree* of economic self-sufficiency. Thus, for example, steel manufactured in the UK would also be engineered into useful products in the UK, rather than being exported for engineering and then re-imported for use in the UK. Similarly the food that is produced in the hinterland of a city, intended to be eaten in that city, would be processed there too, rather than at the other end of the country. Increasing self-reliance means redirecting the economic and social functions of the city primarily into the service of the people of the geographic urban system of which it is the focal point.

In summary, the optimum path to the more sustainable city has two immediate implications for the future. First, it places emphasis on the resourceful, self-reliant city, minimising waste of resources by energy conservation and recycling, and reducing its dependence on imports. Second, it places emphasis on enabling the people who live in cities to increase their control over their own future development, by encouraging bottom-up urban revival based on local community initiatives.

Social change

One necessary but not sufficient contribution to the solution of social and related environmental problems is increased access to economic and political power for the least powerful in society. This means providing the disadvantaged with access to housing, employment and facilities; and the regeneration of local communities, or at least local interest groups, that can identify with and therefore conserve their 'place'. Tackling discrimination is a complementary approach, necessary to enhance economic equality and thus promote economic involvement by all groups.

As noted earlier, a key dimension of development is that it is intended to at least raise the absolute standard of living and quality of life of the least advantaged in society (as part of the process of increasing the sum of general well-being). It is increasingly clear that this cannot be achieved through continued economic growth along traditional lines, if only because continued pollution emissions will further damage planetary systems on which we all depend. To achieve development we must redistribute resources. Increased equity is also necessary if the poor are to become qualitatively less environmentally damaging. Thus the disadvantaged must be a key target of economic development.

In the case of inner cities, McLaren argues that:[22]

> *it is only possible to improve the urban environment by empowering all the people that live in it.* Attracting the wealthy and powerful into new parts of it cannot solve [its] problems. The poor and powerless will continue to suffer disproportionately from environmental problems. Thus it is crucial that any efforts to promote urban regeneration involve a specific social element, designed to assist the poor and powerless to share in the benefits of that regeneration.

In addition to sharing in the benefits of regeneration, the people of the area should be involved in the planning and decision-making about that regeneration.

Transport is critical in achieving a socially cohesive environment within cities and in promoting community regeneration, and yet in the UK there is no coherent transport planning. Cities such as Paris have excellently integrated public transport systems, working well and at a high standard in contrast to the chaos and neglect which exist in London and other UK cities.[23]

Community regeneration also requires consideration of conservation of the psychological environment, retaining familiar landmarks and

forms of housing,[24] in the same way that built environment
Conservation Areas have been established in Britain:[25]

> The need to sustain the familiar attachments and
> understanding, which make life meaningful, is as profound
> as other basic human needs ... the townscape ought to reflect
> our need for continuity, and the more rapidly society
> changes, the less readily should we abandon anything
> familiar which can still be made to serve a purpose.

There is an important territorial argument here; people who identify
with their 'place' are more likely to conserve it, as shown by initiatives
in, for example, arts-led regeneration. A lack of this 'sense of place' has
haunted many of the estate housing schemes of the 1960s and 1970s, and
contributed to abnormal user behaviour such as littering and vandalism,
as well as crime.[26] The reason for this failure in practice is identified by
Hansen as:[27]

> a fundamental misunderstanding among architects about
> what makes a community work. It has been a cardinal belief
> for years that communities can only flourish if they are small
> and well defined; and if architecture creates separation as a
> way of establishing identity [through] small, highly
> localised living areas. But traditional urban communities
> were never like this ... They were unstructured and diffuse
> ... what made them safe was the fact that you would never
> know who you might meet in the street, but that you could
> be fairly sure you would meet someone. Strangers ...
> policed public space, while inhabitants knew each other
> well enough to police the strangers.

Jacobs observed that 'The public peace, the sidewalk and street peace,
of our cities is not kept primarily by the police, as necessary as the police
are, but by an intricate, almost unconscious, network of voluntary
controls and standards among the people themselves, and enforced by
them'.[28] Wedmore and Freeman suggest that:[29]

... this kind of community involvement is inconsistent with
great size and with concrete canyons, filled with dangerous
torrents of vehicles, but rather that it is associated with the
alleys and courts, the small squares and cosy bars and cafes
that were the best aspects of urban centres of the past.
Community consciousness goes with the sense of place,
where there are chances for accidental encounters to occur,
all within an identifiable area.

Freeman, in looking for a way forward, suggests that urban
communities require:[30]

a social matrix in which a worthwhile quality of life and
work can grow. This objective is not mere whimsical
folksiness, but would regain a milieu that can be a very
efficient one for conducting business and other essential
activities.

Direct community involvement in the planning and management of
the locality can develop into a commitment to sustainability, starting at
the local level but visible in a number of dimensions. Local people will
have the opportunity to reflect local needs, for example in building local
parks, workshops and so on, with the result that demand for transport
is reduced. And although not motivated originally by questions of
resource-saving, the efforts of self-build housing groups, for example,
contribute to conservation in a variety of ways. The work provides jobs
and satisfaction, the houses are often built on waste land, and, reflecting
self-interest, they are likely to be energy-efficient and long-life.[31]

Socio-economic self-reliance

Considerable advances towards sustainable urban development,
with concomitant social benefits, could be made through community
regeneration, particularly of a form which is also aimed at increasing
the economic self-reliance of those communities.

Conventional economics is based on an artificial divide between the economic and social aspects of life. Not only is work also a social activity, but even laying this aside, it is difficult to maintain such a distinction in the local economy, especially in disadvantaged localities where the informal sector is often very significant. There it is clear that the need for better housing, health, education, job prospects, incomes and above all an improvement in the capacity and confidence of local people to do more for themselves, is a single constellation of need. It is not a collection of distinct and separate needs to be met in distinct and separate ways, some of them economic and some social.

Arguably, it is in the local economy that real progress must be based, through support of locally self-reliant, smaller, co-operative and community businesses. Currently, community life is unsustainable because of imports of labour and materials which significantly reduce local independence. Sustainable urban development needs, wherever possible, to make use of the available local resources, especially human resources, and consume local products.

Such a proposal presents difficulties for the top-down perspective of conventional governmental, business and economic thinking. It also raises the question of how to balance an enabling approach which directly aims to empower local people and local communities to take more control over, and responsibility for, their own economic and social destinies, with the conventional top-down or 'trickle-down' approach to local community revival, for example in the inner cities.

Robertson argues that a shift towards greater local economic self-reliance requires revival of households and neighbourhoods as active centres of production of goods and services by people living in them for themselves and one another. In most cities this would include substitution of locally produced goods and services for those now provided from outside. For example, in the supply of energy, continued reduction of consumption of heat, light and power through modern conservation methods could be complemented by local supplies such as district heating from co-generation and solar panels on roofs.[32] But home-work on the conventional British model is, at present, one of the lowest paid and lowest status jobs, carried out almost exclusively by women tied to the home by children and the lack of decent local employment and childcare facilities. Alternatively, home-work can be based on a role for the worker as an independent contractor or sub-contractor, which tends to be less discriminatory.

Another field in which import-substitution could clearly contribute to greater local economic self-reliance is suggested by Robertson. When a local community owns a business, at least some of its profits would circulate in the local economy. The same consideration applies to a wide range of services, including public services, now administered to deprived local communities by employees of outside organisations who almost all reside elsewhere. There is scope here for using 'community contracting' to provide public services now delivered conventionally, thereby bringing into local communities the work and the incomes involved in providing these services.

The inner city provides scope for moves to self-managing residents' associations, and then potentially to the collective self-provision of a growing range of goods and services through associated community enterprises. Such projects are already taking place in several inner-city areas such as Pleck in Walsall and Easterhouse in Glasgow. This does not mean that social support mechanisms need to be removed, but rather that mechanisms should be introduced to ensure, firstly, that training and support are available to community 'entrepreneurs' and, secondly, that buildings and land are available for such initiatives.

Change towards greater self-reliance in our cities should take place on a number of fronts, some social, some economic. Three lines of development in this direction can already be identified, each being pursued more or less separately by its own constituency of professionals and activists, and all important for self-reliance. The immediate way forward is a matter of building on these initiatives.

The first is *local employment initiatives* which are happening in all industrialised countries, while both the European Community and the OECD are playing an active part at the international level. The second concerns the *decentralisation of social services*, together with the increasing emphasis being given by the World Health Organisation, national governments and local authorities to the role of community initiatives in health promotion. The third concerns the concept and practice of *social investment*; in recent years, companies and individuals in the US have been showing increasing interest in investing in socially valuable projects, an example that already shows signs of being followed in other countries, including Britain. Government measures to encourage local community initiatives, for example in the fields of local employment and economic regeneration, and local health promotion and community care, are beginning to be seen as public sector social investment to be financed and managed as such with a view to saving social costs and creating social wealth.

Local economic development

Although there is little or no firm proof that local economic development has environmental advantages, there are reasons to assume that locally self-reliant, smaller, co-operative and community businesses will have a significant influence on sustainability. As has been outlined above, they can form the basis for increased local circulation of capital, strengthening the potential for local sustainability.

In general, labour-intensive businesses will have less environmental impacts because they have a high ratio of output to capital and machinery: they therefore inflict less impact on the environment in their demands for energy and other resources. Community business often has the specific goal of creating employment. The principle of substitution of labour for capital does not mean increasing drudgery, but the use of human labour to reduce the generation of pollution, for example. For instance, shops with assistants do not have to resort to excessive packaging to maintain security.

Alternatively the raison d'être of many community businesses is environmental improvement. Such activities increase the stock of environmental capital and thus contribute directly to sustainable development, or, as argued by Pearce *et al.*, can be promoted as 'shadow projects' within a development programme.[33]

Energy efficiency on the part of a firm can be encouraged by the workers having a share in the profits, particularly where the firm is small enough for the results to be visible to the individual. Thus, in theory, co-operatives are likely to manage the use of energy and other finite resources better. Resource conservation is also promoted by increasing self-reliance: if the resource base on which the business depends is visible, and the environmental effects of its exploitation have an impact on the quality of life of the community, efficient use of the resource will be promoted. The general point is that local people have the capacity to recognise more clearly aspects of value of the local stock of environmental capital. Indeed the World Commision on Environment and Development also argue for decentralisation of the management of local resources to local communities.[34]

Locally-based business reduces the travel required by its workforce (who can shift to cheaper and environmentally less damaging modes), by its raw materials or inputs and by its outputs. Community businesses are more likely to try to develop local sourcing, and are likely to be responding directly to a local market need.

The overall principle in local business is not just employment but employment that creates what Morris calls 'new wealth', extracting the maximum sustainable amount of work from the local resource base. He describes the model of the Emilian region in northern Italy which:[35]

> relies heavily on co-operatives and small scale enterprises. Thirty percent of its workforce is self-employed. The vast majority of its manufacturing firms have fewer than 20 employees. Manufacturing firms spin off from one another to specialise. They make custom goods in small batches for a wide variety of customers, thereby insulating themselves from the loss of any one customer. They give a lie to the so-called economies of scale. Sebastiano Brusco, Professor of Economics at the University of Modena notes, "with certain technologies, there is no advantage in producing all the components of a product under a single roof; whether they produce similar or different pieces, twenty lathes have substantially the same productivity whether they are gathered together under one roof or spread out under twenty roofs".

> This of course is economic heresy in most countries. But northern Italy has perhaps the most dynamic economy in the world, one that extends back a thousand years. Its region depends on cooperative firms. Its central city, Bologna, is one of the original city states. Its universities

work hand in hand with artisan groups. Northern Italy has
its share of business failures, and more than its share of
business start ups. But it is proof that a post-industrial
economy can be based on small, collegial firms, that
specialisation can occur not within one factory but within a
community or a region.

Ward's examination of the Italian case places emphasis for its success
on the credit funds which provide finance at low rates even to
home-workers, on the co-operatives that carry out administrative work
such as payroll management for many of the small firms, and on the
effective communication networks. He also notes the benefits it
provides for individuals in terms of providing them with multiple
employment sources both within and between activities. For example,
labourers may work in both agriculture and industry at different times
of the year.[36] Thus this model is likely to be resource efficient,
particularly through effective use of the labour force, but also through
the lower rate of technological redundancy resulting from co-operative
or individual (rather than corporate) ownership of capital equipment.
However, this sector of the Italian economy is still dependent on
sub-contracting from larger concerns.[37]

Buying co-operatives are at the other end of the spectrum from
producer co-ops, but can also contribute to sustainability. Irvine refers
to the Seikatsu Club in Tokyo, which is a purchasing co-operative of
150,000 households (500,000 people) with a turnover of £160m. per
annum. It not only bulk purchases commodities such as soap powder
from less environmentally damaging producers but has also established
a dairy linked to organic farms to provide healthy milk.[38]

On the other hand, the local nature of economic development does
not preclude certain problems arising. Externalities may still be
generated, particularly pollutants which have a limited local impact, but
a serious global one, such as carbon dioxide or CFCs.

Also, larger companies may have some environmental advantages;
for instance, energy conservation or pollution abatement technology
may be relatively cheaper as a result of economies of scale. There is also
a strong argument for a degree of national specialisation: intensive
research and development is necessary to produce technical

intermediate-term solutions for environmental problems, such as CFC refrigerant recycling techniques, and much pollution control technology.

These issues underline the need for regulation by central government to assist economic incentives for sustainability. Local government is already developing a role in the promotion of local economic development, expanding on its role in the provision of a basic physical infrastructure. The new activity of local authorities, in the UK and elsewhere, has been in response to locally high levels of persistent high unemployment, starting in the 1970s. In the past decade local involvement in local economic policies has been developing step by step.

Kuenstler has identified some common policy trends in local government:[39]

i) seeking to diversify economic activity, particularly in older industrial areas which have depended on one industry only;

ii) upgrading the environment, a policy which may have two levels of objective, firstly the economic activity involved in making those improvements, and secondly to improve the 'image' of the area, making it appear more attractive to economic development, as well as strengthening the 'self-image' and self-confidence of the local people;

iii) supporting and promoting small and expanding businesses, which research findings indicate make a disproportionately large contribution to the number of new jobs created. A second issue is that a high proportion of small firms are local enterprises contributing to local economic multipliers and likely to produce more secure and higher quality employment than mobile and 'footloose' industry from elsewhere; and,

iv) developing high growth industry.

Of these, all but the last can contribute significantly to sustainable development. However, so far, local authorities have had difficulties in defining their vision and developing clear-cut policies.

Most began by developing strategies to attract new employers into the locality to provide jobs in place of contracting or closing firms. Such an approach is still being pursued in many places even though relocation is normally at the expense of other areas and involves corporate reorganisation often with reductions in workforce.[40] These employers are by definition 'foot-loose' and locate simply where the package of inducements is most attractive, and may move on again once they have reaped the benefits. Relocating firms often bring employees with them and may continue to use existing sub-contractors elsewhere, thus creating little new local employment and generating more transport movements.

More recently, increasing numbers of local authorities have attempted to generate 'bottom-up' local development: initiatives to create local work to meet local needs with local resources. Loan funds, economic development units, and enterprise agencies have been established for this purpose, while some authorities have attempted to introduce purchasing policies that discriminate in favour of local enterprises although this has been discouraged by central government. Local employment initiatives have also been adopted at the national level in some countries and both the OECD and the European Community now have investment programmes with the same objectives. Adequate technical and financial support for locally based development must be provided. However, the UK government does little to encourage such development through expenditure through the Department of Trade and Industry and on inner-city renewal, and indeed has introduced legislation which generally prevents local authorities treating local contractors preferentially and, through local government financial reform, has discouraged investment in local companies.

Also the emphasis of local employment programmes has shifted and widened from just conventional profit-making businesses. Although support for such businesses has remained important, support for co-operatives and community businesses has been increasing. Some of the more advanced initiatives include even 'potential enterprises' such as people on training or work experience programmes, which may be able to develop into viable enterprises. In some places, with growing problems in state delivery of welfare services, scope has been identified for community enterprises to provide services hitherto provided by the public sector.

However, it is crucial to recognise that, except in a few localised cases, such as some Scottish communities, these types of initiative currently account for a mere 1-2 per cent of economic activity (there are currently some 1,000 worker co-operatives in the UK employing over 11,000 people). In the short term they cannot be expected to have a significant impact on the development of the economy as a whole, and thus the development of urban areas.

Community businesses and co-operatives are the most widely embracing type of community enterprise but there are other forms of community economic activity which are playing an increasing part in local affairs: credit unions, neighbourhood service co-ops, food co-operatives and various forms of housing co-operatives and associations. There is increasing interaction between these various forms of community-based economic activity: credit unions beginning to think about setting up a community business; housing co-operatives establishing sister community businesses to undertake housing development work and landscaping; community businesses sponsoring food co-operatives and credit unions. Development trusts are the flavour of the moment; they offer a model of a 'non-profit-making' body meeting local needs, including employment, with local involvement. The development trust model is of particular value because it can expand to span a whole range of activities.[41]

John Pearce lists the three important facets underlying the value of community enterprises, particularly in regard to their role in economic regeneration of the poorest communities:[42]

> First, by allowing and encouraging people to create a community business structure they are empowered to act in the economy, to create work, to create wealth, to provide services. Without that structure they remain powerless and dependent.
>
> Second, the structure also provides a mechanism for government (central and local) and the private sector to target investment at poor communities with a greater certainty that the target population will benefit.

Types of 'enterprise in the community'

Worker co-operative
A trading organisation owned and controlled by its employees, on the basis of one person one vote. Co-ops usually have 'common ownership', the assets being held collectively not individually. This means that when a worker leaves, she or he cannot pull out a proportion of the company's capital. Income can only be raised through loans, not voting or variable profit-earning shares.

Community business or community enterprise
A trading organisation owned and controlled by local people in a particular area, or people with a 'common bond' (eg women, black people), with both commercial and social objectives. Membership is open to all people in the community; benefits and profits go to the whole community. Community businesses are often 'multifunctional', with a range of activities, and often act as umbrella organisations for other sorts of enterprise. They may be partially subsidised. Employees and supporting organisations such as funders may also have some rights of control.

Community co-operative
Similar to a community business but with the benefits and profits going to the members of the enterprise, not the whole community it serves.

Development trust
Independent not-for-profit organisation which takes action to renew an area physically and socially, often through refurbishment of buildings or provision of employment opportunities. They encourage substantial involvement by local people and are managed by a voluntary board, often involving representatives of local business and local government. Often initially funded by local authorities but obtain financial and other resources from a wide range of sources including the generation of revenue from their activities.

Credit union
A financial co-operative, owned and controlled by people sharing a 'common bond', either a geographical area or a common affiliation. Members save a regular amount by buying shares and earn a dividend on this. They are then able to borrow a multiple of their savings at a fixed interest rate.

Community trust (or community chest)
An independent financial trust which exists to assemble funds to channel into community projects.

Sources: Co-operative Advisory Group and Civic Trust

Third, we must recognise that by far the majority of the unemployed do not want, will not want and do not have the capacity to become self-employed; they want to work for someone else. The community business can be that 'someone else' and with the added perspective of aiming to employ the long-term unemployed.

The Homegrown Economy project in the city of St Paul, Minnesota demonstrates one possible way forward.[43] The goal of job creation is just part of a project which attempts to improve the management of all local resources: human, natural and technological. The aims are increased local wealth and employment, a more durable and diverse economic base, increased citizen involvement and increased self-reliance in local institutions. Support is given to new enterprises which involve local ownership, generate economic diversification, and meet local needs. These have included a revolving loan fund and an investment fund from local insurance companies which provides venture capital at preferential rates. The companies recognise that they have a direct economic stake in their own local economy.

Other city councils, including Barcelona in Spain and Bradford, Sheffield and Glasgow in the UK, are also reported to be moving in this direction. However, UK financial institutions are less deeply rooted in their localities, and their profitability does not depend upon the maintenance of local land values, unlike the situation in many US cities.[44]

There are very few examples of local financial institutions which enable local people to invest local funds for local well-being. A large proportion of local incomes (including national government public expenditures paid into the locality, on welfare for example) leaks out of the local economy via consumption. Local expenditure can be made to circulate locally to a greater degree by seizing opportunities for import substitution, substituting locally produced products and locally provided services for those now being brought in from outside.

Systematic analysis is also needed of ways in which a greater proportion of savings (including insurance premiums and pension contributions) could flow into local investments or loans which would contribute to local economic development. New institutions, such as local credit unions, would facilitate this process. A number of consultancy organisations and academic institutes on both sides of the Atlantic are already beginning to build up expertise in these areas.[45] Innovative methods of financing local development such as development trusts show increased concern for direct social investment, which, according to Pearce *et al.*, is a key element of sustainable development.[46]

Public sector opportunities for the development of social investment largely present themselves in the area of 'community contracting', whereby public authorities encourage local people to set up community enterprises from which the authorities then contract the provision of services (previously provided by public service employees) to their own communities. In this growing area of activity it is recognised that there can be particular benefits for certain services to be delivered by local people as well as providing a means of achieving local job creation at the same time. However, on a city scale care is needed to ensure that jobs are not lost in the process.

Robertson believes that:[47]

> This type of social investment of public funds in local self-reliance, in place of expenditure programmes that perpetuate and even increase dependence on publically provided social services, [could] play an increasingly significant part in housing, health, education and social services, and even in the maintenance and enforcement of law and order, for example through neighbourhood watch and community probation schemes, over the next ten or fifteen years.

The growth of such public sector local social investment could bring important changes in patterns of local income, expenditure and money circulation:[48]

> Local incomes in deprived areas [could] rise, with the transfer of pay from public service employees who live elsewhere to residents in the local community. This, together with the resulting increase in local community

activity, [could] lead to increased local circulation of local
incomes. It [may even] lead to some increase in local savings
available for use in the local community, and to increased
motivation to use them for local purposes that are socially
and economically useful.

This raises the question of private sector social investment. There are
at least four different potential sources of funds for private sector
investment in local economic development:[49]

i) the national financial institutions, such as the banks, the insurance
    companies, the pension funds, the unit trusts and the housing
    finance institutions such as building societies;
ii) local financial institutions. But in all the industrialised countries
    today the financial system has become highly centralised; local
    financial institutions are virtually extinct and the local branches of
    national financial institutions retain little commitment to the local
    economies in which they operate. The significant exception to this
    is still the US where local banks, local insurance companies and other
    local financial institutions retain strong local commitments;
iii) large non-financial companies operating in particular local
    economies; and
iv) personal savers and investors, especially local residents.

There is a growing demand for channels through which savers may
invest in the kinds of projects and enterprises which they themselves
wish to support (reflected in the growing number of social, ethical and
environmental investment funds now being set up in the US, Britain and
some European countries), and to a lesser extent for local investment
funds for local employment initiatives. This may place some pressure
on large financial institutions to examine the practicalities of channelling
increasing investment into self-reliant local economic development.
Robertson concludes that either existing financial institutions will have
to decentralise or new local financial institutions will emerge to compete
for their local business.[50]
There is some evidence of the emergence of a variety of local financial
initiatives, competing (in a limited sense) with existing institutions for

local business. They encompass arrangements for channelling into local development funds originating outside the locality, funds raised from local institutions and corporations, and funds mobilised directly from local people. Recent examples in the public sector in Britain include the London Development Capital Fund, through which the Greater London Council pension fund, ten London Borough pension funds, and two public corporation pension funds have invested in unquoted companies in London, and the West Midlands Regional Unit Trust, run by the West Midlands Enterprise Board and a merchant bank, through which 12 pension funds in the public and private sectors have invested in local companies needing capital for expansion. Counterparts in the US include the local venture capital fund and revolving loan fund set up in St Pauls, Minnesota under the Homegrown Economy project mentioned earlier and the ACTIVE Fund (the Allegheny Targeted Investment Vehicle for Employment) set up by the Allegheny County Pension Fund.

There are non-profit-making community development banks launched by individuals and local groups in the private sector. US examples include the revolving loan fund of the Institute for Community Economics, the South Shore Bank in Chicago, and the Local Initiatives Support Corporation, all of which allow private foundations and corporations (including local banks and churches) to invest in local enterprises. In France a network of small local investment clubs called 'Cigales' has been set up in association with ALDEA (Agence de Liaison pour le Developpement d'une Economie Alternative), which support small local enterprises with risk capital.

Co-operative banks and loan funds are a source of investment for local co-operative enterprises that has been attracting increasing attention in recent years. Probably the best known active example is the Caja Laboral Popular, which is at the heart of the Mondragon Co-operative in Spain. It is a fully fledged deposit-taking bank, unlike some other sources of finance for co-operatives, such as the Co-operative Development Agency and Industrial Common Ownership Finance (ICOF) in the UK, which depend on grants of public funds and gifts from the private sector.

Finally, credit unions are financial co-operatives which extend preferential loans to their members. As a general rule, they have not been used to finance local development. In Ireland 20 per cent of the population save with 460 credit unions. In the UK there are just 83 with 25,000 members, and their scale and levels of savings and loans are limited by regulations made under the Credit Union Act of 1979.[51] But the international credit union movement has a potentially valuable part to play in future local development.

Nevertheless, the combined total of all these local financial institutions is a tiny fraction of the total investment in the economy. Centralised financial functions will not simply dissolve, and the development of a relatively small parallel financial sector is all that is likely even in the medium term. In the context of 1992 and the Single European Market the trend towards polarisation of the financial market can be expected to increase. Thus policies for sustainable urban development need to influence the investment trends and strategies of the giant financial institutions. The vested interests of such institutions lie in ever faster capital circulation, which conflicts with the development of a durable urban form and the development of industries producing durable capital goods.[52] These interests must be challenged. The market cannot be expected to provide spontaneously for the environmentally optimum level of local economic development, and regulatory mechanisms are required to direct private investment both geographically and sectorally. At a minimum, effective planning controls are needed to distribute investment into the pattern of decentralised concentration and to reduce the frequency of the demolition and rebuild cycle in the urban form.

Conclusion

In the UK community regeneration and promotion of local self-reliance have yet to obtain whole-hearted support from government and financial institutions. During industrialisation the UK moved more than any other country towards the establishment of large-scale concentrated industry. Government at all levels supports these huge dominant units at the expense of small businesses. At the same time, when central government talks of small business it does so in terms of businesses with up to 500 employees, while the focus should be on helping those with far fewer employees. Equally, government inner-city aid must be redirected so that it benefits urban residents, particularly local residents in the most deprived areas, rather than landlords and developers.

But the major obstacle to realising sustainable urban development involves the central conceptual assumption about the workings and aims of the economic system: the notion of economic growth. This concept, now largely discredited by the Pearce Report,[53] flies in the face of sustainable development. Increasing local investment, including local social investment, runs counter to the dominant trend in current national and international development. There the emphasis is all on new organisational structures and technical procedures that will enable people to make money from moving investments around rapidly, rather than using their money in more directly useful ways. Rather than any tendency towards decentralisation, the emphasis is still mainly on mergers between different types of financial institution, and on further centralisation and internationalisation of both public and private finance. Thus we need to focus on the way in which funds are directed by institutions. In part this could be achieved by the imposition of taxes and regulations such that unsustainable development was not a profitable investment.

David Cadman insists that the present economic imperative, the well-being of 'the monster Homo Economicus', must be placed back into the context of the city as a whole.[54] He believes that we need to challenge 'the dominance of the view of the city as no more than a market place, a place to be determined only by a narrow form of financial accounting'. He calls for a 'broader vision of what might be regarded as possible', emphasising that in the search for a better understanding of the city, 'our vision must be of the city in its entirety, the whole city'.

References

1. Pearce, D., Markandya, A. and Barbier, E., *Blueprint for a Green Economy*, Earthscan, London, 1989.
2. Cadman, D., (ed.) *The Living City*, Routledge, London, 1989, 'Introduction'.

3. Massey D. and Meegan, R., *The Anatomy of Job Loss*, Methuen, London, 1982.
4. Pahl, R., *Divisions of Labour*, Blackwell, Oxford, 1984; Harvey, D., *The Urban Experience*, Blackwell, Oxford, 1989a.
5. Freeman, H. (ed.) *Mental Health and the Environment*, Churchill Livingstone, London, 1984, 'Introduction', p. 16.
6. Grieco, M., 'The impact of transport investment projects upon the inner city', (typescript), 1987.
7. Freeman, *op. cit.*, p. 14.
8. Braverman, H., *Labour and Monopoly Capital: the degradation of work in the twentieth century*, Monthly Review Press, New York and London, 1974.
9. Hall, P., *London 2001*, Unwin Hyman, London, 1988.
10. McLaren, D.P., *Action for People: A critical appraisal of government inner city policy*, Friends of the Earth, London, 1989.
11. Harvey, *op. cit.* and SERPLAN, *Into the next century, review of the south east regional strategy* (consultation paper), SERPLAN, London, 1989.
12. Harvey, *op. cit.*
13. Freeman, *op. cit.*, p. 204.
14. Wedmore, K.K. and Freeman, H., 'Social Pathology and Urban Overgrowth', in Freeman, H. (ed.) *Mental Health and the Environment*, Churchill Livingstone, London, 1984, p. 307.
15. Wistrich, E., *The Politics of Transport*, Longman, London, 1983.
16. Freeman, *op. cit.*, p. 199.
17. Morris, D., 'Free Trade, Self Reliance and the Health of Cities', paper delivered to the *UK Healthy Cities Conference*, Liverpool, March 1988.
18. Robertson, J., *The Economics of Local Recovery*, New Economics Foundation, London, 1986.
19. Harvey, 1989a, *op. cit.*, and *The Condition of Post Modernity*, Blackwell, Oxford, 1989b.
20. Frobel, F., Heinrichs, J. and Kreye, O., *The new international division of labour*, Cambridge University Press, Cambridge, 1980.
21. Grey, A., discusses the social audit in 'Community Initiatives in Waste Management and Recycling', in the proceedings of the *SEEDS Green Plan for the South East Environment Conference*, Stevenage, SEEDS, 20 October 1989.
22. McLaren, *op. cit.*, pp. 7-8.

23. Hall, *op. cit.*
24. Freeman, *op. cit.*
25. Marris, P., quoted in *ibid.*, p. 13.
26. Coleman, A., *Utopia on Trial*, Hilary Shipman, London, 1985.
27. Hansen, J. quoted by Wedmore and Freeman, *op. cit.*, p. 306.
28. Jacobs, J., *The Death and Life of Great American Cities*, Penguin, Harmondsworth, 1965.
29. Wedmore and Freeman, *op. cit.*, p. 301.
30. Freeman, *op. cit.*, p. 14.
31. Davidson, J., and MacEwen, A., 'The Livable City', in *The Conservation and Development Programme for the UK*, Kogan Page, London, 1983.
32. Robertson, *op. cit.*.
33. Pearce *et al.*, *op. cit.*
34. World Commission on Environment and Development, *Our Common Future*, Oxford University Press, Oxford, 1987.
35. Morris, *op. cit.*
36. Ward, C., *Welcome Thinner City*, Bedford Square Press, London, 1989.
37. Harvey, 1989b, *op. cit.*
38. Irvine, S., *Beyond Green Consumerism*, Friends of the Earth, London, 1989.
39. Kuenstler, P., *Local Employment Initiatives and Local Employment Development*, New Economics Foundation, London, 1987, pp. 12-3.
40. Massey and Meegan, *op. cit.*; Vanke, J., PhD research at the University of Aston, Transport Engineering Department, 1989.
41. Ecotec, *Good Practice in Urban Regeneration: Creating Development Trusts*, London, HMSO, 1988.
42. Pearce, J., 'Community Enterprise: What is it?' in *The First Ten Years: A Decade of Community Enterprise in Scotland*, Community Business Scotland, Glasgow, 1988.
43. Robertson, *op. cit.*
44. McLaren, *op. cit.*; Cowie, *The Phoenix Partnership*, Building Materials Producers, London, 1985.
45. Robertson, J., *Socially Directed Investment, and its potential role in local development*, New Economics Foundation, London, 1987.
46. Pearce *et al.*, *op. cit.*

47. Robertson, 1986, *op. cit*, p. 16.
48. *Ibid.*, pp. 16-7.
49. *Ibid.*, pp. 17-8.
50. *Ibid.*
51. Dauncey, G, *After the Crash*, Greenprint, London, 1988.
52. Harvey, D., *Social Justice and the City*, Blackwell, Oxford, 1973.
53. Pearce *et al.*, *op. cit.*
54. Cadman, *op. cit.*

Chapter 8: Synthesis

The economical, livable and equitable city

This study has concentrated thus far on the concept of sustainable development, and what it might mean in the context of the future development of cities. This reflects the political shift triggered by publication of the report of the World Commission on Environment and Development in 1986.[1] As a result, economic growth is being superseded as a policy objective by sustainable development, with its emphases on resource conservation and environmental protection.

The first part of the present chapter summarises the ways in which these emphases run as common themes through the topics considered in preceding chapters using the concept of resource *economy*. This means the conservation and efficient use, not only of finite resources but also of renewable resources in terms of their protection from degradation. Of course, environmental protection does not just mean the conservation of those resources with an economic function. Protection of the environment has an important related social function in that it provides for an improved quality of life, whether through access to green space nearby, or through the knowledge that, for instance, there are still whales in the oceans of this planet.

The chapter therefore proceeds to examine the parallel but related development in government policy in which improvement of the *quality of life* enjoyed by the individuals, families and groups that make up society is increasingly being recognised as a central objective. Environmental improvement is considered here in terms of its contributions to 'livability' and to health. The section attempts to demonstrate the ways in which the pursuit of sustainable urban development can meet these political objectives. In other words, how, by adapting our paths of urban development to promote sustainable development, we can improve the quality of life of city dwellers.

However, as noted earlier, there is a further aspect to sustainable development. The process is meaningless without the integration of the concept of equity, not just between generations, but also within the present generation, providing for the needs of the least advantaged in society. The Pearce report argues cogently that the latter is integral to any definition or form of 'development'.[2] Equally we should not consider development without considering the distribution of those goods contributing to the quality of life. The preceding chapter has demonstrated that the needs of the least advantaged are unlikely to be met by the continuation of current patterns of economic growth.

Sustainable (urban) development, on the other hand, has the capacity not only to tackle the widespread resource abuse which exists in our cities but also to contribute to the solution of many of the socio-economic problems that bedevil particularly the inner areas of cities. This chapter therefore concludes with an examination of how goals of equity can be met in, or in some cases are necessary to, the adoption of a path of sustainable urban development.

Sustainable urban development and the economical city

The city depends on a wide resource base. An economical city is one which is not wasteful and makes efficient use of those resources which it does exploit, including energy, minerals, land and natural resources. The common themes are conservation, that is, the minimisation of damage to a resource through consumption or other use (eg as a medium for pollution), and efficiency, that is, increasing the welfare derived from each unit of the resource. One way of achieving the latter is through re-using or recycling the resource, either directly or as energy. Increasing efficiency and conservation is likely to ensure that human activity does not breach ecological sustainability constraints.

Ensuring that economy in the use of one resource in one activity does not lead to increased depletion or degradation in another is central to sustainable urban development. For example, economy in the use of land for agriculture can increase the use of energy and chemicals.

However, substitution can act in either direction. In the past the tendency to substitute capital or machinery for labour in all sectors of both the domestic and the commercial economies has acted contrary to the promotion of sustainability. This trend can be reversed, as can be clearly demonstrated in transport, where human energy, in terms of walking or cycling, is a direct substitute for use of the car for short journeys.

It is easy to see how the use of renewable resources might be sustainable in that the rate at which the resource is renewed dictates its rate of exploitation. A forest can yield only a certain amount of timber each year without felling of immature trees (thus reducing future production). A reedbed can only treat a certain amount of domestic sewage each day before being polluted beyond use, (although the accumulation of heavy metals from household products and plumbing also creates a longer-term limit to the use of reedbeds in this way). The global carbon cycle can only take a certain amount out of the atmosphere each year to balance the carbon dioxide being added to it. On the other hand, resources such as fossil fuels which are renewed only on geological timescales (if at all) are more difficult to conceptualise in terms of sustainable use. The key is to consider their use as providing time to develop ways of meeting the needs that they currently meet with more easily renewable resources.

Energy is the basic physical resource; some use of energy is required to meet all needs and aspirations. These are currently met almost exclusively from finite sources. It is not possible to predict, with any degree of certainty, when the UK's, or indeed the world's, finite resources of fossil fuels will be exhausted; only that there will come a point at which they can no longer be used because of the pollution effects of burning them and the direct impacts of their extraction, particularly on fragile ecosystems such as those of polar regions. This point will arise before physical exhaustion, and indeed is likely to arise before economic exhaustion. In particular, the threshold to the burning of fossil fuels with the resultant emissions of carbon dioxide has already been passed. Carbon dioxide, the main contributor to global warming, is accumulating in the atmosphere. Likewise, uranium is running out, and in any case, we cannot continue to use it for environmental reasons.

It is therefore clearly desirable that the rate at which we use these resources should be reduced, simultaneously lengthening their 'lifespans' in order to allow for a smooth transition to patterns of lower energy consumption and for research and development of less damaging alternatives. In all sectors, transport, buildings, industry and domestic, we need to be economical in our use of energy. Design can be especially conscious of the potential for energy-conserving forms and methods of construction, while a compact, self-contained city minimises energy consumption by greatly reducing the need for motorised travel. At the same time, dense urban development can improve energy conservation in buildings while offering potential for economical district heating on a block scale.

The same thinking is essential in the use of other material resources. Mineral resources, including metals, are consumed in the city, not just in the production of material goods, but also as construction materials for buildings and for transport infrastructure. In the latter case doubts must exist about policies aimed at keeping pace with the output of the motor industry. The availability of metals and minerals for motor manufacture, and aggregates and land for road construction, is declining. The built environment needs to be seen as a capital resource, to be conserved and used economically. The need for new aggregate quarries, with all their associated pollution and nuisance, can be minimised. Conserving existing buildings minimises the demand for building materials. When buildings do need to be demolished, it is essential to recycle the maximum possible proportion of the building material rather than extract new material.

Recycling is essential in reducing the rate at which resources are exploited, whether potentially renewable resources such as wood-pulp or finite such as bauxite. This produces a number of benefits. Reductions in the rate of renewable resource exploitation to below the maximum sustainable rate allow for less environmentally damaging methods of exploitation to be used in forestry and agriculture, for example, or provide an opportunity for substituting the renewable resource for a finite resource.

Sustainable urban development recognises that waste is a resource. Currently we recycle only a small proportion of our domestic waste, whereas a figure of 60 per cent is possible.* Huge reductions can be made in the demands for materials by adopting recycling as a primary criterion not just in methods of waste management but in product and packaging design as well. There are also likely to be significant benefits in terms of reduced energy demands. Recycling materials requires less energy than production from raw materials, and although there may be increased energy demands in the collection of materials from dispersed sources, this can be overcome by adapting existing distribution networks to function in both directions. Recycling in fact tends to substitute human energy for fuel or electricity. This is borne out by the fact that recycling creates jobs. Canadian studies indicate that six times as many jobs are created by recycling as by landfilling.[3] Many of these jobs would be attractive for unskilled and semi-skilled workers, who represent the hard core of the structurally unemployed – a major problem in the inner cities.

Recycling of renewable resources does not stop with paper. Nutrient recycling is a case where a renewable resource can be substituted for a finite one. Organic materials in the domestic waste stream are typically landfilled while sewage sludge is still dumped in the sea. These practices are not only directly or indirectly polluting, but are also a loss to soil fertility, which is maintained instead with chemical fertilisers.

Pollution is the main way in which urban development continues to degrade existing natural resources, both within and outside the built-up areas. Yet these provide vital functions for the city which could be significantly expanded, as outlined in Chapter 4 on the natural

---

* Higher proportions may be possible through the use of anaerobic digestion, but it is debateable whether this process can be described as recycling.

environment. In many cases, economical use of these natural resources provides a way in which finite resources can be substituted.

There are still natural resources in our cities, such as air, water, green space, wildlife and fertile soils. Sustainable urban development would not only prevent their degradation by pollution or built development, but would also protect similar resources outside the urban area. The impact of the city on the natural resources of its site and surroundings can be ameliorated.

One example is in the prevention of flooding downstream from the city. This is often met by chanelisation of the river(s) downstream, with consequent loss to wildlife. Alternatively the proportion of permeable land within the urban area can be maintained at a level adequate to absorb rainfall and reduce the run-off peak to a manageable level through downstream land use in traditional floodplains. Furthermore, many urban drinking water supplies are dependent on local aquifers so that any pollution of the land overlying the aquifer is potentially disastrous. Loss of existing open space also damages wildlife and amenity values which contribute to quality of life.

More broadly, myopic use of natural resources affects urban food supplies, notably through the destruction or impoverishment of agricultural land, via soil erosion, degradation of soil fertility and structure, and the widespread use of pesticides and artificial fertilisers.

Land is a scarce resource in a country as heavily developed as the UK. There are numerous competing uses, including food production and nature conservation. Policies to achieve a greater degree of self-sufficiency in food production are not furthered by the loss of fertile acres to road building or low density car-oriented residential development. Although the proportion of England and Wales' land area under built development in 1980 was little in excess of 11 per cent,[4] this has been increasing at a rate of over 6,000 hectares per year[5] and the land at the fringes of built-up areas is that most under pressure: this is often the most fertile land, and where it is not in agricultural use it is often of significant value for wildlife or amenity. New building or road construction does not just take the land of its site, but also the land required for extraction of rock, gravel and sand. Efficient use of land in cities requires relatively dense development.

As well as economising in the use of material resources, sustainable urban development can also be economical with financial resources. Recycling is cheaper than waste disposal. Energy conservation is cheaper than new power plants. However, such measures are often logistically more complicated. Politicians know that energy conservation is cheaper than building new power plants. They recognise that preventative medicine and health education are cheaper than building new hospitals. But they also know that such policies require a very different emphasis. They require working with thousands of individual households and working with the city dweller, rather than the engineer. It is a labour-intensive strategy. It is community-based. There is no doubt that it is much harder to accomplish, but in the long term it is also much cheaper, and builds a conserving and self-reliant city.

Resource conservation is promoted by increasing self-reliance: if the resource base on which a business is dependent is visible, and the environmental impacts of its exploitation impact on the quality of life of the local community, efficient use of the resource will be promoted. The general point is that local people identify more clearly the value of the local stock of environmental capital.

Sustainable urban development and the livable city

The concept of livability has been explored by a number of authors.[6] In the context of this report a livable city is seen as one which provides for a high quality of life. This depends on creating an urban environment conducive to well-being. Health is such a crucial component of this that it is considered in a separate section below. The present section concentrates on social contact and diversity of experience, access to (and quality of) services, facilities and green space, psychological identity of places, safety and security.

Cities are about human contact. As Cadman has suggested, 'to understand the city, we have to *be* there, to experience the comings and goings'.[7] James Hillman stresses the importance of such a personal relationship with the city. Criticising the straight grid-like pattern of city roads and streets that currently favour the car against the pedestrian, he says 'cities depend on walking for their vitality'. At once he draws us into a direct and intimate relationship, 'meeting faces by walking among the crowd' and jostling in the streets.[8] Mayer Hillman blames the motor car too:[9]

> In cities today, where transport is based on the motor vehicle social contact, particularly incidental social contact is lost. The substantial rise in traffic and its ubiquity have had many adverse social and environmental consequences. Wide roads and streams of motor vehicles destroy the function of the street as a locus for social interaction and break community ties, particularly for children. Cars are more responsible than any of the other main methods of travel for a reduction in environmental quality and a distortion of preferred travel patterns. And they are available, on an exclusive basis, to only a minority of the population.

Women in particular suffer from reduced social contacts as a result of these factors.

The need for diversity in social contacts is in part met through a range of informal and formal types of entertainment. People meet socially in the public house, at the sports centre or at the discotheque or any one of a hundred different forms of entertainment. For many people these are what makes living in towns and cities preferable to village life. But people want these facilities to be accessible. They also meet socially in the streets and public spaces of the neighbourhood, particularly when young. Where these facilities and meeting places are not available the environment is rather less than livable.

It is therefore likely that the deleterious effect of traffic on the quality of urban life is in some measure responsible for encouraging migration to more spacious suburbs and rural areas. This residential mobility, however, has undesirable features relating to livability: the congenial surroundings in the suburbs can only be enjoyed by incurring additional traffic costs for those left behind, thereby reinforcing the disadvantages of erstwhile neighbours. Moreover, people commuting in uncomfortable conditions become tired and irritable, lowering levels of performance at work.[10]

Because of its environmental impacts reduced dependence on the car is required for sustainable urban development. In all respects, public transport, cycling and walking are the preferable modes of travel from the viewpoint of the community as a whole. Both the relative and absolute efficiency and attractiveness of these modes can be increased by the use of area-wide traffic calming. This has the effect of greatly reducing the impact of motor vehicles on both residential and through-streets, so that they are again recognised first and foremost as places. The quality of life of people living and working on those streets is greatly enhanced. Road safety will also be improved, primarily through significantly reduced vehicle speeds. Hillman discusses the importance of the street for children:[11]

> The residential street used to be the traditional play space and social milieu for children and provided an introduction for them to the world beyond their family. Now children are largely confined to the home or have to be taken to a playground which rarely provides the same freedom and unpredictability which are essential parts of the process of informal learning.

Traffic calming in residential areas can make it safe for children to play outside their front doors and to cycle to school.

Social contacts between adults are also increased as the severing effects of roads on communities are reversed. In shopping and commercial areas, even when they are on a main road, pedestrians gain priority. The appearance of the environment can be improved through tree and verge planting with additional benefits in pollution control. As walking and cycling become more attractive modes of transport, they will also regain the role as social activities which they have lost in modern cities because of the unpleasant, noisy and dangerous street environment. Walking provides particularly for increased informal social contacts, which help build up a sense of community. Such contacts are particularly lacking in newer residential areas, where walking is also discouraged by the lack of accessible local facilities.

Sustainable urban development promotes such facilities, with the aim that as much daily activity as possible can be conveniently transacted on foot. A sustainable city has the advantage of compactness. An emphasis on 'urban' housing densities should ensure the survival of local facilities like shops, pubs, schools, doctors' surgeries, open spaces and bus stops within walking distance of everyone's front door.

If a living and livable environment is to be created and the use of cars discouraged, it is important that facilities are not only local but meet the needs of local people in a high-quality way. People who discount the real costs of car travel will choose to travel to better quality facilities, whether cheaper shopping or safer or more diverse recreational facilities. In many cases high-quality provision requires effective local planning and development control decisions and central regulation to level the playing field for local service providers.

Excessive zonal separation of uses has destroyed the vitality of cities. Living, working, trading, shopping and playing all gain from being linked. Mixed uses make for lively, safe environments, environments where the mere presence of people reduces the threat of attack or abuse, which is so often experienced by women, the disabled and ethnic groups in our cities. Much has been written in recent years on private and defensible space. Often this has triggered an excessive reaction, such as new inner-city housing estates with high fences around them, as in London's Docklands. In many continental cities such as Berlin, a balance has been struck: tenement-style houses and flats lead onto public streets while defensible garden spaces are shared among several families.

At the same time planning techniques are used to improve security. In Amsterdam, the city's structure plan includes policy guidelines designed to improve personal security. These include:

- that the ground floor of building blocks should contain dwellings;
- that long blank facades should be avoided;
- that public transport stops should be situated as close as possible to dwellings;
- that cycle routes should be overlooked by dwellings; and
- that facilities and services should be located where they can be used after dark.[12]

The increasing separation of home, workplace and recreation, encouraged by the planning process, also threatens basic human identity needs: people are far less likely to be concerned about their local environment if they spend most of their time outside it. Instead of dispersed buildings, separated from each other by highways and left-over tracts of land, the result of a sustainable development path should be attractive, intricate places related to the scale of pedestrians, not people in cars. Such development considers *places* as a whole rather than focusing on a city made up of individual buildings and by creating a sense of place provides for people's identification with their physical places. This simultaneously promotes environmental protection and enhancement while contributing to the fulfilment of psychological needs. It is important to recognise that some social groups, notably women with children and the unemployed, are rarely able to spend time outside that local environment. Women in particular have to tackle the problems generated in such areas: problems of poor quality, damp housing, of lifts that don't work and so forth. An improved environment would be more equitable for these groups.

If we look at the city from a biological perspective, we need to bear in mind that humanity has evolved in small groups, suggesting that there is a biological need for malls, piazzas and other public spaces where human encounter can be enriched by contact with strangers.[13] This is the spiritual element our cities so often lack, as recently enunciated by Prince Charles:

> We have created somewhat godforsaken cities from which nature, or at least the spiritual side of life, has almost been erased.

This spiritual dimension underpins our responsibility to our planet and its stewardship. This relationship must be forged in cities where most people live. A first step is to recognise people's strong need for nature, which may be a very deep emotion: the need for something green and wild or a place to go for sanctuary or solitude, a place to experience 'wilderness' in the city. The need for such places, whether in the form of ecology parks, city farms, allotment gardens or just neighbourhood wildspace, lies at the heart of the livable city. And it is not just a white middle-class need. Harrison and Burgess found that all groups, regardless of social class, income or place of residence viewed urban green space as an integral part of the urban environment.[14]

Retaining familiar landmarks and forms of housing in the built environment also reinforces the sense of place in the city. Sustainable urban development requires us to build to last and adapt. Buildings need to be 'robust' and provide for continuity in our urban surroundings. Traditionally, buildings in successful urban areas have had a remarkable ability to adapt over time to changed circumstances and different uses and opportunities. Georgian town buildings are an example. The materials of which they are built were selected for their permanence, their mellowing and enduring qualities as well as for ease of maintenance.

Long-life buildings add interest to the townscape and are often of heritage value. The emphasis on conservation has encouraged the retention of cherished buildings and areas, in contrast to the comprehensive redevelopment schemes of the 1950s and 1960s. Building to last prevents the need for such wholesale destruction of areas of the city and its attendant social disruption and pain. The city also needs old buildings because of the need to provide the venue for the many less profitable 'downtown' activities that are essential to its commercial vitality but which cannot support the market rent of new accommodation.

Yet the urban aesthetic is not just about conserving old buildings. It relates to scale: it means that buildings should be comprehensible on a human scale. This does not mean that large buildings are undesirable, just that they should have many entrances and exits on the street[15] and that they should be architecturally detailed on smaller as well as larger scales. Public art can contribute to making building scale seem more appropriate, while art in the form of murals and sculptures also contributes to the pleasure people (both residents and visitors) find in the urban environment.[16] The physical greening of cities also has aesthetic, as well as ecological, psychological and educational roles.

All these aesthetic features are degraded by pollution, particularly acid rain, and the soiling effects of diesel fumes from vehicles. Building cleaning costs resulting largely from these causes total some £80 million a year in the UK at present.[17] Urban traffic routes, particularly motorways and road widening schemes, also degrade the appearance of a city. Generally the flow of traffic along them interrupts the urban form of linked views, while the size of new roads and often even the road signs and lighting standards on them are visually intrusive and out of human scale.

Sustainable urban development and the healthy city

The health of people in the city cannot be divorced from the city's own health. Health is bound up not just with personal lifestyles but with the economic, social, built and natural environment in which people live. This section will consider the issues of healthy food, unpolluted air and water, physical risk and mental stress.

The links between diet and health are undisputed. A healthy diet should include a high proportion of fresh vegetables, providing fibre in particular. Yet city dwellers, especially those without access to a garden, are much more likely to base their diet upon highly processed convenience foods. In addition, there is growing evidence to suggest that the contamination of food with chemicals, antibiotics and hormones is a potential risk to health. Many urban dwellers either cannot afford the premium prices charged for organically produced food, or may lack the opportunity to supplement their diet with healthy home-grown food because urban soils are widely contaminated as a result of air pollution.

We are now paying a price for our dependence on the motor vehicle: pollutants such as lead manifest their harmful effects on health not just through the air but also through the diet. In spite of recent initiatives in the promotion of unleaded petrol, a survey carried out by the Association of London Chief Environmental Health Officers indicates that all central urban sites, and other sites close to main roads, are likely to be so affected that the probability of finding uncontaminated produce in these areas is negligible.[18] Derelict open land is often even more severely contaminated with pollutants from waste disposal and industry.

Only by greatly reducing pollution and by positive action to decontaminate soils in the city region can we have access to locally grown healthy food. Local production has the advantage that fresh foods can be supplied to the city with minimum transportation. Food grown within the city itself, in gardens, allotments, and commercial city farms and market gardens, provides both recreation and local employment, as well as improving the urban environment by increasing the proportion of open space.

City pollution takes many forms: ubiquitous noise nuisance results from our increasingly complex technological society and in particular from traffic. Air and water are polluted by industry, by power generation, by transport systems and by agriculture. The internal environment of buildings can be polluted by fumes from manufactured products and through the bacterial contamination of air-conditioning systems, while the so-called sick building syndrome seems to have a range of contributory factors. Overall, pollution problems in the workplace, for local neighbourhoods and for the public at large, still exist and in many cases are increasing.

Traffic is perhaps the single most important source. Despite reductions in atmospheric lead mainly triggered by reducing the lead content of petrol, rising traffic levels have increased the health risks from nitrogen oxides, carbon monoxide, hydrocarbons and ground level ozone, particularly for vulnerable individuals, such as the elderly, and the chronically exposed such as traffic policemen. Holman has catalogued a range of health risks from air pollution.[19] The potential health risks from water pollution include illness caused by sewage bacteria being thrown out of power station cooling towers. Contaminated drinking water can also constitute a health risk, particularly where existing treatment methods are inadequate, such as in the removal of industrial solvents and pesticides or of cryptosporidium organisms which need to be removed by slow sand filtration.

The World Health Organisation defines health as embracing the physical and mental well-being of the individual and not merely as the absence of disease or infirmity. This requires a wider consideration than polluting factors, and the general stresses and strains of city life must be included.

Nowhere is this more obvious than in relation to transport. Many of the health problems faced by city dwellers derive from the fact that today's cities have been planned as much with the car in mind as the human being, imposing huge environmental stress both on communities and on individuals.

City dwellers in the UK are clearly at increased risk through the prospect of accidents involving cars. In 1988, 2,446 people were killed in accidents on built-up roads, out of a total for all roads of 5,052, and 1,413 (or 58 per cent) of these casualties on built-up roads were pedestrians. Of this figure more than 400 were children, while other groups highly represented among pedestrians are women and the elderly. Every year there are over 20,000 reported accidents involving cyclists and cars. These figures are in a context where a meagre 2.3 per cent of journeys of over one mile are undertaken by cycle and 10.4 per cent on foot.[20] Porritt underlines the tragedy of the situation:[21]

> People are so used to these statistics that they no longer recoil at the appalling suffering that is caused by such accidents. The victims are not just a much loved child, a squashed cyclist, a bus queue hit by a lorry outside a school, it is the whole of society. We are all losing out. We are all victims of pandering to the whims of the vehicle manufacturers, the car advertisers, the road lobby and the bloody-minded, selfish and dangerous road users who provide us with this toll of fatalities every year.

Moreover, as Hillman points out, transport is detrimental to health in a wide variety of ways other than the physical ones of injury and death. It is detrimental psychologically, for distress and bereavement are occasioned in road accidents, the risk of these occurrences causes fear and traffic conditions can produce harmful stress. It is detrimental pathologically, as pollution from motor vehicles is the source of some diseases and mental impairment. For example, it should not be ignored that lung cancer rates are higher in urban areas; although not entirely proven, there can be little doubt that vehicle emissions are contributing to urban lung cancer deaths. It is detrimental in terms of practicality and personal autonomy, as a substantial proportion of the population have diminished opportunities for leading lives not dependent upon being driven or being accompanied to and from desired destinations. Finally, it is detrimental in respect of health promotion, for current patterns of traffic and planning deter people from using their own feet as means of getting regular exercise by walking or cycling to their destinations.[22]

People are also exposed to physical and chemical risks at work. Many environmental hazards have the same source as health and safety hazards: an inadequate control of the risk in the workplace. Improving health and safety standards both within the workplace and in the relationship between the workplace and the city is vital. A contribution can be made by the promotion of community businesses and co-operatives, as current experience suggests that they tend to maintain higher standards on health and safety issues.

The physical appearance of cities also influences the health and quality of life of residents. The current public debate, brought to prominence largely by Prince Charles, lays stress on the need for far greater consideration to be given to the wishes of all city dwellers in planning and designing the built environment. This has particular relevance for those groups at risk of abuse or even assault in public spaces. Poorly lit and unfrequented bus-stops and road underpasses (for example) are a source of mental stress as well as physical risk for women and the elderly in particular.[23]

The development 'machine', largely concerned with speculative investment, has different priorities and ambitions from those of local residents. New development is only rarely designed for the local population. The imperatives of the investment company can often give rise to development which is not required locally. Thus local people are forced to go outside their area to meet their needs, creating increased demand for motorised transport, and the employment opportunities for women with children are effectively reduced.

It is important to provide people with the opportunity to shape situations, places and activities that affect their lives. A recent study suggests that active participation is an especially important factor in strengthening resistance to disease and 'unless people can, in some way, create, manage, change or participate in activities that affect their lives, dissatisfaction, alienation and even illness are likely outcomes'.[24] Pressure for development often means that natural areas and green space are lost under concrete and tarmac. Sustainable urban development would reverse this process, and provide ways in which people could relate more closely to nature in cities, both by the protection of the surviving vestiges of the natural world, and by the creation of completely new opportunities for natural flora and fauna to flourish in an urban setting.

The development process reflects a vision of the city as no more than a market place, a place to be determined by a narrow form of financial accounting. This conventional economic outlook makes an artificial distinction between the creation of wealth and the creation and maintenance of health. Not only are conventional economic policies and conventional business goals uninterested in the promotion and maintenance of health, they can also be positively damaging to health. There are many examples. Poor living and working conditions and pollution of all forms can threaten people's mental and physical health. These problems are most severe in the inner city.

High rates of unemployment create poverty and thus damage health. The Black Report recently documented the adverse effects of poor socio-economic conditions on accidents, illness and mortality. Poorly paid jobs are often associated with poor working conditions and thus increased health, as well as environmental, risks. But there is also mounting evidence of the adverse effects of involuntary unemployment itself on the workers affected and their families, not only on mental but also on physical health.[25] The development of locally self-reliant, smaller, co-operative and community businesses not only creates employment, it can also provide individuals with a greater sense of self-fulfilment and self-reliance, both of which contribute to mental well-being.

The idea that the development of healthier people, and the creation of a social and physical environment which enables people to be healthy, might be treated as productive investment in a society's capital assets, as the development of its most important resources: its people, is largely alien to conventional economics. However, in sustainable (urban) development the creation of wealth, in terms of an increased stock of total capital, includes natural and human capital. One way in which the stock of capital to be passed on to the next generation can be increased is by 'creating' health. This leads us on to the consideration of equity issues, as those who are disadvantaged by income or as a result of unemployment tend to suffer more from occupational or environmental ill-health.

Sustainable urban development and the equitable city

Several of the policies advocated as ways of promoting sustainable urban development could, at least in a transitional period, have a more severe impact on the poor. The clearest examples are the effects of taxes on non-luxury items: notably fuel. Fuel-poverty is already an important issue, especially for the elderly and those with disabilities, particularly those who live in older properties. This report does not advocate that such policies should be allowed to cause increased hardship.

It has already been argued that 'development' by definition involves an element of improving the welfare of the less advantaged elements of the population. Now that it is clear that there are limits to existing patterns of economic growth, this can be achieved only by a degree of redistribution. Therefore sustainable urban development must equally involve such a dimension. Unless 'environmental' policies which would have regressive effects contain an effective counter-balancing mechanism, development will not be achieved. Without this the result will be not only increased and intensified poverty, but continued problems in achieving sustainability, problems that, following on the example of fuel-poverty, result from the high investment needed on the domestic scale to reduce consumption. Thus in this case, at least some of the proceeds of a tax on fuel should be directed into compensatory measures such as government investment in improved insulation and more efficient heating systems, and if necessary, fuel subsidies for those subject to fuel-poverty.

This is one example of an equity issue which is essential to sustainable urban development. These issues fall into two areas: those necessary to sustainability which must ensure that a maintained environmental capital stock is passed on to the next generation; and those necessary to development, as outlined above. Several of these issues have been discussed in the preceding chapter on socio-economic organisation. A central issue is distributive equity. The poor are often qualitatively more environmentally damaging; we may therefore need to improve their incomes, or subsidise environmentally beneficial purchases, especially of capital goods such as insulation. The greater levels of consumption of the rich are quantitatively more environmentally damaging; their consumption of environmental resources must therefore be reduced in both qualitative and quantitative terms.

Sustainable urban development will not always threaten equity. In fact there are many aspects of sustainable urban development that will directly contribute to improving equity. Access is a key element of equality. Our proposals should significantly reduce many of the physical obstacles to access which currently result in incidental discrimination against many groups. Indeed access to facilities independent of the ability to afford a car will be the major outcome of changes proposed in Chapters 1 and 2 on the built environment and transport.

Improved access to lively mixed-use town centres will benefit women in particular. Significant numbers of employed women work in town centres, in clerical, office, retailing and personal service functions. For such women, who travel on foot or public transport, shopping (and using other facilities) in the town centre is an efficient means of fitting in the time demands of paid work, domestic work and family care.[26] These women have therefore been losing out as facilities have been centralised or moved to out-of-town sites. A reversal of this trend will have an associated equity benefit.

Not just physical, but also institutional obstacles to access to employment must be challenged. Sustainable development requires rational use of human, as well as natural resources. Women, members of ethnic groups and people with disabilities are currently more likely to be unemployed or in a low-paid job such as homeworking as a result of direct or indirect discrimination. Yet such people are not less capable of doing the jobs which they are denied. The breaking down of institutional obstacles to their obtaining employment which makes best use of their abilities (including potential abilities), must therefore form part of any policy for sustainable development. Appropriate local jobs, which reduce transport requirements, are especially valuable for those women also involved in bringing up a family.

Sustainable urban development depends equally upon the development and maintenance of sustainable agriculture. The main policy strand of Chapter 5 on food and agriculture is to reduce chemical dependence in agriculture with concomitant benefits in the provision of healthy food. The widespread promotion of such agriculture could relatively quickly reduce the often excessive prices currently charged for such produce and spread its potential health benefits to all groups in the population.

Perhaps the most important issue is the improvement of the urban environment, both generally and specifically in terms of housing quality. Degraded areas are currently the only locations where many of those disadvantaged by income – the elderly, one-parent families, the unemployed – are able to find affordable accommodation. Women in particular have to cope with the domestic problems of poor accommodation on a day-to-day basis. Improvements in the housing stock have largely bypassed 'the bulk of dwellings in the poorest condition, which are strongly associated with low incomes, the elderly, single parents and simply, poverty.'[27]

The emphasis on refurbishment in Chapters 1 and 3 on the built environment and energy would, if carried out, have a significant impact on poor housing. Improved urban design and planning can assist those women who bear the domestic responsibility and who have to cope with poor management, poor design, lack of open space and community facilities and the isolation engendered on many urban housing estates. Increasing and improving green space, particularly on derelict land, will improve those environments. Reducing urban pollution will also help.

But once again, if this action is to constitute development, the beneficiaries must be those who live there, rather than the property companies which then see an opportunity for the development of offices or executive housing. A combination of public support with strong planning is the only answer here as in many of the issues discussed above. The planning system can be powerful, as was witnessed by the planning 'disasters' of the 1960s, but it need not always produce less livable and equitable environments. This will be much less likely if the planning system involves all the communities living in an area in an on-going process; and will also help to overcome the incidental discrimination likely to arise from the gender, race and ability composition of the profession.

Conclusions

This chapter has highlighted some of the potential benefits for the individual of urban life in the 'living city', if the path of sustainable urban development is taken. These complement the clear benefits to society as a whole, in terms of sustainability, of a high level of urbanisation. Both groups of benefits can be shared amongst the whole population if true development is pursued.

The chapter has also highlighted many of the challenges that exist at all levels if a successful transition from the concrete jungle of the present to the living city of the future is to be achieved. The final chapter summarises how these challenges might be met.

References

1. World Commission on Environment and Development, *Our Common Future*, Oxford University Press, Oxford, 1987.
2. Pearce, D., Markandya, A. and Barbier, E., *Blueprint for a Green Economy*, Earthscan, London, 1989.
3. Morris, D., 'Free Trade, Self-Reliance and the Health of Cities', paper delivered to the UK *Healthy Cities Conference*, Liverpool, March 1988.
4. Best R.H., *Land-use and Living Space*, Methuen, London, 1981.
5. Department of the Environment, *Land-use change in England*, Statistical Bulletins 1987(7), 1988(7) and 1989(7).
6. Most recently Cadman, D., (ed.) *The Living City*, Routledge, London, 1989.
7. *Ibid.*, 'Introduction'.
8. Hillman, James, 'Paradise in Walking', *Resurgence*, No.129, 1988, pp. 4-7.
9. Hillman, M., 'Social Goals for Transport Policy', in Institute of Civil Engineers, *Transport for Society*, ICE, London, 1975.
10. *Ibid.*
11. *Ibid.*
12. Van Wijk, J., 'Making safe the streets of Amsterdam', *Town and Country Planning*, Vol. 56, No. 10., 1987.
13. Macdonald, R., 'The European Healthy Cities Project', *Urban Design Quarterly*, April 1989, pp. 4-7.

14. Harrison, C. and Burgess, J., 'Qualitative research and open space policy', *The Planner*, Vol. 74, No. 11, 1988.
15. Hillman, Judy, 'The importance of the street': paper presented to Town and Country Planning Association conference on *British towns and the quality of life*, London, 28 November 1989.
16. Bianchini, F., Fisher, M., Montgomery, J. and Worpole, K., *City Centres, City Cultures*, Centre for Local Economic Strategies, Manchester, 1988.
17. Mansfield, T., PhD research at the Centre for Urban Pollution Research, Middlesex Polytechnic, 1988.
18. Denton, D., 'Lead in London Soils and Vegetables', *London Environmental Supplement* No.16, 1988.
19. Holman, C., *Air Pollution and Health*, Friends of the Earth, London, 1989.
20. Department of Transport, *National Travel Survey 1885/6 Part 1*, and *Road Accidents in Great Britain 1988*, HMSO, London, 1987 and 1989.
21. Porritt, J., *Healthy Cities: Environment Action Area*, Department of Community Health, University of Liverpool, 1988.
22. Hillman, M., 'Transport and the Healthy City'; paper presented to the *UK Healthy Cities Conference*, Liverpool, 1988.
23. Bowlby, S., 'Planning town centres for women', *Town and Country Planning*, Vol. 56, No. 10, 1987.
24. Macdonald, *op. cit.*
25. Smith, *Unemployment and Health*, OUP, Oxford, 1987; Robertson, J., 'Health is Wealth', in *The Living Economy*, Routledge, London, 1986; *Inequalities in Health: Report of the research working group*, (The Black Report), Department of Health and Social Security, 1980.
26. Bowlby, *op. cit.*
27. SERPLAN, *Review of the regional strategy, background paper: Housing*, SERPLAN, London, 1989.

Chapter 9: Policy Recommendations

Many pundits would have us believe that there are realistic choices for the future development of our urban systems. Most of them would make the assumption that the current patterns of use and access to resources *could* remain, subject to relatively minor adjustments. In the UK the maintenance of these patterns and trends could be expected to lead to the development, in physical form, of a spread or dispersed city, possibly with an internal green belt. Such a city would be dependent upon personal motorised road transport and would be highly energy-intensive. The social and environmental consequences of such a development can be clearly seen in the current state of certain cities in the USA.

Friends of the Earth does not believe that current patterns of use and access to resources can be maintained. In contrast, we argue that an alternative course is the only option in which cities have a future. This is a choice based on a fundamental reappraisal of resource use, especially in the areas of energy, transport, land, materials, food and waste.

Current patterns of material and environmental resource use and abuse in our urban systems are inherently unsustainable. The scale of contemporary urbanism means that it is now a major threat to global sustainability. This is demonstrated most clearly by the issue of global warming. The use of resources in cities contributes greatly to emissions of greenhouse gases. And over two-thirds of the world's fifty largest cities will be forced to adapt their patterns of resource use within a few generations, either to deal with the rising sea-level resulting from global warming, or to prevent or delay that consequence. However, those resources will not be available for long if the process of global warming is allowed to continue. Radical changes are therefore necessary in all sectors of society, beginning with immediate short-term priorities while laying the ground for more fundamental longer-term changes.

This chapter identifies the different sectors which have a role in the transition to sustainable urban development and outlines their roles in terms of the mechanisms available to them to effect change. The key elements of a strategy for the future sustainable development of the city as a whole are then outlined, concentrating on the role of central government in creating a framework in which all the different sectors identified can act effectively.

Individuals

The individual has roles as consumer, citizen, worker and participant in environmental action. The consumer, through the market, can reduce or direct consumption so as to encourage producers to protect the environment. The individual can take personal action, beyond that as a consumer, for instance in recycling or gardening. In his or her job, individuals can influence their employer, colleagues or employees.

The citizen can not only exercise a democratic choice in favour of environmentally responsible government, but can also act more widely in the political process, by direct or indirect lobbying of his or her representative(s).

The voluntary sector

The voluntary sector is diverse, including pressure groups and those who undertake action, such as recycling projects or derelict land reclamation, which other agencies are unable or unwilling to do. By demonstrating the efficacy of these projects or through research, voluntary organisations can construct a basis for raising consciousness in, educating, lobbying and otherwise influencing all the other sectors considered here.

As pressure groups, voluntary organisations represent a body of opinion that is able to influence the governmental sectors (even between elections). They cover many issues of direct relevance to sustainable urban development including energy conservation, pollution, transport, traffic calming, food quality, and recycling.

The professions

Several professional groups have central roles in the movement towards sustainable urban development, primarily planners and architects, but also teachers and many (other) local and central government officers.

The planning profession must draw up development plans based on the principles of sustainable development, both in their policies and their proposals. Planners must also develop criteria for the development control process which will allow them to reject development which damages sustainability. Architects must design buildings in such a way as to reduce energy consumption and dependence on air conditioning and must specify less environmentally damaging construction materials. Transport planners and engineers must design and build transport systems which promote accessibility and reduce dependence on private motorised transport.

But to achieve these goals, all the professions need new information and education. A basic understanding of sustainable development must be taught in all professional education, such as business management courses, as well as forming a focus of environmental and scientific education in schools and colleges. Professionals also need information related to their disciplines and should collaborate to reach a common understanding of how to progress toward sustainable urban development.

Trade unions

Trade unions have always had legitimate interests in the urban environment, in that the health and safety of the workforce is dependent on many of the same factors as the health of the environment. Thus the major role of the unions in sustainable urban development is a continuation of this interest. Unions can ensure that environmental and health and safety regulations are met in workplaces, and can legitimately lobby for improved regulations.

In the longer term, the effects of environmental *degradation* are likely to include job losses and poorer working conditions generally.

Unions also have an educational role as far as their members are concerned with regard to environmental hazards and needs. For example, unions can promote energy conservation and recycling in the workplace, and should consider the implications of such issues for working practices.

The private sector

In the past, the private sector has been slow to exercise leadership on environmental issues, but today the Confederation of British Industry (CBI) is calling for improved environmental regulation to 'level the playing field'. The private sector has more than a lobbying role, however, it is the source of most of the investment in built development and in research and development of products and processes. Such investment can pursue sustainable development, or continue along destructive paths of environmental and resource exploitation.

The construction and property development industries, including agents, funding and investment institutions, thus have a special responsibility to further the process of sustainable urban development. Despite efforts by some individual companies, the need to conserve the environment poses a fundamental challenge to the development industry, which, if embraced, could allow it to meet or exceed high standards of environmental protection and significantly raise the quality of the built environment.

Commerce and industry must develop their environmental concern beyond a response to green consumerism to a long-term commitment to invest in more sustainable production and distribution systems. This will require far higher levels of investment in energy conservation, pollution control and recycling. It could be extended to investment in the locality, through the development of local sourcing to encourage small, local enterprises. Where new processes or practices are developed, for example in building construction, the private sector can demonstrate and advertise their effectiveness widely. The private sector is also a major consumer of goods and services, which can be specified according to environmental criteria.

Local authorities

The role of the urban local authority is perhaps the broadest. It encompasses the operation of the planning system, both in the drawing up of development plans and in the operation of the development control system, both of which need to be informed by principles of sustainable development. It has a role too in regulation, in areas such as environmental health, pollution control and trading standards. Here national legislation must be enforced more effectively and authorities should use their limited powers to the full to maintain and improve standards.

Local government is also a major consumer of goods and services, and as a bulk buyer (particularly through purchasing consortia) it is able to influence suppliers to a much greater degree than individual consumers. Similarly it should include environmental criteria in specifications for services carried out for it, including those to which compulsory competitive tendering applies, while it should modify the services it provides directly to take into account the needs of sustainable development. Such modification can include economic development functions which should be used to promote the local economic sector through the provision of appropriate local facilities.

These specific tasks are underpinned by the special relationship between the local authority and the community, in which the local authority can act in an enabling capacity, catalysing community (or private sector) action; for example, in nature conservation, recycling or local economic enterprise. Finally, local authorities also have the ability, particularly through their associations, to influence central government policy.

Local authorities need to adapt policies and actions in all spheres to promote sustainable development, and thus need to change existing structures and invest in staff training.*

National government

The role of national government is central to the process of sustainable development which cannot occur in a totally free-market situation. This role involves the introduction and reform of legislation and regulations, and manipulation of the market by fiscal measures. It also involves effective enforcement of legislation through adequately staffed and empowered inspectorates (whether the tax inspectorate or the pollution inspectorate), investment in public infrastructure such as railways, and the further development of the system of regulations, circulars and guidance notes used to improve the performance of legislation in, for example, development planning. These activities all form part of the provision of the legislative and economic framework necessary for sustainable urban development.

Internal changes in the operations of central government are needed to ensure that the actions of all government departments in implementing policies take full account of environmental consequences.

International bodies

The global nature of environmental problems necessitates international co-operation. International authorities must play a role through regulation, and enforcement of legislation. Britain is most directly influenced by the European Community, but other important bodies include the United Nations and the Organisation for Economic Co-operation and Development (OECD). Effective international

---

*   For details of the policies and practices that authorities should adopt see Friends of the Earth, *The Environmental Charter for Local Government - Practical Recommendations*, FoE, London, 1989.

regulation or agreement through conventions are often the only ways in which concerns about national competitiveness can be assuaged.

Major recommendations

These roles can be grouped into three main functions which must be fulfilled by the various sectors outlined above:

• the creation of an adequate regulatory framework for the actions of individuals and companies, which provides disincentives to unsustainable action and incentives for positive sustainable action;
• individual and corporate action which positively promotes sustainability;
• generation of pressure for the creation of that framework and the promotion of such action.

The following recommendations deal primarily with the first of these functions and thus relate primarily to the role of central government. Specific recommendations are made relating to each of the major topics covered by the preceding chapters.

Built environment

An explicit urban planning policy is needed, based on the concepts of decentralised concentration and high density mixed land-use. The policy must also influence the nature of the future development of the built environment so that it is based on the need to conserve resources and provides secure and attractive public and private spaces.
This requires:

a) the removal of the presumption in favour of development on greenfield sites, and the imposition of a particularly strong presumption *against* commercial development in 'out-of-town' locations;

b) a requirement for development plans to provide for decentralised concentration and high density mixed land-use in urban areas to promote accessibility and safety and reduce the need for motorised travel; planning guidance on urban densities and design that will ensure that development plans do not set maximum densities at undesirably low suburban levels; and encouragement for the use of design briefs for housing that promote high-quality medium-rise terraced housing;

c) the extension by legislation of the definition of material considerations in development control so that issues such as wider traffic generation, energy implications and wider resource and environmental impacts have to be considered; and the revision of the Use Classes Order to prevent over-specialisation of urban areas and to protect mixed uses;

d) improved specifications for construction funded directly or indirectly by public authorities, including environmental criteria in the provision of all grants given for urban development;

e) revised Building Regulations which cover all buildings and a wider range of issues, notably life-span, and which provide higher environmental standards relating to energy and construction materials; and

f) improved enforcement of planning control and building regulations to ensure that environmental standards are met.

Economic activity

National policies should not be designed to promote economic growth *per se* but should promote environmentally sustainable economic development, particularly through the development of sustainable local economies and increased self-reliance in cities.

This requires:

a) the provision of technical and financial support for locally based development (including community business and co-operatives) and incentives for locally based investment by the private sector;

b) a requirement for development plans to provide for a mixture of scales of economic activity and in particular to protect and promote locally based activity; and
c) the redirection of policies for inner-city renewal such that they renew the local social infrastructure and the local employment base as first priorities.

Transport

A balanced national transport policy and development programme is needed, based on the promotion of walking, cycling and mass transit, the reduction of total road capacity for private vehicles, particularly within cities, and enhanced safety for all road-users. Higher technical standards of fuel economy and emission control are also required to reduce the environmental impact of the remaining vehicles.

This requires:

a) the extension of fiscal and regulatory mechanisms to restrain private motorised transport and increase the relative costs of long-distance travel;
b) reduced public investment in private road transport and at least equalisation of the criteria for investment in road building, in mass transit and in provision for cyclist and pedestrian travel;
c) improved direct support for mass transit provision and powers for local authorities to support mass transit financially on environmental grounds;
d) improvements in the travel environment for pedestrians and cyclists, notably cycle and pedestrian priorities, traffic calming and pedestrianisation and lower speed limits; and
e) the inclusion of the minimisation of travel needs and the promotion of accessibility as statutory elements of development planning and development control.

Energy

Within national energy policy it is necessary that priority is given to energy conservation and efficiency and to the development of supply based on cleaner and more efficient technology and renewable sources.

This requires:

a) strengthening of the Energy Efficiency Office in order to promote and co-ordinate conservation efforts based on new, wider and more stringent energy efficiency regulations for equipment and buildings;

b) introduction of tax differentials to favour energy conservation, such as mortgage relief on energy-efficient buildings and the placing of insulation materials into the lower (currently zero) VAT band. In addition, the potential for increasing the level of taxation on all fuel must be examined;

c) direct investment in energy-saving refurbishment of the housing stock;

d) prohibition of the use of electricity for heating in new buildings and (where suitable safe alternatives exist) in refurbished buildings;

e) reform of the legislation affecting energy supply companies to dissociate profits from energy supplied, such that energy demand reduction can be in their commercial interests;

f) revision of the statutory obligations of the energy supply companies to include 'least-cost planning' and to prevent regressive pricing;

g) increased support for research into, and regulation to promote, alternative energy supply, notably renewables and combined heat and power; and

h) introduction of energy considerations as a statutory element in development planning and provision of guidance to enshrine the status of energy consumption as a material consideration in development control.

Natural environment

National and urban policy mechanisms are needed to protect and enhance the existence of the 'natural' environment in cities and to minimise the interference of cities with ecological processes.

This requires:

a) absolute statutory protection for valuable existing habitats and amended planning guidance to increase protection for existing 'natural' open spaces and designated sites through a presumption against development;

b) criteria for all schemes promoted or supported by public authorities (such as transport investments or derelict land reclamation) which take into account the full environmental value of open space both for amenity and conservation;

c) a requirement for development plans to include nature conservation strategies based on regular surveys; and

d) promotion of native, naturalistic and productive landscaping in schemes funded directly or indirectly by public authorities.

Food and agriculture

National agricultural policies need to promote a system of sustainable food production which provides healthy and uncontaminated food without damaging the environment in its production or distribution. In particular, the use of chemicals in agriculture needs to be reduced and localised production promoted.

This requires:

a) the linking of agricultural subsidies to conservation and reduced use of chemicals and the modification of the Common Agricultural Policy to promote more sustainable agriculture, for example through the introduction of non-transferrable nitrogen quotas;

b) increased direct support for research into sustainable agricultural methods and conversion to alternative production systems;

c) improved regulation on chemical residue standards in food;

d) a requirement for development plans (at minimum) to protect land for local production within and on the margins of urban areas, including allotments and urban gardens; and

e) more stringent regulations on intensive livestock rearing to encourage mixed agriculture.

Waste and pollution

National policies are needed which minimise the generation of waste and pollution, through the application of absolute polluter liability, with the aim of eliminating emissions of persistent, accumulative and dangerous pollutants, and basing ambient standards for other pollutants to well below global, regional and local critical loads or levels.

This requires:

a) promotion of re-use and recycling of waste through source separation for recycling, assisting or promoting investment in reclamation technology, introducing a resource tax on relevant raw materials and promoting stabilisation of the market for recyclable materials as an interim measure;

b) promotion of waste reduction and clean technology;

c) extended regulations and incentives for pollution control, based on absolute retrospective producer liability and use of the best available technology;

d) more stringent environmental quality standards designed to force progressive improvements in production technology with the aim of eliminating pollution;

e) extended and improved monitoring and enforcement systems, both nationally and through local authorities, and provision for unrestricted public access to information about pollution, including the detailed results of monitoring;

f) an adequately resourced requirement on local authorities to carry out surveys of contaminated land, and introduce absolute retrospective polluter liability as a legal charge on the land (where the polluter can be identified); and

g) promotion of the composting of sewage sludge and regulation to minimise industrial contamination of human sewage. Assistance for local authorities to separate compostable waste from the waste stream and provide composting sites at civic amenity centres and parks and gardens.

Conclusion

The adoption of these policies at national levels will not instantly solve all our urban and environmental problems but should provide a context in which effective action can be taken.

The decision to make these reforms cannot be delayed. According to the Inter-governmental Panel on Climate Change (IPCC), the threat of global warming requires global cuts in carbon emissions of 60 per cent merely to stabilise atmospheric carbon concentrations. Carbon emissions are still increasing and thus corrective action will become increasingly costly. And global warming is only one of the most pressing threats to our planet.

Immediate action must be taken on energy conservation, on recycling, on planning and pollution legislation. By the end of the 1990s, renewable energy supplies should be on stream, mass transit systems constructed, much of our building stock refurbished, the necessary infrastructure in place to prevent contamination of sewage, and the return of facilities to central but accessible facilities begun.

The modern city is unhealthy, inequitable, and an intolerable burden on the planet. However it can be revived. By 2020 the benefits of the above-mentioned policy changes will be clear. The revived city will be greener, less polluted, denser and reclaimed from the car, giving urban dwellers improved access to jobs and other facilities. On top of these benefits within the city, its impact on the global environment will be reduced to a sustainable level.

Subject Index

Place Name Index

Author Index

Other Friends of the Earth publications

■ All prices are inclusive of postage and packing
■ Payment must be received with order
■ Please allow 28 days for delivery
■ Cheques should be made payable to Friends of the Earth
■ Send order and payment to: Friends of the Earth, 26–28 Underwood Street,
                                 London N1 7JQ

The Environmental Charter for Local Government, November 1989,	£13.00
Beyond Rhetoric: an economic framework for environmental policy development in the 1990s, September 1990,	£3.00
Action for People? A critical appraisal of government inner city policy, March 1989,	£5.00
Stealing Our Future, September 1989,	£6.00
An Illustrated Guide to Traffic Calming, January 1990,	£5.00
Air Quality and Health, August 1989,	£6.00
Getting Out of the Greenhouse, December 1989,	£3.00
The Good Wood Guide, January 1990,	£5.00
Reviving the City, January 1991,	£13.95

Order Form

Title	Quantity	Price
Name _____	Total Cost	
Address _____	Donation	
_____	P&P	FREE
Telephone No _____ Date _____	Total Sent	

The Earth needs all the friends it can get.
And it needs them now.

For thousands upon thousands of years our planet has sustained a rich diversity of life. Now, one single species – humankind – is putting the Earth at risk.

People the world over are suffering the effects of pollution, deforestation and radiation. Species are disappearing at a terrifying rate. The warming of the atmosphere threatens us all with devastating change in climate and food production.

But it needn't be like this – we know enough to reverse the damage, and to manage the Earth's wealth more fairly and sustainably. But the political will to bring about such a transformation is still lacking.

And that's exactly where Friends of the Earth comes in.

IT'S TIME YOU JOINED US

I'd like to join Friends of the Earth. Please send me your quarterly magazine. I enclose:

£12 ☐ individual   £17 ☐ family   £250 ☐ life

I'd like to donate £50 ☐   £35 ☐   £15 ☐

Other £ _____

I enclose a cheque/PO for total of £ _____
payable to **Friends of the Earth** or debit my Access/Visa No:

_____   Card expiry date: _____

Signature _____   Date _____

Full Name _____

Address _____

_____

_____

_____   Postcode _____

Send to: Membership Dept, Friends of the Earth, FREEPOST, 56–58 Alma Street, Luton, Beds LUI 2YZ.

081 200 0200 to join/donate anytime

F8I LADL